The
Idea of Race

MICHAEL BANTON

The Idea of Race

TAVISTOCK PUBLICATIONS

First published in 1977
by Tavistock Publications Limited
11 New Fetter Lane, London EC4P 4EE
Printed in Great Britain
at the University Printing House,
Cambridge

ISBN 0 422 76170 2

Contents

Acknowledgements

Some friends and colleagues have kindly read certain of these chapters in draft and given me the benefit of their criticisms. Several of them will remain critical of my arguments, but they have helped me to formulate more clearly my views on both the points on which we agree and those on which we differ. I would particularly mention my indebtedness to Michael Biddiss, Steve Fenton, Michael Lyon, David Mason, and Hannan Rose.

M. B.

University of Bristol
October 1975

1

The intellectual inheritance

On the fourteenth of August 1862, Abraham Lincoln summoned to the White House a group of black Americans to explain to them his despair about the future of black people in the United States and his interest in schemes for sending them back to Africa. He began:

> 'You and we are different races. We have between us a broader difference than exists between any other two races. Whether it is right or wrong I need not discuss, but this physical difference is a great disadvantage to us both, as I think your race suffer very greatly, many of them by living among us, while ours suffer from your presence . . .'

Congress had appropriated funds to colonize blacks outside the country. Lincoln emphasized that 'on this broad continent not a single man of your race is made the equal of a single man of ours'. In his judgement they were suffering 'the greatest wrong inflicted on any people'. The President did not spell out his explanation of why they were treated in this manner. Apparently he thought that for some unspecified reason white Americans were incapable of behaving with justice towards blacks. Criticizing the colonizationists, a contemporary had asked if it was conceivable that Christ had commanded men to love one another without giving them the power to do it. Lincoln did not refer to this objection. He seems to have regarded racial prejudice as in part a moral issue, but not entirely. What he called 'this physical difference' apparently marked a boundary within which communal sentiments operated (Sinkler, 1971: 37—53).

Lincoln's remarks reflect the belief that there is something about relations between people of different race that distinguishes them from relations between people of the same race. That belief was nurtured by the theory of racial types formulated in the middle years of the century, and it lingered on to give plausibility to the view that race relations constituted a special field of study. Today it would be generally agreed that the subordinate position of blacks in the United States in 1862 did not spring from differences in the biological nature of blacks and whites but from political, economic, and social causes. According to this interpretation race relations are relations between members of social categories that happen to be identified by racial labels.

This book explores the intellectual context within which the old conception of race relations arose, and goes on to discuss the main lessons to be learned from changes in the way of looking at these matters. It deals with the study of race relations as a general body of knowledge which tries to bring together in a common framework studies of group relations in different countries and in different periods of history. If such a framework exists, it is at present far from adequate. Indeed it is worth considering whether the attempt to improve it shows any promise since many scholars would consider this a misconceived enterprise. They maintain that 'race' has meant different things in different circumstances and the categories to which the label has been applied in particular circumstances have been so varied that the scholar can do no more than write the history of particular societies and particular conflicts. For example, at the beginning of this century a reference to race relations in South Africa was usually a reference to relations between Afrikaans-speaking whites and English-speaking whites, whereas today it would surely refer to relations between blacks and whites. When a group starts to regard its relations with another group as 'racial' this may well betoken a change in the nature of those relations, and may merit attention on that account. Equally, an understanding of Lincoln's beliefs about the nature of race may help the historian interpret the President's actions, but no one today who asks what American race relations were like in 1862 would be justified in starting from Lincoln's assumptions about the nature of race. The student of race relations must not limit himself to the participants' conceptions of what was racial, even though his material has always to be considered in its historical context.

To ask what we have learned about race relations is therefore to pose a complex question. It entails, first, the study of the growth of knowledge; second, it examines knowledge about a changing subject matter which appears to be transformed as peoples' conceptions of race have

changed; third, it requires study of the work of scholars who did not stand apart from their subject matter but shared understandings about the nature of race with the people whom they were studying. For this last reason at least it is unwise to separate the sociology of race relations sharply from the history of the idea of race. Sociological theory is built with ideas, and these ideas have their histories, so that the relationship between the theory and the histories is something the sociologist must keep under examination.

As people can understand their history only through the concepts of their own time, it is continually necessary to rewrite history in the light of new concerns and understandings. Equally, people interpret their own time in the light of their beliefs about the past, and if they misunderstand their past they cannot properly understand their present. In human affairs there is a continual inter-relation between the present and the past which is reflected in all the social sciences and has a special relevance to a field like race relations which has to build on uncertain foundations.

It is also unwise to study the idea of race in isolation from two other ideas that were likewise reborn in the early years of the nineteenth century. The modern ideas of race, of class, and of nation, arose from the same European milieu and share many points of similarity. All three were exported to the furthest parts of the globe and have flourished in many foreign soils. In so far as men have believed that it was right to align themselves on the basis of race, class, and nation, or have believed that these would become the major lines of division, so these ideas have proved their own justification. But events have not borne out the predictions very closely. Nation has been the most successful of the three. The idea promised that every man possessed a nationality as a natural attribute and that he had a right to be ruled only as a member of his nation. This implied that a state must coincide with a nation and that minorities should separate and join up with their fellow nationals. That promise has not been fulfilled. Some states, like the United Kingdom, include more than one nation. Almost every state includes one or more minorities (Iceland, Europe's oldest nation, is an exception that scarcely upsets the generalization). If one state seeks to expel one of its minorities, as Uganda has recently done, it adds to the minority problems of other states. The idea of class promised an ever-widening patterning of group alliances based upon common relations to the ownership of the means of production. Yet instead of sharper discontinuities, social stratification in most industrial countries today is characterized by a continuous distribution of positions along a scale of status. There are occupational communities that show a sense of collective identity but across the broad social range class consciousness is a feeble force compared with the consciousness of status differentiation. The third idea, that of race, promised at first that each racial type would take command of the territory to which it was naturally suited, but this gave place to the belief that the whites had inherited a superiority that would enable them to establish their rule in all the regions of the world. In neither form has the prediction been fulfilled. The self-confidence of the Anglo-Saxons has been shattered and the appearance of a biological basis for racial theories has disintegrated.

One approach to the study of social relations starts from Marx's grandiloquent assertion that 'the dominant ideas [of any age] are nothing more than the ideal expression of the dominant material relationship' (Marx, 1956: 93). This declaration can be taken in either a weak or a strong sense. In the weak sense, that of advice to examine the relationship between the popularity of particular ideas and the structure of political and economic relations in the society, it is of the greatest importance. In the strong sense, it can be taken as an insistence that race, class, and nation are political ideas that arise from underlying economic and political structures. Race and nation could be seen as propagated by ruling classes, whereas the idea of class would emerge from an awareness among the subordinated of the structure that promotes their exploita- more problematic than the quotation acknowledges. The sentiment of and has changed in character, but all along it has been related to a uni- many considerations independent of social structures, and this must demonstrate that the definition of what constitutes an idea is much more problematic than the quotation acknowledges. The sentiment of nationality is obviously influenced by the natural boundaries of geography, by shared language, outward appearance, and culture. Nor can race be regarded as a purely political idea; it has appeared in diverse forms and has changed in character, but all along it has been related to a universe of biological knowledge where the understanding of race has been less subject to political influences. Those who would argue for a strong interpretation of Marx's claim have made little attempt to demonstrate that it can be satisfactorily applied to the understanding of racial categories.

'Class' became a central concept in the sociological tradition, but 'nation' has been neglected and the problems in the use of 'race' have been evaded. Since some social relations have been generally defined as race relations, it is not surprising that this has been regarded as a more or less distinctive field of political concern and social enquiry. Scholars have for many years been plagued by doubts about the legitimacy of de-

fining an area of social study in terms of an apparently contentious concept on which the biologists are the authorities. The argument of this book is that the student who wishes to understand the nature of the field of race relations study (including its recent shift in the direction of 'ethnic relations') should approach it from the standpoint of the growth of knowledge. This will give him a grasp of the character of the field and what has governed that character. It will also help him formulate his views upon what the field might or should become.

There was no clear-cut nineteenth century idea of race. There were many classifications and theories, and much controversy. But in so far as one simple conception caught popular attention and led to a notion of race relations, it was the doctrine of permanent human types reflected in Abraham Lincoln's words. This doctrine was slowly constructed in the first half of the century and attained its most systematic statement in a book called *Types of Mankind* which was published in Philadelphia in 1854. The influence of this school of thought is apparent in Lincoln's belief that there is a finite number of races or types (blacks and whites being the most distant); that the differences are permanent; and that the differences have a decisive influence upon the kinds of social relationship possible between members of different races, perhaps because each race is situated to a particular part of the globe. There is a little more to the doctrine, but Lincoln had certainly seized some of its chief features. In Chapter Three I shall show that it is useful to return to the distinction between race and type drawn by many nineteenth-century anthropologists and shall show that the view that influenced Lincoln constituted a theory of racial typology. Before doing so, I shall, in Chapter Two and part of Chapter Three, discuss some of the sources of this theory which have received insufficient attention in earlier writings.

The theory of racial typology ushers in the beginning of the study of race relations, for though it was a theory about race, it held that the nature of races determined the relations between them. If one seeks an event and a date to mark this development, the best is the publication in 1850 of Robert Knox's *The Races of Men*. Earlier books had advanced racial classifications and some of Knox's contemporaries made contributions to the theory of equal or greater importance, but Knox was the first to come forward with an exposition that was comprehensive even if jumbled and confusing. However, Charles Darwin's work almost immediately cut the ground from under the feet of Knox, Gobineau, Nott, Gliddon, and the other typologists, by showing that in nature species were not permanent entities but were subject to evolution by adaptation and selection. Darwin's studies raised questions which no one at the time was able to answer, concerning such matters as the source of variation and the unit upon which selection operated. Adaptive characteristics are transmitted, and tend to come in clusters, like the skin colour, hair form, nose and lip shape of Negro West Africans. It was difficult to banish the misleading concept of racial type until something to comprehend such clustering was ready to be put in its place.

It took more than seventy years for this to be achieved and for the nature of Darwin's revolution to become fully apparent. Only in the early 1930s with the establishment of population genetics was it clear that the concept that had to take the place of racial type was that of population, and that populations had to be studied statistically instead of typologically. Populations are always changing, not because of the nature of the whole, but because their individual members are subjected to the pressures of selection as they adapt themselves to changing environments. If this has been scientifically demonstrated does it mean that the study of race relations is founded on a ghastly error and that wherever the word race appears we should now substitute that of population?

Such a substitution would indeed reflect the lessons that the studies of geneticists have to teach, but there are several sets of circumstance that tell against so simple a solution. First, the populations with which we are concerned in many cases constitute what have been called geographical races. They draw upon gene pools which include at high frequencies genes that ensure that nearly all the members of each succeeding generation display the appearance that causes ordinary people to ascribe them to particular races. The appearance persists of what ordinary people believe to constitute race and the general public is bound to lag behind the more sophisticated understandings of the scientist. Second, the nineteenth-century idea of race has been threaded into the tapestry of world history and has acquired a social and political significance that is largely though not completely independent of the significance that can be given to the concept of race within biological science. For these reasons also, the substitution of the word 'population' would be of little assistance. The third set of circumstances turns on questions of another kind. When it appears that a concept is no longer sufficiently accurate and is causing misunderstanding, the main task is not to ban a bad label but to find a better one to put it its place. The geneticists were able to make better progress by putting 'population' in place of 'race' but social scientists have different interests. They must identify what for their purposes are the key features of the kinds of social catego-

ries that have been designated races. Though this is not a completely satisfactory solution, it looks as if for social science purposes it would be better to use the concepts of majority and minority in this connection. The arguments in favour of this conclusion are brought together towards the end of the book.

Some of the nineteenth-century writers who attempted to synthesize the new knowledge about man's social nature reasoned as if individual men possessed attributes of race, nationality, and class, which, when allowed free expression, brought them together with others of their kind, so that the history of mankind, in the past and the future, was the product of this inner nature working its way through to the surface of human affairs. Contemporary social science sees races, nations, and classes as social groups, the outcome of a process whereby individuals join with one another to form coalititions, factions, and cliques as well as larger units. This social process of alignment is inter-related with a psychological one whereby individuals are conditioned to identify themselves with certain others and to perceive the social world in terms of shared associations. An English child brought up among children who are all of pinkish complexion is likely to categorize children of another complexion as socially different. Many characteristics become associated with racial distinctions and are passed on to successive generations as part of a cultural process. This includes not only unfavourable judgements of others but also the ways in which individuals conceive their own groups. Ideas about race have been woven into such categorizations and judgements in ways that differ from one part of the world to another and are sometimes quite different from those of racial typology.

Those who preached nationalism in the nineteenth century were anxious to bring together into single political units people whom they thought belonged together. Intermediary groups and national minorities upset such schemes. Instead of their being eliminated in one way or another, such groups have multiplied and have become more significant. Revolutionary changes in transport, and the cost of travel, have made it possible for men to move to other continents in search of work. Members of minorities can now keep in touch with their homelands, revisit them, and maintain their homeland ties with a facility previously impossible. For a far longer period they can entertain the thought of returning to the country of their birth and do not have to contemplate a future in which assimilation seems the only outcome. From the declining importance of nationality in such circumstances springs the enhanced significance of ethnicity. If nations are populations that have come together, or are disposed to come together in nation states, ethnic minorities are groups possessing national attributes that are willing to live within states that do not put at the centre their customs, language, religion, and values. Notions of race have become so closely involved with the affairs of ethnic minorities that it is frequently unproductive to try to demarcate the study of race relations from the study of ethnic relations. Examination of the history of many minorities shows that it is impossible to separate the influence of race, ethnicity, class, religion, and so on, as if these were factors in an algebraic equation. Human history is not that simple.

Today race relations have to be understood as the outcome not of biological qualities, but of the way individuals in different situations align themselves with those they perceive as allies, and in opposition to others. Just how they align themselves depends upon many things; not only political oppositions, economic interests, beliefs about the nature of social groups, and other general circumstances, but also human choice, leadership, and responsibility in the critical situations that mark the beginnings of new periods in political history.

Though Darwin's discoveries spelled the end for the concept of the permanent racial type, it took several decades for their import to be appreciated. During this period it appeared as if the theory of natural selection had given new life to some elements of the earlier theory of race. A new school of thought arose, often called social Darwinism, in which race once more featured as an important biological category, but which nevertheless differed in important respects from its predecessor. There is no obvious date signalling this new phase, but one as good as any is 1875, when Ludwig Gumplowicz's *Rasse und Staat* was published. Gumplowicz's initial enthusiasm for the biological explanation of social relations faded with the years, but there were may others who developed this line of thought with greater stridency, maintaining that race was the key to race relations. Their influence, like that of the typologists, can still be discerned today.

With the rise of sociology in the United States another approach extricated itself from the coils of social Darwinism. The change was gradual but is signalized best by the appearance in 1921 of an influential text book edited by Robert E. Park and Ernest W. Burgess entitled *An Introduction to the Science of Sociology*. Park advanced a general conception of race relations as the product of European expansion. They were to be seen in a historical context, the outcome of the same forces as those that generate other features of human history. American scholars chiefly developed those aspects of this approach that could be applied in a domestic context. Sociology took over decisively as the leading discipline in this field and the emphasis was moved to the study of social relations distinguished by race. This was the work of Charles S. Johnson, John Dollard, W. Lloyd Warner, Allison Davis, Burleigh Gardner, Gunnar Myrdal, Oliver C. Cox, E. Franklin Frazier, Everett C. Hughes and their generation, many of them Park's pupils. It established a tradition of enquiry located within American sociology. Separate smaller and affiliated traditions (which I have had to omit from this book) can later be detected in the influence of scholars such as Max Gluckman, who approached the problems from a South African background and looked more towards social anthropology, and Roger Bastide who has joined a French view of sociology to psychiatry and has exercised a major influence on race relations studies in Brazil. But so far the research in South Africa and Brazil, like that started by Kenneth Little in Britain, has not been adequately related to the American work so as to constitute an international discipline which can benefit from the variety offered by different local situations instead of being confused by its great complexity.

A tradition of study incorporates sets of ideas of how to go about the task, what topics to investigate, and what methods to use. Any successful book tends to be taken as a model by research workers who subsequently start in the same field. A successful teacher cannot help but indicate to his student that there are recommended questions to ask; often the students concentrate upon trying to improve upon the answers which their teachers have advanced. When several scholars are at work on similar topics they tend to sharpen one another's wits and there are advantages to be gained from the occasional appearance of distinctive 'schools' of interpretation. A whole generation of scholars may concentrate upon a particular line of study until suddenly someone comes along with a new kind of question and new sorts of answers. If the new approach finds favour, new criteria are adopted in place of the old and the tradition is re-orientated. Such changes in the study of race relations can be located round about 1875 and 1921. New theories were advanced then which claimed not only to account for all that the previous theories had explained but to do so more convincingly and to solve new problems as well.

It is more than usually important to examine the intellectual inheritance in this field because race relations is an area that people consider of urgent political concern. They rightly believe that if only men were sufficiently determined they could significantly reduce the hostilities and the lack of understanding so often associated with racial divisions. This has given and still gives the study of race relations a preoccupation with contemporary affairs and with the prediction of future developments. But haste does not always mean speed. One reason why the sociological study of race relations has not made better progress is that it lacks an adequate critical tradition. In other related branches of study the classical works have been subject to frequent re-analysis. Later writers have found in the material on the Trobriand Islands and the Hawthorne factory evidence for conclusions undetected by Malinowski or by Roethlisberger and Dickson. Students cut their sociological teeth by chewing on the mistakes in the Yankee City research. But where is the critical literature on Dollard's *Caste and Class* or Cox's *Caste, Class, and Race?* Where are the re-interpretations of the rich material in *Deep South* or *An American Dilemma?* What has passed for criticism in race relations studies has too often been abuse and denunciation.

Traditions exist for students to react against as well as to provide an orientation for those who accept their predecessors' assumptions. In any subject there is a place both for the textbook that seeks to give an up-to-date picture of the subject as it is at present, and for the textbook that teaches the student to master, and perhaps advance, his subject by showing him how understanding of its principles has been obtained. If the second course has been followed it is important not to take contemporary knowledge as a starting point, ignoring the false trails and judging earlier writers by their relative success in contributing to a set of theories that — who knows? — may require radical revision in a few years' time. The study of the history of a subject is more valuable to the student if the work of earlier scholars is examined within the context of their generations; by reconstructing the problems with which they were faced, and reviewing the reasons some proferred solutions succeeded and others failed, he can get a perspective onto his own problems. He can learn from their mistakes, and by studying their assumptions can be more aware of his own. The study of mistakes is central to any review of the growth of knowledge and can be rewarding because it is easier to recognize error than truth; by discovering why a conjectural solution is unsatisfactory, one moves a step closer to the truth.

Any scholar working in a field must stand in some relation to the dominant tradition. He must seek either to extend it or to change it. If he studies his inheritance he becomes more aware of his own position and of how he situates himself in relation to others. He gains an extra measure of self-awareness. The writer who does not read his predecessors' work runs the risk of repeating their mistakes. The student who examines the tradition that has come down to him has something valuable on which to sharpen his own intellect. He has to examine the existing tradition if he is to go beyond it and if (for this is an important addition) he is to be able to explain to other people in what ways his solutions are better than those he wishes to supercede.

The tradition of study pioneered by Park was preoccupied with the racial problems of the United States. Seeking social instead of biological designations for the black and white categories, many of the writers mentioned earlier thought it better to call them castes than races. All of them assumed that the future of black Americans lay in their right to full American nationality and citizenship. Oliver Cox's book *Caste, Class and Race* was the first major challenge to this tradition. Cox did not question the assumptions about nationality, but he attacked the parallel with caste with all his might. More important, he outlined a mode of analysis that subordinated both race and nation to class. It was in the relations between exploiting and exploited classes that the dynamic of history was to be found. Ultimately white workers and black workers would see through the rationalizations of the capitalist system and unite to overturn it.

Cox's book did not receive in American universities the attention it deserved, but when in the nineteen sixties the cry 'black power!' evoked its enthusiastic response the race relations tradition of study encountered so strong a challenge that the re-orientation of scholarly work was almost too precipitate. The three phases I have so far described (racial typology, social Darwinism, and the proto-sociological studies that began with Park) can be identified by changes in the thought of scholars. The first two stemmed from discoveries within the biological realm, the third from the attempt of American scholars to formulate sociological explanations of what they believed to be sociological problems. The new phase started differently, being inaugurated by changes in the behaviour of the people who had been seen as constituting a major portion of the subject matter if not of the problem. The change of mood quickly communicated itself to black peoples everywhere, to other minorities, and to the women's movement. The vocabulary of race had been an idiom of exclusion used by the dominant social category. The black movement adopted the vocabulary of nationalism and used it as an idiom of identification for the dominated. Its intellectuals challenged the assumptions about assimilation and nationality in sociological orthodoxy that had been left untouched even in Cox's onslaught. They put the blame for bad race relations upon the majority society. That was the white man's problem; their energies were to be devoted to mobilizing the black man's strength, cultivating his pride, and teaching him to prefer to be black. Blacks came to be more of an ethnic minority like other groups that were struggling to preserve their distinctive inheritance and combat the influences making for cultural uniformity.

In the analysis of ethnic minorities the ideas of race, class, and nation meet once more. Notions of race have left their mark upon the way many minorities are regarded and on how some minority members regard themselves. The belief in national distinctiveness is often central to the image ethnic minority members have of themselves. But class is important in another way. The most effective examples of ethnic minority organization relate to minorities that find themselves occupying a lower position in the system of social stratification than their self-respect will tolerate. So long as they feel unfairly placed they collaborate in the attempt to improve their position. Once they have attained their goal the impulse to minority organization is gone and minority members disappear into the status structure of the majority. For those who have been committed to minority organization worldly success brings bitter disappointments. For such reasons it is today particularly interesting to study developments amongst Afrikaans-speaking white South Africans. They became a distinctive people during the years of British colonial rule; they fashioned their own language; they fought a bitter war for their independence; brought back into an English-dominated state as a relatively poor, rural, people, they mobilized their strength, captured the government, and cultivated their economic power. Today their success is qualified only by external threat and their internal bonds are weakening. The Afrikaners' story suggests questions to be asked of minorities that at present appear very different from each other. The comparison of variations in ethnic consciousness in different minorities, of changes in the character of minorities, and of the relations between these and majority structures, could help provide firmer sociological foundations for the kinds of research with which race relations are now concerned.

The chapters that follow are presented as a contribution to the study of how the idea of race has interacted with the growth of sociological knowledge. They discuss the categories that sociologists have developed in the attempt to understand the phenomena that have been regarded as falling within the field of race relations, and point to alternative conceptualizations which I hope to improve and utilize in studies of the contemporary situation. Though I attempt to place the beginning of the story in a historical context, the book is not a history of the idea of race. Too little of the basic work (especially on the period following 1870) has yet been carried out for anyone to write a satisfactory history of the idea of race, but when it is attempted the influence of sociology will probably prove a central theme in the period spanned by the last hundred years.

2

The racializing of the West

It is sometimes assumed that contemporary Western conceptions of race arose out of the contacts between white people and black people that followed European voyages of exploration to America, Africa, and Asia in the fifteenth and sixteenth centuries. This is too narrow a perspective and underestimates the significance of social changes within Europe. Race, like class and nation, was a concept developed first within Europe to help interpret new social relations. All three should be seen as modes of categorization which were increasingly used as greater numbers of Europeans became aware of more and more persons overseas who appeared to be different from themselves. Because their continent went through the process of industrialization first and was much more powerful than others, Europeans unconsciously imposed their social categories upon other peoples who now have, in many cases, adopted them as their own.

Obviously the contacts between the European adventurers and colonists and the peoples of America, Africa, and Asia were important to the development by Europeans of racial categories. Obviously, too, the material interest of the Europeans in the exploitation of these contacts is likely to have influenced those categories. Noticing the absence of racial consciousness and antagonism in the classical and mediaeval worlds, some writers have suggested that it is possible to date the origins of racial prejudice as a characteristic of European culture, and to attribute its appearance to specific causes. The same causes, in their view, would influence Europeans' ideas about themselves. Oliver C. Cox seizes on the years 1493–94 when Spanish and Portuguese spheres of influence in the New World were delimited, as marking the beginning of modern race relations. He pictures the capitalist spirit as causing fundamental changes (1948: 331–33). Marvin Harris thinks that racial prejudice arose as an ideological justification of the interest that European nations had in the exploitation of black labour (1964: 70). Arnold Rose dated it in 1793 when the invention of the cotton gin gave cotton planters a new interest in slave-holding (1951: 17). But attempts to trace racial prejudice back to a single 'root', 'source', or historical cause are not very persuasive. It rather looks as if consciousness of racial difference has grown gradually and that the nature of the phenomenon to which we attach the label 'prejudice' has changed significantly.

There has always been a tendency for people to prefer those of their 'own kind' and to be wary of strangers. In mediaeval Europe white had a positive and black a negative value (Hunter, 1967). In Arabic culture blackness came to be disparaged when the Arabs acquired black slaves (Lewis 1971: 27–8). The great age of English exploration in the century before the revolution of 1640 was an age driven by the twin spirits of adventure and control. Society at home was in ferment. The upper classes were anxious about the apparent dissolution of social and moral controls, while 'masterless men' who earlier had a proper place in the social order were wandering about begging, robbing, and raping (Jordan, 1968). The loosening of controls released new energies and many men were out to make the most of their opportunities at home and abroad. These were the generations that represented Africans as radically different. Europeans seem to have displaced onto them some of their own anxieties. George P. Rawick contends that the capitalistic organization of society required a new outlook on the part of its members. They had to discipline themselves to a more demanding work schedule and because they had to suppress much that had previously been important in their lives, they had greater need of scapegoats. Black men met this need (Rawick 1972: 128–33). It looks as if there were many influences that contributed to the gradual growth of prejudice. Its story is the history of Western Europe itself and it is impossible to separate the various items in a unique sequence of events.

In the creation of racial doctrines of the nineteenth-century variety, a crucial part was played by anthropology. Seventeenth and eighteenth-century biologists believed that God had in the beginning created a limited number of species which were unchanging. Each had its place in the divine scheme. One consequence of this doctrine was that when mammoth bones were first found in the United States it was argued that there must be living mammoths somewhere, for God would never have created a species unless there was a permanent place for it in Nature's simple plan. Those writers who first propounded the theory of polygenesis, that several different races had existed from the beginning, were persecuted. The orthodox doctrine was that all men descended from Adam and that the world was about six thousand years old. How then was it that some peoples were much more backward than Europeans and lacked such essentials of civilization as the art of writing? What were the causes of barbarism? Two kinds of cause were discussed, physical or biological, and moral, by which was meant the factors of history, geography, and way of life, which we would today put under the heading of 'culture'. One strand in the thought of the Enlightenment was hostile to explanation in moral terms. Linnaeus, for example, believed that whereas man lived according to custom, he could live according to reason. Our ideas about the world could, in the modern phrase, be de-mystified. Men did not really need myths. Reason could provide the ground for a conception of Man independent both of God and of Nature. Less emphasis was put upon man's moral status, more upon new knowledge about human nature conceived in physical terms. When, therefore, the anthropologists ceased writing in Latin and, after some hesitation, picked on the word race to denote natural varieties of mankind, the development was momentous.

Other authors have assembled and reviewed evidence about the relations between peoples of European and non-European descent in the fifteenth to the seventeenth centuries and the contemporaneous development of anthropological theories (most notably Curtin, 1964 and Jordan, 1968). While I do not wish to travel along the same paths neither do I wish to minimize the importance of these authors' conclusions. Instead I want to draw attention to a thread running through the historical evidence which I think may prove more significant than has hitherto been appreciated. This concerns the way Englishmen came to think of themselves as belonging to a race and reasons behind this that were independent of their contacts with non-Europeans.

When a large group of people answer the question 'who are we?' they usually reply with a genealogy, a historical account of where they came from and how they have reinforced their unity (this argument has recently been advanced at greater length by Leon Poliakov in a study which reinforces and extends the arguments of this chapter). For several centuries up to the beginning of the nineteenth, Englishmen's notions about themselves, and about all men, were dominated by the anthropology of the Bible. The head of the Englishman's genealogy was therefore Adam. Yet three-quarters of the way through that century at the head of the genealogies of many well educated English gentlemen stood Hengist and Horsa, the Saxon chieftains who landed on our shores in AD 449. This re-working of Englishmen's images of their own origin was an important element in the change in the relations between them and the rest of the world.

Many of the ingredients necessary to the construction of a racial doctrine had been present for some time. Jacques Barzun (1932; cf. Poliakov, 1974: 17–36) shows how an opposition between Teuton and Latin ran through much French historical writing from the sixteenth to the eighteenth century. In the last two decades of the fifth century, Clovis, ruler of a small Frankish Kingdom, conquered Gaul and established a new empire. By the end of the seventh century the Franks and the romanized Gauls had been fused into a single people, but later historians persisted in arguing that the Franks and the Gauls were distinct races for a further three hundred years. The motive power behind the dispute about origins was political. The Franks were barbarians of German origin (though some writers maintained that they were descended from the Trojans!). The name 'Frank' was supposed to mean 'free'. The nobility claimed to be descendants of the Franks and derived their claim to privilege from the right of conquest. This version of history was countered with claims that the Gauls invited the Franks to help repulse the Romans (as by Hotman), that Clovis came not as a conqueror but with the authority of the Roman Emperor (as by Abbé Dubos), and that no special privileges were granted to leading families. Historians combed the writings of Caesar and Tacitus to see what these could tell about the original Frenchmen as if the earliest customs had the greatest claims to legitimacy. Though the word 'race' is used in these writings in a way that is compatible with notions of natural distinctiveness, it does not at this time have any biological connotations.

A remarkably close parallel can be found in English political writing of the seventeenth century. Faced by the ambitions of the Stuart monarchs to weaken the power of Parliament and rule by divine right, some defenders of the Parliamentary cause turned to the historical record. They maintained that the English were descended from the Germans described by Tacitus. Richard Verstegan in a book called *Restitution of Decayed Intelligence*, first published in 1605 and in its fifth edition by 1673, gave scholarly backing to such claims. He opened his first chapter with the proclamation that 'Englishmen are descended of German race and were heretofore generally called Saxons' and went on to explain why 'the Germans are a most noble nation'. Tacitus had testified of the Germans that 'the authority of the kings is not unlimited'; 'on minor matters the chiefs deliberate; on larger questions the whole tribe'; and 'the King or chief . . . is attended to more because of his authoritative persuasion than of any power to command'. The Germanic race came to England in AD 449 in Hengist, Horsa, and their followers who were Saxons, Jutes, and Angles. In seventeenth-century England the adjective 'Germanic' was not commonly used; 'Gothic' was employed sometimes to identify the Jutes but more generally to refer to all peoples of Germanic stock as opposed to the Romans and their culture. Later it became more common to refer to the fifth century invaders as the Anglo-Saxon branch of the Germanic race (cf. Kliger, 1952).

Just as Boulainvilliers believed the Frankish age of Charlemagne to have been a golden age for Frenchmen, so there were Englishmen who believed that the Anglo-Saxon centuries prior to 1066 had been such an age for their forebears. It was embodied in the myth of the Norman Yoke resting on the Anglo-Saxon's neck. This is truly a myth in the correct sense of that currently much abused word, for though it claims to be historical, its essence lies in its much more general message. It implies that inequality and exploitation date from the Norman Conquest; that they were absent before 1066; and that by reversing the Conquest men could return to a life of liberty and equality. The ruling class is pictured as the descendants of an alien oppressing race, who have no right to be in the country and no claim to the obedience of Englishmen. This myth had its own appeal for those who would reform the church, for they liked to think that Englishmen practised a pure faith before the papal grip tightened upon them. Equally, it could unite the third estate against the Crown, the church, and the landlords. Christopher Hill reports that the myth was first used in the thirteenth century, then rediscovered in the seventeenth. David Douglas observes that by many early English historians the Conquest was represented as a national tragedy, and even as a national disaster. He suggests that because it was seen as a cause for shame it was not used by Shakespeare as a theme for one of his historical plays. For a long time the Whig interpretation of English history was hostile towards William (Douglas, 1946). The French experience has its parallel here too, for English writers like Philip Hunton in 1643 and John Hare in 1647 held that 'Duke William pretended the grant and gift of King Edward, who died without children; and he came with forces into this kingdom, not to conquer, but to make good his title against his enemies' (Kliger, 1952: 132). However, Parliament won the trial of strength and this interpretation was not needed by the democrats of the next century. The events of 1066 to 1215 remained a story of conquest, perhaps colonization, by an invading people. It was so easily turned into a story of racial conflict that it set a special stamp upon ideas of the origins of the English as a nation.

There was a more philosophical aspect as well. Scholars of the seventeenth century were fascinated by the murky prophecies in Chapters Two and Seven of the book of Daniel. Two centuries later Dean Stanley was to call these chapters the first attempt at a philosophy of history, for they appear to describe a sequence of four kingdoms, of gold, silver, brass, and iron, to be followed by a fifth kingdom, established by God and eternal. The statement that the saints of the most high were to take this fifth kingdom and possess it for ever and ever inspired the 'fifth monarchy men' of Cromwell's era. The Gothic interpretation, however, was that the Roman empire had been the fourth kingdom and that the succession was now passing to the Teutons. Thus an embryonically racial theory was built into English interpretations of history at a very early date.

Both in France and Britain the word 'race' starts to change its significance round about the year 1800. Previously it was primarily used in the sense of 'lineage'; differences between races resulted from the circumstances of their history and though they were maintained over the generations they were not fixed. In England this usage may have been strengthened by Biblical modes of speech, for though the King James' translation of the Bible does not use the word race in referring to men, by 1570 Foxe was writing of 'the race and stock of Abraham', and Milton a little later of the 'race of Satan'. Why the word apparently came into increasing use merits separate study, but it may have been associated with the widening range of human contacts made possible by improved modes of transport and communication. In the nineteenth century race comes to signify an inherent physical quality. Other peoples are seen as biologically different. Though the definition remained uncertain, people began to assume that mankind was divided into races. They therefore had to explain why there were racial differences. Did these mean that some races were superior to others? or that races succeeded one another in leading humanity? or that each had its distinctive contribution to make to humanity? In any event, one of the major problems was to uncover the nature of race.

The new use of the word 'race' represented it as a physical category. It led to neglect of the way in which race was socially utilized as a category for organizing peoples' perceptions of the populations of the world. There was a social process, which can be called racialization, whereby a mode of categorization was developed, applied tentatively in European historical writing, and then, more confidently, to the populations of the world. Though much has been said about the evils associated with racial classification, there has been little systematic study of this process (cf. Guillaumin, 1972, for a pioneering contribution). This chapter suggests that the first applications of the concept of race to European affairs have to be related to contemporary political struggles. The political utility of racial classification to late nineteenth-century colonialism is so obvious that it leads some students to overlook the extent to which the course of racialization was influenced by the inspirations and mistakes of intellectuals trying to make sense of the new and bewildering information that was coming to hand. Nor have there yet been many systematic comparisons of the ways in which racial classifications were utilized in the government of different regions, of the transformations that the original conceptions of race have undergone, and the ways in which they have been related to recent developments now that the world seems to have entered a period of de-racialization in which many politicians and educators seek to correct the mistakes of the past.

The present-day concerns suggest that it is of some importance to ascertain what kind of change occurred in the use of the word race in the course of the nineteenth century. A good way of tracing this in English usage, which also shows how the changes are related to the self-conceptions of Europeans, is to look at contemporary historical writing. In his 1754 *History of England* David Hume uses 'race' in the sense of a line of descent, but he calls the Germans a nation, the Saxons a tribe of the German people, and the Normans a people also. He has no obvious criteria for classifying social units. Neither has Sharon Turner, who published the first volume of his *History of the Anglo-Saxons* in 1799. He says that Europe has been peopled from the East by three great streams of population: the Kimmerian and Keltic race; the Scythian, Gothic, and German tribes; the Slavonian and Sarmantian nations. He derides the 'fanciful but unscientific opinion that there have been several aboriginal races' and the idea of 'seventeen primaeval races' advanced 'by some Parisian dreamers'. The chief interest in Turner's volumes, which ran to their fifth edition in 1828, is the testimony to the 'patriotic curiosity of readers' and to a theme that was to be heard with growing insistence in nineteenth-century historiography. The author marvels how, from so inauspicious a beginning 'a nation has, in the course of twelve centuries, been formed, which, inferior to none in every moral and intellectual merit, is superior to every other in the love and possession of useful liberty' (1828, vol. 3: 1). Nineteenth-century Englishmen continually celebrated their liberty and thanked providence for giving them political institutions so much better than those of other countries. They looked to their history to discover where that liberty and where those institutions had come form. They found their answers in the Anglo-Saxon heritage.

Christopher Hill declares that by the nineteenth century the myth of a Norman Yoke was no longer used by political radicals. When it was no longer dangerous to the state, this theme was taken up by new story tellers and a new audience. 'Only when Saxon freedom had ceased to be a rallying cry for the discontented masses did it begin to be enthusiastically taught in the lecture rooms of Oxford' (1958: 118). This generalization cannot be sustained (Briggs, 1966: 6–8) but the central notion became a vehicle for the new ancestral myth that the chief English virtues derived from their Anglo-Saxon forebears. Sir Walter Scott got this idea from a play about Runnymede and made it the theme of one of the best-selling novels of the century, *Ivanhoe; a romance*, published in 1820. Scott's story is set in England while Richard the Lionheart is away on a Crusade to Palestine and the country is being ruled by his brother John (about 1194). The theme is that of the ill-feeling between the resentful Saxon peasantry and their cruel oppressive Norman rulers, summed up in an old 'proverb' quoted by one of the characters:

> Norman saw on English oak,
> On English neck a Norman yoke;
> Norman spoon in English dish,
> And England ruled as Normans wish;
> Blythe world to England never will be more,
> Till England's rid of all the four.

One of the heroes of the English resistence is Robin Hood, and there is a subsidiary plot centering upon a Jewish money-lender and his beautiful daughter. But a striking feature of the novel is that Scott presents the opposition between Saxon and Norman as a struggle between two races. By my count he uses the word 'race' fifty-seven times. On two occasions he uses it in the loose way of earlier literary men to refer to 'a race of clowns or jesters' and to the younger generation as 'the younger race'. On twenty-six occasions he employs it to refer to Normans, Saxons, or occasionally, other comparable peoples; on eighteen occasions to refer to the Jews, frequently as an accursed or despised race (indeed the way he depicts Isaac is far from sympathetic); while in a further eight instances he makes it denote a lineage as in 'the race of the immortal Alfred' or 'the race of Hengist'. Sometimes races are represented as possessing particular attributes: the Saxons have a special skill in interpreting physiognomy; Normans are 'not an intemperate race at the table' and 'being a mixed race . . . had lost most of the superstitious prejudices'. Finally, when considering the effect that Scott had upon his readers, it should be noted that he has his characters speak as if they thought of themselves and others as members of racially as well as culturally distinctive groups so that they talk of 'my race' and 'thy race'.

Scott's historical romances were an inspiration to Edward Bulwer-Lytton, a prolific novelist and Tory politician. In 1843 Lytton published *The Last of the Barons*, a story based on the events of the 1460s and 1470s when there was an uneasy relationship between the powerful Earl of Warwick and the young Edward IV which resulted in the former's rebellion and his death on the battlefield. It is a three-cornered struggle between 'the King, his Norman gentlemen and his Saxon people' with the people further divided into the agricultural populace and the trading towns. There is an explicit reference to the myth of the Norman Yoke when Warwick is made to say:

'Ye know well that ever in England, but especially since the reign of Edward III, strange, wild notions of some kind of liberty other than that we enjoy, have floated loose through the land. Among the commons, a half-conscious recollection that the nobles are a different race from themselves feeds a secret rancour and mislike, which, at any fair occasion for riot, shows itself bitter and ruthless — as in the outbreak of Cade and others.'

Lytton uses 'race' eight times to designate either the Normans or the Saxons, and as many times again in the sense of lineage. Twice he uses it to refer to the young generation, once to the effect that the queen's kin had introduced a literary race into royal favour and once to say that Warwick's proud retainers appeared 'as if they belonged to another caste, another race, than the herd of men'. The opposition between Norman and Saxon is not presented in so clearly racial terms as in *Ivanhoe*, but Lytton can write of the 'still half Norman race, of which Nicholas Alwyn and his Saxon class were the rival antagonistic principle' and some of his characters are very conscious of belonging with one or the other.

The ideological content of the novel is striking. Lytton represents the trading towns as sympathetic towards the king and antagonistic towards the aristocracy. 'The recent revolution was one in which the towns *had had no share*. . . . Classes in all times have a keen instinct of their own class interests. The revolution which the earl had effected was the triumph of aristocracy.' Warwick saw the king as the first of the nobles, believing that they together depended on the support of the agricultural population. What happened, says Lytton, was that the king separated himself from the nobility and developed a despotic rule based on an alliance with the merchant class. 'The true spirit of the age fought for the false Edward, and against the honest Earl.'

Five years later Lytton published a historical romance entitled *Harold: the Last of the Saxon Kings* which treats events up to the Norman Conquest. He uses 'race' fifty-two times, on thirty-two occasions to refer to ethnic groups, mostly Saxons, Danes, and Normans, but also 'the mixed races of Hertfordshire and Essex' and on one occasion 'pirate races'. Sixteen times it refers to lineage and four times when designating shared attributes: Normans are poets by race, Saxons a clean race, and an anti-Norman chief came from Kent 'where all the prejudices of his race were strongest'. 'Race' is mostly used to refer to divisions within the English population. Normans are divided by class, for their settlement in Normandy was so recent that there was none of that 'amalgamation between class and class which centuries had created in England'. Once again the characters are conscious of their racial identities and a Norman can say to a Dane 'We Normans are of your own race'.

Lytton's *Harold* was a model for Charles Kingsley's *Hereward, last of the English* published in 1866 and repeating Lytton's two representations of the hero as the last of his kind. Kingsley uses 'race' on eleven occasions. At the beginning of the story we are told that 'the Anglo-Saxon race was wearing out'; at the end the English are dejected to see 'their race enslaved'. Sometimes the word still has the sense of lineage though a new note may perhaps be discerned in expressions such as that of an 'appeal to the antipathies of race'. In later writing Kingsley denied the myth of the Norman Yoke, asserting that the conquerors were the civilizing branch of the Norse race. Yet in describing the use of historical themes in literary romanticism I am running ahead of developments in more serious historical work.

Scott's *Ivanhoe* influenced an imaginative French historian, Augustin Thierry who, discontented with French political life, looked favourably upon English institutions and wondered where they had sprung from (it was he whom Marx called 'the father of the "class struggle" in French historical writing'). Thierry concluded that English institutions were the fruit of a conquest, and wrote in 1825 a *History of the Conquest of England by the Normans* which sympathized with the conquered people and stressed the agonies they had to suffer. This book was later republished in the popular Everyman's Library. Thierry opens it by expressing the hope that these novel researches may contribute to throw light upon a question which is not without importance in moral science — 'that concerning the different varieties of the human species in Europe, and the great primitive races from which those varieties have sprung'. He makes continuous use of the word race in interpreting the relations between groups. 'I considered what I was doing was really conducive to the progress of knowledge, in construing (if I may use the expression) the history of the Welsh, of the old Irish, of the Scotch, whether of the old or the mixed race, of the Britons and Normans of the continent . . .' Thierry does not say that this history is determined by the biological qualities of the races, but his manner of writing is compatible with such an interpretation. It is not far-fetched to see Thierry's book as an academic under-pinning and expansion of Scott's *Ivanhoe*.

Another step in the growth in 'patriotic curiosity' in national origins is marked by John Mitchell Kemble's *The Saxons in England* of 1849 which has the interesting sub-title 'a history of the English Commonwealth till the period of the Norman Conquest'. Mitchell is capable of racial hyperbole, as when he writes 'Then first, dimly through the twilight in which the sun of Rome was to set for ever, loomed the Colossus of the German race, gigantic, terrible, inexplicable; and the vague attempt to define its awful features came too late to be fully successful'. That attempt was mainly Tacitus'; his short chapters were still examined with the greatest care by historians of early Europe. Kemble continued, 'Let us confine our attention to that portion of the race which settled on our own shores. His volume was presented as a 'history of the principles which have given her empire its preeminence among the nations of Europe', but what were these principles? Kemble's chapters bear titles like 'The Mark', 'The Gá or Scír', 'Landed Possession. The Eðel, Hid or Alod', 'The Mutual Guarantee. Maegburh, Tithing. Hundred', 'Fæhðe Wergyld', 'Folcland, Bócland. Láenland. For Kemble these constituted a grave and solemn subject 'the history of the childhood of our age — the explanation of its manhood'. But the explanation is not there. The connection between such recondite matters and Victoria's success is not established. Any reader other than the specialist must have had a high tolerance of tedium and most must have taken the connection on trust.

In 1848 appeared the first edition of Thomas Macaulay's *The History of England to the Accession of James II* which treats the Conquest in terms similar to Scott's. The battle of Hastings gave up the whole population of England to the tyranny of the Norman race, the foremost race of Christendom. The subject race were trodden under foot so that during the next century and a half 'there is, to speak strictly, no English history'. England was ruled by French kings until the Normans discovered that they had to choose between making a home in Normandy and in England. The first pledge of reconciliation was Magna Carta. Then common interests grew. 'In no country' says Macaulay, 'has the enmity of race been carried farther than in England. In no country has that enmity been more completely effaced.' He writes of an amalgamation of races, suggesting a biological process though he himself may not have so conceived it, for he explains 'Moral causes noiselessly effaced, first the distinction between Norman and Saxon, and then the distinction between master and slave' with the result that 'our fore-fathers were the best governed people in Europe'. The first volume, in which this theme is proclaimed, had sold 133,653 copies by 1875 (Altick, 1957: 388).

Kemble and Macaulay were employing racial categories in writing the history of England, but some years earlier, in 1841, Thomas Arnold, the headmaster of Rugby, had used them on a much grander scale in his inaugural lecture as professor of modern history at Oxford. For Arnold 'the great elements of nationality' were 'race, language, institutions and religion'. The first of these could be crucial, for

> 'if we consider the Roman empire in the fourth century of the Christian era, we shall find in it Christianity, we shall find in it all the intellectual treasures of Greece, all the social and political wisdom of Rome. What was not there, was simply the German race, and the peculiar qualities which characterize it. This one addition was of such power, that it changed the character of the whole mass.' (Arnold, 1842: 26–27).

We, this great English nation, he intoned, whose race and language are now over-running the earth, are of Teutonic or German stock, for 'though our Norman fathers had learned to speak a stranger's tongue, yet in blood, as we know, they were Saxons'. Europe was the third great civilization, but was it also the last? 'Now looking anxiously round the world for any new races which may receive the seed (so to speak) of our present history into a kindly yet vigorous soil, and may reproduce it, the same and yet new, for a future period, we know not where such are to be found'. If there was no successor race and we were in the latest period then the study of modern history must be especially significant (cf. Faverty, 1951; Forbes, 1952: 68; and for a corrective to simple interpretations, Barksdale, 1957).

It looks as if by 1850 a significant section of the English upper classes subscribed to a rudimentary racial philosophy of history. Benjamin Disraeli is a special case because he wished to claim superiority on these very grounds. The English aristocracy, he remarked, is 'sprung from a horde of Baltic pirates who were never heard of during the greater annals of the world'. The Jewish genealogy was far longer. This is one of the components of his trilogy, *Conningsby*, *Sibyl*, and *Tancred*. In the last of these, published in 1847, a leading character explains that the historical success of England is 'an affair of race. A Saxon race, protected by an insular position, has stamped its diligent and methodic character on the century. And when a superior race, with a superior idea to Work and Order, advances, its state will be progressive, and we shall, perhaps, follow the example of the desolate countries. All is race; there is no other truth.' Five years later Disraeli repeated 'In the structure, the decay, and the development of the various families of man, the vicissitudes of history find their main solution. All is race.'

Some periodical publications took up the theme, and the idea of race entered upon a new phase of its career, but something still was missing. Evolutionary ideas were commonplace prior to 1859 when Darwin explained how evolutionary processes could actually operate. Racial philosophies were widespread, but they lacked a satisfying explanation of what made one race superior to another. In this connection it is important to notice what some of the contemporary writers fail to say. Thomas Arnold, despite his emphasis upon the historical significance of race seems to have inclined to the belief that the superiority of particular races was accidental and temporary (1842: 156–57). Consider, too, the case of Bulwer-Lytton who was later ennobled and served as Secretary of State for the Colonies. Like so many others he harked back to Tacitus when he told the House of Commons 'It was in the free forests of Germany that the infant genius of our liberty was nursed. It was from the free altars of Germany that our Constitutional Monarchs came' (quoted Curtis, 1968: 11). In 1854 he told the Leeds Mechanics Institute that 'out of all Europe there are only three great races which are in the full vigour of progressive life — the great Germanic race, the people of France, and the people of Great Britain'. The nearest he comes to an explanation is when later he suggests 'the difference between one race and another appears to be according to the mental organization by which any given race can receive ideas from a more civilized race by which it is subdued, or with which it is brought into contact . . . England never seems to have been inhabited by any race which did not accept ideas of improved civilization' (Lytton, 1874 vol i: 175, vol ii: 196).

On other occasions Lytton argued that mountain life made races robust and vigorous. They then swept down and conquered the plainsmen. Presumably they later yielded place to new hordes from the mountains. But he seemed to leave a place for moral causes. In Canada men from different countries but kindred race came together, taking the stamp and colour of the land in which they settled: 'no matter where men come from, place them in ground covered by the British flag, overshadowed, though at a distance, by the mild British sceptre, and they will soon be British in sentiment and feeling'. Members of Parliament had a common interest 'to fulfil the mission of the Anglo-Saxon race, in spreading intelligence, freedom, and Christian faith wherever Providence gives us the dominion of the soil' (1874 vol i: 92–7; vol ii: 92, 96).

In this light it becomes possible to accept the otherwise startling statement of Luke Owen Pike in his book *The English and their Origin* of 1866 that

'There are probably few educated Englishmen living who have not in their infancy been taught that the English nation is a nation of almost pure Teutonic blood, that its political constitution, its social custom, its internal prosperity, the success of its arms, and the number of its colonies have all followed necessarily upon the arrival, in three vessels, of certain German warriors under the command of Hengist and Horsa . . . when Germany is in distress, we are invariably reminded that Germans are our kinsmen.' (1866: 15–16)

In the latter part of the century the strengthening of this pedigree became the basis for an historical industry in which Seeley, Freeman, Stubbs, and J. R. Green led the field. Freeman had read Lytton's *Harold* and his enthusiasm caused him to announce that he would gladly have fought against William at Hastings. Douglas observes that Freeman treated the eleventh century struggle almost as a matter of present day politics; but this is a later age and a different chapter of the story.

3

The racializing of
the world

The previous chapter has discussed some of the factors in the history of
Europe that encouraged people to think of themselves as belonging to
races and paved the way for the elaboration of a form of classification
which assigned all the peoples of the world to racial categories. In the
eighteenth century the word 'race' was used primarily to identify the
common descent of a set of people; their distinctive characteristics
were taken for granted and the category 'race' was used to explain how
they came by them. In the nineteenth century, 'race' came to be a means
of classifying people by these characteristics, as can be seen in the quotation from Abraham Lincoln at the beginning of Chapter One. As that
quotation also suggests, racial categorizations could then be used without commitment to any theory about the origins of such distinctions.
Behind Lincoln's remarks can be seen the doctrine that mankind was
divided into a series of distinct and permanent racial types, or, to put it
another way, that blacks and whites were different species. This chapter discusses the growing significance of racial categorizations in the
nineteenth century up to the time when Darwin's work brought about a
re-orientation. A great many writers in France, Germany, Britain, and
the United States, theologians, anatomists, physiologists, ethnologists,
poets, and travellers contributed to the vigorous and confused debate
about race and the historical examination of it is still far from complete.
Because 'race' meant different things to different writers, and was the
source of much of the confusion, it is more helpful to use the concept of
'type' as a clue that leads through the maze. In the sense that is relevant

here, the concept of type originates with Cuvier in the early years of the nineteenth century. It comes into English through one of the major figures in the study of race, James Cowles Prichard, and quickly spreads, especially in the United States where it is built into the new doctrine systematized in Nott and Gliddon's book *Types of Mankind*, published in 1854. Whether Gobineau should be seen as an expositor of this doctrine is less straightforward. In his *Essai sur l'Inégalité des Races humaines* he made some use of the doctrine of type, and in many books his essay on the inequality of races is interpreted from this standpoint; but his essay has also been interpreted as extending the romantic conception of the complementarity of races and as a personal manifesto which developed a concept of race in the course of expounding a pessimistic political philosophy.

The notion of type was a convenient one because it was not tied to any particular classificatory level in zoology, so that it was easy to refer to the physical types characteristic of particular nations, to 'types of cranial conformation', or to say that a skull 'approximates to the Negro type' without having to establish just what that type was. This was appreciated at the time, for W. F. Edwards in his important essay of 1829 observed

> 'In identifying a combination of well defined characters as a type — a word which has the same sense in ordinary speech and in natural history — I avoid all discussion about the rank which a group so characterized will occupy in a general classification, since it suits equally well the distinctions between variety, race, family, species, genus, and other categories yet more general.' (1829: 125)

As the evidence about the diversity of human forms accumulated, more and more writers tended to refer to various kinds of type, and, indeed, the construction of typologies of various kinds became a characteristic of nineteenth-century scholarship. The conception of racial types is more central to the debate about race than is the attempt to classify the peoples of varying regions. It contrasts sharply with the conceptual apparatus that Darwin made necessary, and it remains at the core of a now discredited ideology of racial determinism which looks like retaining some political significance for the remainder of the twentieth century.

At the beginning of the controversy the word 'race' does not appear at all. In the eighteenth century there had been a strong tendency to rank all the things in the world — mineral objects, vegetables, and animals from the lowest to the highest — as constituting a 'great chain of being'. It was argued that each form shaded imperceptibly into the next one so that it was arbitrary and misleading to separate them into distinctive categories. The Swedish botanist Linnaeus, however, produced a classification which won very general acceptance. Plants and birds were identified first as members of classes, then orders, then genera, and finally species (though there might be varieties within species). Linnaeus introduced the practice of naming species by two words of which the first is the name of the genus. Each genus and each species has only one correct name. Many scientists of his day thought that a more systematic understanding of God's creation took them one step nearer to the Creator. Knowledge was growing rapidly and there was a desire for synthesis that reached its height in the middle of the nineteenth century. Medical studies of the anatomy and physiology of Europeans were becoming more systematic. Better reports were coming in about the physical character and the culture of men in distant parts of the world, and scientists were beginning to make sense of the previously confusing evidence about the higher apes and the reputedly lower varieties of *Homo sapiens*.

If there was a finite number of species on the earth then it was not difficult to believe that God had made each one for a particular purpose. In that event, why had he created so many different kinds of men? Was mankind one genus divided into species or one species divided into varieties? Linnaeus had included man in his scheme in only a tentative fashion. How his line of enquiry could best be continued was problematic, for the Bible clearly represented all humanity as descendants of Adam and Eve and therefore as being of common stock. Biblical chronologies suggested that the earth was about six thousand years old, yet geologists were uncovering evidence that pointed to a much longer history. They were also discovering fossil remains of creatures that had become extinct. Increasing scepticism was being expressed about the value of the Old Testament as evidence concerning the earth's history, so that orthodox Christians felt under an obligation to explain how, if mankind had a common origin, the different branches of humanity could have diverged so greatly. Inevitably, they suspected that differences of climate and habitat must have led to changes, but they could not satisfactorily explain how the changes had come about or whether their general direction was one of progress or decline.

If there is one man whose work reflects the attempt to organize new knowledge about human diversity within a framework compatible with Old Testament conceptions it is James Cowles Prichard (1786–1848) the Bristol physician who in his day was considered the world's leading authority on race. His M.D. dissertation *De Generis Humani Varietate* was the seed bed from which rose two works, a *Physical History of Mankind* and a *Natural History* each of which grew over the years until in their fourth editions the one ran to five volumes and the other to two. In his first work Prichard is concerned both to defend the Mosaic account by criticizing suggestions that human diversities have been constant from the very beginning, and to argue that there is no good evidence to indicate that acquired characters can be transmitted by heredity to the next generation. Both these arguments return again and again in his later books. First comes the question whether the races of mankind 'constitute separate species or are merely varieties of one species'. Species are to be identified by 'peculiarities of structure which have always been constant and undeviating'. He uses race to refer to physically distinctive nations but is equally content to write of 'the tribes of men' (cf. 1826: 90). Faithful to the traditional interpretation of *Genesis* Prichard believed that the Creation occurred some six thousand years earlier; his problem was to explain the appearance of racial differences within this period by some hypothesis other than that of the inheritance of acquired characteristics, and, in the current state of knowledge he could not do this. Always he was led back to antecedents, as when he wrote 'in some instances . . . the forms of several animals seem to be so modelled on a particular type, that they have all been imagined to have arisen from the same race' (1826: 91), or when he explained how the word race ought to be used:

> 'races are properly successions of individuals propagated from any given stock; and the term should be used without any involved meaning that such a progeny or stock has always possessed a particular character. The real import of the term has often been overlooked, and the word race has been used as if it implied a distinction in the physical character of a whole series of individuals. By writers on anthropology, who adopt this term, it is often tacitly assumed that such distinctions were primordial, and that their successive transmission has been unbroken. If such were the fact, a race so characterised would be a species in the strict meaning of the word, and it ought to be so termed.' (1836: 109)

While rejecting the claim that acquired characters could be inherited, Prichard was conscious that children did not resemble their parents in any predictable manner; he contended that the more accurate our researches into the ethnography of the world became, the less ground could be found for the opinion that the characteristics of human races were permanent. So he enquired 'has man received from his Maker a principle of accommodation by which he becomes fitted to possess and occupy the whole earth? He modifies the agencies of the elements upon himself; but do not these agencies also modify him? Have they not rendered him in his very organization different in different regions . . .? (1843: 3–4). At one time Prichard came quite close to what we now know to be the answer. He remarked that whole colonies of individuals may perish when moved to climates for which they are not adapted. Horses and cattle when transported to Paraguay and allowed to run wild underwent an alteration, but domesticated breeds did not. Perhaps, he said, there was an analogy with the races of man, and that once varieties were newly established in a stock they might continue there long after the race had been removed from the climate in which they originated (1826: 581–83).

From his anatomical studies Prichard concluded, tentatively, that there were three types of skull: prognathous, pyramidal, and oval. Every type showed deviations and shaded into the others by insensible gradations. All three types of cranium were found amongst Negroes and the types seemed to be associated with degrees of civilization rather than geographical populations. Each species, said Prichard, had a psychological character, but the type was preserved in the individual varieties, so he studied the psychological make up of human races and concluded that this supported the evidence of external characters, and that mankind constituted a single species (cf. Stocking, 1973).

The industry with which Prichard assembled evidence from so many sources, and the sobriety of his judgements, gave his books a special authority, but much turned on the definition of species, which was problematic. Usage varied. In 1826 Desmoulins, a Paris anatomist, was putting forward a classification of man into sixteen species; certain of these were divided into races, which made race a sub-specific category. More than two decades later a cautious English ethnologist was writing 'a race is a class of individuals concerning which there are doubts as to whether they constitute a separate species or a variety of a recognized one. Hence the term is *subjective* . . . The present writer . . . has either not used the word race at all, or used it inadvertently' (Latham, 1850: 29).

The course of the nineteenth-century debate about race was affected by the assumptions different writers felt able to make about the age of the earth. If man had become so differentiated in the course of some six thousand years, as Prichard believed, his physical structure could not be a stable determinant of his culture or way of life. His culture might well determine his physique. Writers who felt free to assume that the earth was much older, were ready to argue that physical structure determined the cultures of peoples. This decisive shift was made most clearly by Cuvier, who, together with a man of very different temper named De-gérando (Moore, 1969) was involved in the preparations for a French scientific expedition to Australasia in 1799 (Stocking, 1968: 13–41). Cuvier's career prospered, and under Napoleon he became one of the dominant figures in French science.

Cuvier was a Protestant who accepted the Biblical story of man's common descent but did not believe that *Genesis* provided a complete chronology. He took up the questions of Creation and classification in a more open-minded manner than his predecessors, believing that a scientist should concentrate on problems where sufficient evidence was available or could be accumulated, and should not concern himself with those that were for the time being beyond reach. Within zoology Cuvier continued Linnaeus' work by compiling a magisterial study of the animal kingdom. He distinguished four principal branches within this kingdom, the vertebrates, molluscs, articulates, and zoophytes, which were further divided into genera and subgenera. Cuvier put great reliance on the concept of biological type, believing that if that had been grasped the essentials of the category could be understood. He emphasized the importance of type in opposition to those who considered that the various forms shaded imperceptibly into one another. Genera and species were both discrete, morphologically stable units, and therefore examples of types. In his extensive study of fishes each volume deals with one genus and the first chapter is devoted to a description of its type. Cuvier is probably better known, however, for his geological theory that there had been a series of natural catastrophies (such as floods) which had killed off large numbers of species and divided natural history into some eight separate epochs. His most recent biographer has concluded that he did not believe, as was often very understandably thought, that each epoch began with a new creation, but that some individuals survived, while migration and the mutual exchange of species between territories accounted for subsequent diversity. In this way he could accept that all men were descended from Adam, suggesting at the same time that the three major races escaped in different directions after the last catastrophe, some five thousand years before, and had developed in isolation (for a contemporary critical review from a monogenist standpoint, see de Salles, 1849). A variant of this theory, sometimes associated with Cuvier (e.g. Prichard 1843: 133) regarded the three major races as stemming from particular mountain slopes: whites from the region of

Mount Caucasus, yellows from the neighbourhood of Mount Altai, and blacks from the southern face of the chain of Mount Atlas.

For Cuvier *Homo sapiens* was a division of the vertebrates and was split into three subspecies: Caucasian, Mongolian, and Ethopian. Each of these three was further subdivided on geographical, linguistic, and physical grounds. Malays, Eskimos, and American Indians remained outside these subdivisions, but, being inter-fertile, all mankind was one species. Two features of Cuvier's conception of human races deserve attention. The first was his representation of them as forming a hierarchy with whites at the top and blacks at the bottom. The second was his contention that differences in culture and mental quality were produced by differences in physique. 'It is not for nothing', he wrote, 'that the Caucasian race has gained dominion over the world and made the most rapid progress in the sciences'. The Chinese were less advanced. They had skulls shaped more like those of animals. The Negroes were 'sunken in slavery and the pleasures of the senses' yet they 'were rational and sensitive creatures', while 'slavery was degrading for both slave and master and must be abolished' (Coleman, 1964: 166).

To argue that man was an animal was scarcely daring. The key question was whether he was just an animal. Man could create his own world, could build a civilization, and study himself. Could this be explained by the same principles as those which accounted for his physical being? Cuvier's affirmative answer to this question is one of the biggest steps leading to the doctrine of racial types. It can also be seen as a criterion for distinguishing between two paradigms in the study of man: the anthropological approach which sought to explain both physique and culture in a unified theory that found the causes of differentiation in biological laws; and the ethnological approach which drew a sharp distinction between man's physical nature and his culture, believing that the latter demanded explanations of a different kind (cf. Stocking, 1973: c). This was not the way in which most nineteenth century writers saw the distinction. Latham, for example, saw anthropology as studying the relations of man to other mammals; ethnology as studying the relations of the different varieties of mankind to each other; both were concerned with physical influences and the study of moral causes was the province of history (1850: 559). Others drew the dividing line in different places still, but it became ever clearer that the key question was the relation of physical to cultural explanation and it is convenient to label the two kinds of answer to it 'anthropological' and 'ethnological'.

A straightforward endorsement of the anthropological paradigm

The Idea of Race

was liable to attract the hostility of those who considered it contrary to revealed religion and subversive of morality. Those who favoured it therefore had reasons other than those of ordinary scientific prudence for avoiding any confrontation and testifying that from a zoological standpoint it was an open question whether man was a single species or had 'sprung successively or simultaneously from a genus having no less than three distinct species'. The quotation is from Charles Hamilton Smith (1776–1859) a disciple and friend of Cuvier who saw military service with British troops in West Africa, the West Indies, and 'on both portions of the American continent' between 1797 and 1807, later translating the works of the master while on manoevres. In 1848 he published *The Natural History of the Human Species* which built on Cuvier's foundations a speculative superstructure about man's origin in three aboriginal normal types springing from a common centre near the Gobi desert 'for this was, approximately, either the seat of man's first development . . . or the space where a portion of human beings found safety, when convulsions and changes of surface, which may have swept away a more ancient zoology, had passed over the earth and were introductory to a new order of things' (1848: 169). He even brought into this scheme ideas about the history of the Goths which derived from sixth century writer Jordanes. The diagram summarizing his theory is reproduced below.

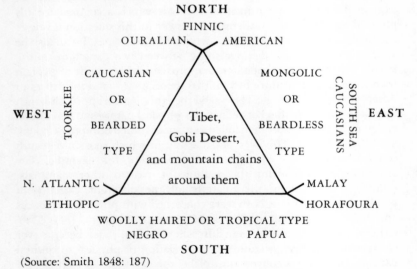

(Source: Smith 1848: 187)

Diagram 1 Charles Hamilton Smith's view of the primaeval location of mankind and the three typical stocks

Smith maintained that zoology limited the possibilities of colonization. A race could have only provisional tenure of a region until the in-
destructible typical form appeared to take over the territory assigned to
it by nature. Conquest entailed extermination unless it was one of the
great typical stocks effecting an incorporation of its own affiliates. Mu-
latto strains were eventually infertile. For Smith the three types were
the woolly-haired or Negro; beardless or Mongolian; and bearded or
Caucasian. The Negro's lowly place in the human order was a consequence of the small volume of his brain (the author had noticed how
even the smallest British army caps issued to black troops in the West
Indies proved too big and required padding an inch and a half in thick-
ness to make them fit; he also stated that white infants who had been
fed on the milk of Negro wet nurses subsequently suffered in appearance and temperament). The Mongolians, 'no doubt with some aid
from the Caucasian elements' had achieved a homogenous civilization.
The Caucasians were Nature's highest achievement. Moreover, Smith
drew upon the work of A.E.R.A. Serres (1786–1868) a French anatomist sometimes quoted as an authority for the permanence of types.
Serres was one of the expositors of the recapitulation theory ('ontog-
eny recapitulates phylogeny') according to which every human as it
developed in the embryo had to repeat the development of a fish, a rep-
tile, a bird, and a mammal before it emerged as a human. M. Serres's discoveries, wrote Smith, showed the conditions of cerebral progress to be
more complete at birth in the Caucasian type: 'the human brain successively assumes the form of the Negroes, the Malays, the Americans,
and the Mongolians, before it attains the Caucasian. One of the earliest
points where ossification commences is the lower jaw. This bone is
therefore sooner completed than any other of the head, and acquires a
predominance which it never loses in the Negro' (1848: 125–27).
Here, then, in lectures originally given to the Plymouth Institution between 1832 and 1837, was most of the theory that occasioned the controversies of the 1850s. It did not touch on racial antagonism and was
couched in less combative terms than the later works, which may help
explain why it seems to have been forgotten more quickly.

It would seem that Cuvier's work had less influence upon the development of racial theories in Germany because of the special link in that
country between the development of what might now be called the 'life
sciences' and the literary movement known as romanticism. This
movement contained many different strands; it can best be identified as
a series of changes in subject matter and approach characterizing much
of literature and the arts between 1760 and 1870. The teachings of Jean-
Jacques Rousseau mark its beginnings, and in this early phase romanti-

cism is reflected in such images as that of the 'noble savage' — which implied that man was naturally good and that evil was caused by faulty social organization. Romanticism has to be seen as a reaction against neo-Classicism, against the assumption that the finest elements in West European culture were to be traced to the Roman heritage, and against the rationalistic orientation of the Enlightenment. Therefore it was associated in some writers with a tendency to look for inspiration to Nordic rather than Latin culture and to recall the barbarian liberties praised by Tacitus. Dissatisfied with the limited nature of cause-and-effect interpretations of the universe, romantics put more reliance on human imagination and interpreted the world through a vision of mysterious forces which they called divine. Instead, like Cuvier, of asking only the questions to which they could obtain certain answers, they tried to explore the relations between the phenomena of Spirit and those of Nature in ways that would lead to the truths of poetry rather than of science. In Germany Goethe combined his literary work with serious scientific enquiries and romanticism had a significant influence upon some of the early nineteenth century theorizing about man's nature.

The significance of romanticism in early German racial theories is well brought out in a study by Hermann Blome which, being published in Munich in 1943, might have been expected to give as much weight as possible to the biological elements. Blome fills in the intellectual genealogy which, after Kant and Blumenbach, passes through a variety of writers, including Schelling, Steffens, to such theories as those of Lorenz Oken and Wolfgang Menzel. Oken asked why there were no blue and green races. He thought colour an unsatisfactory basis for ordering differences and advanced a five-fold classification of races based on the human senses: eye men, nose men, ear men, etc. Menzel described the sun, moon and stars as symbolic realms to which the divisions of mankind must correspond. This approach resembles the attempt of Greek philosophers to explain the world in terms of the elements of fire, earth, air, and water, rather than the empirical method of science. The high point of romantic thought about race, Blome says, is represented in the work of Carl Gustav Carus who advanced a philosophy of man which comprehended both his physical and spiritual dimension and detected an underlying symmetry in the relations of races (cf. Poliakov, 1974: 239–42).

Carl Gustav Carus (1789–1869) was a man of talents almost as varied as Goethe's. A physician to the royal family, privy counsellor, professor at Dresden, friend of Goethe, art critic and landscape painter, he also published important works on medical topics, on psychology, on the symbolism of the human form and an account of his travels in England and Scotland. In nine of the books he published between 1835 and 1861 Carus has something to say about race but it occupies a relatively small place in the mass of his writing and he is rarely remembered for his racial theory. Carus was impressed by the influence of great men on the course of history and wondered whether their prominence revealed anything about more general differences in human capacity. This explains why his one-hundred-page essay 'On the Unequal Capacity of the Different Divisions of Mankind for Higher Spiritual Development' (his chief statement about race) was published as a memorial to Goethe on the centenary of his birth. Carus was acquainted with earlier racial classifications and the work of Klemm and J. C. Prichard, but he was dissatisfied with classifications based solely on external physical form. He thought he had found a better basis in the relation of the divisions of mankind to the earth as a planet, and in particular to the sun. This separated the earth's peoples into those of the day, of the eastern twilight, of the western twilight, and of the night. He refers to a recognized but not yet explained law that progress follows a path from east to west; the great human migrations have gone in this direction and so have epidemic diseases. But no argument is advanced as to how the sun could have had a differential effect upon humans: the terminology is metaphorical. Carus himself represents it on occasion as dealing with symbolic relationships and makes no attempt to deal with the obvious difficulties inherent in such a theory. He draws on Morton's measurements of cranial capacity but instead of maintaining that physique determines culture, he regards them both, physique and culture, as manifestations of the whole entity.

Carus writes 'The day peoples, who achieve a specially pure form in the region of the Caucasus, have spread out their type, sometimes in greater, sometimes in lesser perfection, over all Europe . . .' but this is the only time he uses the word 'type' and his theory does not depend on such a conception to the extent that Voegelin's exposition would suggest (Carus, 1849: 17; Voegelin 1933a: 155–57). The Eastern twilight peoples are the Mongolians, Malayans, Hindus, Turks, and Slavs; the Western twilight peoples are the American Indians; the night peoples are the Africans and Australians. Carus opens his discussion of the day peoples with a statement of the recapitulation theory, listing the most notable twelve: Caucasians, Persians, Armenians, Semites, Pelasgians, Etruscans, Thracians, Illyrians, Iberians, Romans, Celts, and Germans. Apparently the last named recapitulate in their embryonic development not only their eleven forebears but also certain peoples from the other three-quarters of humanity. From this, Carus says, emerges an important phenomenon, 'that the big movements in the history of peoples, if they stem from a special stock, always demonstrate the special energy of this stock . . . in the childhood of peoples the material force is dominant but in more developed circumstances the spiritual principle comes to the fore' (1849: 81–2). It is the duty of the day peoples to guide and help the less favoured ones. Though he is not explicit on this point, Carus implies that in the right circumstances a people can civilize itself and in this he provoked Gobineau's dissent.

The other great German racial theorist of this period also lived in Dresden. This was Gustav Klemm (1802–67) who spent most of his life in charge of the royal library in that town. In the years 1843–52 he produced a ten volume study, *Allegemeine Cultur-Geschichte der Menscheit*, synthesizing ethnographic accounts of the peoples of the world; in it he distinguished three stages of cultural evolution: savagery, domestication, and freedom. He divided mankind into active and passive races, stating that peoples differed in mentality and temperament. Much of the argument is summarized in an address of his on the fundamental ideas of a general science of culture (Klemm, 1851). Klemm's conception of culture history is of a philosophy of history of the kind envisaged by Herder and Kant; it emphasizes environmental and cultural influences upon human development and is opposed to the more idealistic orientation deriving from Fichte in which different aspects of culture are subordinated to political evolution (Voegelin, 1933b: 159). In politics Klemm was a liberal democrat who found the decline of the ancient regime congenial, while the rise of egalitarian democracy appeared to him as the crowning peak of history.

One problem is to decide whether Carus and Klemm were advancing a conception of races as permanent human types or were using the terminology of race in a metaphorical fashion. It has been asserted that Klemm, at least, was 'deeply involved in biologizing history' (Harris, 1968: 101–102), but this seems to be no more than prejudiced guesswork based on a secondary source. There are many passages in the original sources that favour the second interpretation but their intention is often obscure to the modern reader. Moreover, the two leading authorities, Erich Voegelin (the refugee from Nazi Germany) and Hermann Blome (who wrote in an intellectual milieu sympathetic to the typological conception of race) are not in complete agreement. Blome is adamant that Carus's conception of race has nothing whatsoever in common with those definitions that are rooted in biological categories; his four races are appearances of similarity which exist only as symbolical manifestations of planetary relations. Whereas Klemm's conception of race is free from romantic influences in its ethnological and culture-historical foundation, his theory of race bespeaks the romantic spirit and philosophy (1943: 221, 253). Blome writes:

'Just as Klemm thought it was from the "marriage of peoples" and from the penetration of the passive by the active peoples that humanity starts upon a general cultural development, so Carus saw the inequality of human races as Nature's summons to interaction, to give-and-take, whereby humanity as a total organism might be served. The tribe of day peoples was "entitled to regard itself as the true flowers of humanity", but for Carus that signified not only that this tribe was the bearer of civilization but also that, because of its superiority, power, resoluteness and perseverance, it had the "duty" to lead the weak and less favoured tribes by lighting their path and assisting them along it; in so doing it would prove true to itself" [quoting Carus 1849: 85]. To the question exactly how this task was given to the day peoples or active tribes, both Carus and Klemm give extensive answers. They see the whole of humanity as one great organism; its unequal parts, the races, have to stand in an inter-acting relationship of exchange and progress, so that under the leadership of the white race the "idea" of humanity can be realized.' (Blome, 1943: 254–55)

The pictures of Caucasian and Ethiopian skulls in Blumenbach's volumes were unsatisfying because the author could not say what their peculiarities meant. In the new romantic visions these pictures become alive. Men belong no longer to abstract categories, but to races whose distinctive physical and cultural characters are related to the basic principles of Creation.

Voegelin also emphasizes the way in which Carus's theory brought body and mind together. He believes that in Christian theology there must be a sharp distinction between these two realms and deplores the way in which biological differences can be used to divide the human community. Consequently he looks more anxiously at Carus's basic philosophy and pictures his synthesis as important to the later development of more ominous racial theories. Voegelin is unimpressed by Klemm's interpretations, describing his racial theory as 'a rather banal conglomeration of all the suggestions which an industrious research worker can receive from his generation' but he goes on to conclude that Klemm and Gobineau were at one in their major theses, namely: (i) all important cultures in history have as their basis a symbiosis of races;

(ii) there are distinct human types called by Gobineau the strong and the weak, by Klemm the active and the passive; (iii) the races migrate, or at least the active do; (iv) migration leads to the conquest of the weak by the strong; (v) as a result of conquest the races enter into a symbiosis which, by mixture or extermination, ends with the dissolution of the active conquering race as a distinct unit; (vi) when the active race dissolves, political tension disappears and an egalitarian society is established (an occasion for Klemm's satisfaction and Gobineau's despair).

This does not do full justice to the differences between the two writers. Klemm did not employ the concept of type; nor is it evident that he did regard racial characters as innate and permanent. He writes of humanity as divided into two kinds of races analogous to the division into two sexes and to the division of the atmosphere into oxygen and nitrogen, so the argument seems to lie on a metaphorical plane. Though he selects Caucasians as exemplifying the active races, and coloured peoples the passive races, and though he pays considerable attention to the expansion of the former, any conception of them as superior is left implicit. Explicitly he emphasizes the complementary nature of the two halves. Active races isolated from their passive partners (like the nomadic Mongols) are incomplete and cannot achieve true culture. On occasion he refers to the active and passive castes. 'First through the mixture of the two races, the active and the passive, I would like to say through the marriage of peoples, does humanity become complete; in this way it first springs to life and nourishes the blossoms of culture' (1843 i: 192–204; 1851: 169, 179).

The romantic world-view of a writer like Carus needs to be explored with the care of a social anthropologist trying to discover the conceptual structure of a strange culture. Its representation of race has more in common with the biblical story of the creation than with the approach of the modern scientist. Though Carus clearly formulates a theory of European superiority, it is within a conception of races as forming a symmetrical whole, and leads to conclusions about how people ought to behave rather than to interpretations of their actions as pre-determined. These considerations are also relevant to one assessment of Gobineau's *Essay*, and need to be examined because that work has often been presented as the poisoned well of all later racialist theorizing without proper weight being given to its antecedents in nineteenth century thought.

Before writing it Gobineau had read widely in German literature, so it should not be surprising to find in his work traces of a similar kind of romanticism. Working on a novel of the kind made popular by Scott's *Ivanhoe*, he had carefully studied the work of Thierry and some of the

French authors whose books were discussed in the previous chapter. Though he did not stand squarely in the line of debate about the two races of France, being anti-nationalist and pro-European, one strand of the Frankish, anti-Roman, genealogy can be traced through Montesquieu, Boulainvilliers and Montlosier to Gobineau. The novel, entitled *L'Abbaye de Typhaines*, dealt with a twelfth century revolt. Characteristically, Gobineau did not take sides between the peasants, bourgeoisie and clergy. He showed a concern for local liberties but implied that mere love of liberty was insufficient to ensure that people would be able to exercise it.

Gobineau's first significant use of 'race' to account for human nobility appears in an epic poem and in the *Essay* he makes relatively little reference to anthropological authorities for his assumptions. His arguments are less original than he claims; many of them were expounded by Victor Courtet de l'Isle (1813–1867), the Saint-Simonian author of *La Science politique fondée sur la science de l'homme* published in 1837. Courtet was elected Secretary of the Société ethnographique de Paris in 1846 and re-elected in 1848; the following year he published his *Tableau ethnographique* and, as many of his associates were well known to Gobineau, it seems certain that the latter borrowed heavily from him without acknowledgement (Boissel, 1972:83, 178–80). Courtet identified the Germans as a superior race which had formerly been spread over Europe 'like the oil of the nations'. Where Thierry had stressed the conflict of races, Courtet saw the mingling of blood as having 'chemical' consequences which he thought must ultimately be beneficial. Gobineau disparages Prichard ('a mediocre historian and even more mediocre theologian') but brings into prominence the table of cranial capacity in different races that Carus had dug out from one of Morton's footnotes. Though he has not had Klemm's book in his hands, Gobineau has heard of his distinction between active and passive races. When he claims that human activities have their origin in the 'male' and 'female' currents within humanity and that civilizations are born from the mixing of races, the resemblance is close, but Gobineau believes that if the two of them were travelling along the same paths it would not be surprising if they came upon the same truths.

In the chapter entitled 'Racial Differences are Permanent' the influence of Cuvier is very apparent. Gobineau observes, 'the reader will not fail to see that the question on which the argument here turns is that of the permanence of types'. He uses the concept of type in two senses. The first is one that relates to the declaration in his dedication of the book in which he says that he is constructing a moral geology that deals only in series of centuries, occupying himself rarely with individuals, but always with ethnic units. The geology spans four periods. The type of man first created was the Adamite but it must be left out of the argument since we can know nothing of its specific character. In his earliest stages, man might have assumed unstable forms and change would then have been easier, producing races which differed from their original ancestor as much as they differed from each other. In the second stage three races were present: white, black, and yellow, though 'it is probable that none of the three original types was ever found in absolute simplicity'. Inter-mixture is the origin, he says, of what we may call tertiary types, though 'our knowledge of the life of these tertiary races is very slight. Only in the misty beginnings of human history can we catch a glimpse, in certain places, of the white race when it was still in this stage — a stage which seems to have been everywhere short-lived . . . to the tertiary races succeed others, which I will call "quarternary" ' (1853: 155–57). A quarternary race could be further modified by the intervention of a new type. Gobineau wrote of the existing races as being descended from the secondary races, as if present-day populations might represent the second, third, fourth, or even a subsequent stage in the process.

The second use of type is that which became important in anthropological theorizing: the assumption that there was, or had been, a pure physical form behind the appearances of diversity. Gobineau never defines race and makes it clear that he regards all the contemporary groups to which that label is applied as having in varying degrees lost their true character through miscegenation. For example, he wrote 'As for the Persian race, it no longer exists in the scientific sense of the word, any more than does the French race, and of all the peoples of Europe we are surely that in which the type has been most obliterated. It is even this obliteration which we accept, in physique and in culture, as being our own type. It is the same with the Persians' (Buenzod, 1967: 558 n38).

The *Essay* begins with a statement that everything great, noble, and fruitful in the works of man on this earth springs from the Aryan family. It expounds his principles for explaining the rise and fall of civilizations and then shows their operation in a lengthy review of the ten most notable (for a summary, see Biddiss, 1970: 112–31). History begins after one of the cosmic catastrophes envisaged by Cuvier: the Aryans are living in small independent communities, unable to see as their equals those other creatures which, with their evil hostility, their hideous ugliness, brutal intelligence and their claim to be the offspring of monkeys, seem to be falling back into the ranks of animals (1853: 442).

From this base the Aryans spread out to create first the Hindu civilization, then the Egyptian, Assyrian, Greek, Chinese, Roman, German, Alleghenian, Mexican, and Peruvian civilizations. The author's preoccupation is with degeneration. He celebrates the vigour of the master race and asserts that 'the irreconcilable antagonism between different races and cultures is clearly established by history' (1853: 181); nevertheless, in order to avoid disappearing into the masses over whom it ruled, 'the white family needed to add to the power of its genius and courage a certain guarantee of numbers' (1853: 393) and consequently lost some of its potency unless reinforced by further migrations from other Aryan populations. The book's most quoted assertion is 'Such is the lesson of history. It shows us that all civilizations derive from the white race, that none can exist without its help, and that a society is great and brilliant only so far as it preserves the blood of the noble group that created it, provided that this group itself belongs to the most illustrious branch of our species' (1853: 209).

But there is a subsidiary theme which can be discerned in places and leads Janine Buenzod in her very full study of the *Essay* to assert that the assertion just quoted simplifies the author's view of the relationship between race and civilization to the point of misrepresenting it. The subsidiary theme deals with the contribution that other races can make to the creation of civilizations, the emergence of élites and the inability of the white race to progress in confined environments (like that of Newfoundland). To the 'moral geology' can be added another evocative expression (which also appears in the Dedication), that of 'historical chemistry'. Gobineau did not think of racial crossing in terms of blending inheritance, as if the progeny inherited equally from both parents. Rather, he regarded the superior race, especially the Aryan, as a catalytic agent, bringing out latent powers in others (as yeast makes bread rise), or, if it was too strong, destroying them (Buenzod, 1967: 328, 384 — but note that Gobineau was inconsistent in this, as in other, respects). The principles of this mixing were not understood, a conclusion which recalls the author's earlier remark that 'the science of social anatomy is in its infancy' (1853: 58).

The elements that go into the historical chemistry are no longer pure and all the races contain their own differences of quality. 'When it is a question of individual merit', Gobineau writes,

'I refuse completely to make use of that mode of argument which runs "every negro is stupid", and my chief objection is that, to complete the comparison, I would then be obliged to concede that every European is intelligent; and heaven preserve me from such a paradox . . . I have no doubt that many negro chiefs are superior, in the wealth of their ideas, the synthetic power of their minds, and the strength of their capacity for action, to the level usually reached by our peasants, or even by average specimens of our half-educated bourgeoisie . . . Let us leave these puerilities, and compare, not men, but groups.' (1853: 182)

It is from the comparison of groups that Gobineau concludes that the Aryans have overstretched themselves and that the chemistry has gone wrong. It is not difficult to accept the conclusion that 'the chief element in the *Essay* is the idea of the decadence of civilizations and not that of the inequality of races . . . The explanation in terms of race is a key; but the door which has to be opened — that of understanding history in its broadest dimensions — comes before the key'. It demands much more to assent to the same writer's statement 'the central idea, the truly fertile idea in the *Essay*, is that of the complementarity of races' (Buenzod, 1967: 328–29, 471). If there were evidence that Gobineau saw the chemistry as Carus saw the phases of day and night, as a whole, as part of a meaningful design for the universe, it would be easier to agree.

If Gobineau derived such ideas from Carus and other writers he gave them little emphasis. The principal passage comes towards the end of the first book when he writes about the advantages that have followed from the mixture of blood. 'Artistic genius, which is equally foreign to each of the three great types, arose only after the inter-marriage of white and black. Again, in the Malayan variety, a human family was produced from the yellow and black races that had more intelligence than either of its ancestors . . . to racial mixtures is due the refinement of manners and beliefs, and especially the tempering of passion and desire' (1853: 208). Elsewhere Gobineau maintains that for the worldwide movement of cultural fusion to stretch out it is not sufficient just that a civilizing milieu should deploy all its energy; it is necessary that in the different regions ethnic workshops should establish themselves to work on their own localities (1853: 867–68). How this fits with other parts of his vision is problematic. It is also difficult to be sure what he meant when in a discussion of Hindu caste he declared

'a light admixture from the black species develops intelligence in the white race, in that it turns it towards imagination, makes it more artistic, lends it larger wings; at the same time it weakens the reasoning power of the white race, diminishes the intensity of its practical faculties, delivers an irremediable blow to its activity and physical power, and almost always removes from the group deriving from this mixture, if not the right of shining much brighter than the whites and thinking more profoundly, at least that of contending against it with patience, tenacity, and wisdom.' (1853: 346)

At times Gobineau pours the new wine of racial typology into the old bottles of romanticism, but he does not always pour it very straight, and the idea of complementarity is, in a crucial passage, clearly subordinated to that of natural aristocracy.

'If mixtures of blood are, to a certain extent, beneficial to the mass of mankind, if they raise and ennoble it, this is merely at the expense of mankind itself, which is stunted, abased, enervated, and humiliated in the persons of its noblest sons. Even if we were to admit that it is better to turn a myriad of degraded beings into mediocre men than to preserve the race of princes whose blood is adulterated and impoverished by being made to suffer this dishonourable change, yet there is still the unfortunate fact that the change does not stop here.' (1853: 209)

He then goes on to sketch the way in which the unions of the degraded lead societies into the abyss of nothingness.

It is remarked time and again that those who write the history of distant periods regularly do so from the standpoint of their own generation. They interpret ancient disputes in the terms that are alive as they write. This observation is particularly relevant to the *Essay*. Gobineau begins with a reference to the revolutions of 1848 which he sees as symptomatic of the decay of European civilization and he continues to write from the perspective of a man out of harmony with his time. As Michael Biddiss explains, his hypothesis is founded in the contemporary world; it is social and political rather than properly biological (1970: 132). Unlike most of those with whom he can be compared, Gobineau does not expound a theory to press a particular solution on his readers. He has no solution, and in his thought the theory works towards the annihilation of political will and purpose. Though his belief in natural aristocracy, and race as one of its forms, runs through other writings, not one of the seventeen books he wrote after the *Essay* develops his compassion of the major races. It is the history of one race that concerns him and his books about it are a very personal declaration.

That Gobineau's use of the conception of type was in accordance with contemporary French scientific usage is suggested by an essay pub-

lished in 1859–60. In it Paul Broca, founder of the Paris Anthropological Society, criticized the view 'that the crossing of races constantly pro-
duces disastrous effects'. This was far too general, for under certain circumstances it had favourable results. Broca insisted on the importance
of distinguishing between race and type. The popular view that people
with hair of different colour did not belong to the same race seized the
true meaning of the term race, whereas only the scientist, studying the
ensemble of characters common to a natural group, could constitute the
type of that group (1864: 8). Human types were abstractions and were
not to be confused with actual groups of men. The use of 'race' as if this
denoted a pure category was to be avoided. 'Every confusion in words',
Broca sternly warned 'exposes us to errors in the interpretation of
facts'.

The weakest point in Cuvier's system was the purely speculative hypothesis that the changes in the fossil record were to be explained by catastrophes for which there was little independent evidence. An alternative explanation was implicit in the theory of Cuvier's former collaborator Etienne Geoffroy Saint-Hilaire (1772–1844) who maintained there
had been but one creation and that one plan underlay the animal universe so that every bone found in a mammal had its counterpart in a
fish. Though Geoffroy was no forerunner of Darwin, his theories were
more sympathetic than Cuvier's to the transformation of species. Cuvier debated with Geoffroy before the Academy of Sciences in 1830 the
latter's claims about the unity of structure between molluscs and vertebrates (Piveteau 1950). Cuvier won. Many biologists followed the controversy with interest, among them Robert Knox who studied in Paris
in 1821 having graduated from Edinburgh in 1814. Knox referred to
the debate in *The Races of Men*, remarking that each of his friends, Cuvier and Geoffroy, was 'partly in the wrong; Cuvier most' (1850: 441).
He went on to observe 'as early as 1827 I proposed a modification, sub-
stituting a doctrine of type for the then existing theories' which makes
it difficult to see what was at issue between him and Cuvier.

Knox's system was one he called 'transcendental anatomy' an expression used by Geoffroy but which Knox said was coined by his esteemed
friend and teacher (and Cuvier's successor) H. M. D. de Blainville.
Knox described it as originating from South Germany and from a mixture of the Slav and Gothic races. Its object was 'to explain in a connected chain the phenomena of the living material world'; to show that
'all animals are formed upon one great plan' (1850: 171). ' "There is but
one animal, not many" was the remarkable expression of Geoffroy; it
contains the whole question. What was, now is, under other forms; but

the essence is still the same'. As there was only one creation, 'in time there is probably no such thing as species' but 'for a few centuries organic forms seem not to have changed'. This theory had been popularized in Britain (and, according to Knox, misstated) by the anonymous author of a best-selling work *Vestiges of Creation*. Geoffroy claimed that the unity of animal forms could be proved by the examination of embryonic forms. Knox also started from the recapitulation theory: 'whatever is irregular in man is a regular structure in some lower animal and was in him a regular structure during his embryonic life. This law . . . is the basis of the law productive of irregular form in man — the law of deformation'. Variety was deformity. It was balanced by 'the law of unity of the organization'. Knox summarized his argument as follows:

'The races of men differ from each other, and have done so from the earliest historic period, as proved —

1. By their external characters, which have never altered during the last six thousand years.
2. By anatomical differences in structure.
3. By the infertility of the hybrid product, originating in the intermingling of two races.
4. By historic evidence, which shows that no distinct hybrid race can ever be shown to exist anywhere.'

But his summary is scarcely complete, for elsewhere Knox insisted on including in his typology of races not only their external characters, but their internal ones as well, that is their morale, temperament and ability to build a way of life (1860: 168, 477, 36, 175, 503).

The distinctive features of the doctrine of racial typology were four, and they can all be clearly seen in Knox's writing. First, that variations in the constitution and behaviour of individuals were to be explained as the expression of different underlying biological types of a relatively permanent kind; second, differences between these types explained variations in the cultures of human populations; third, the distinctive nature of the types explained the superiority of Europeans in general and Aryans in particular; fourth, friction between nations and individuals of different type arose from innate characters. Disregarding Prichard's warning, the typologists used racial type as a synonym for species, whereas modern zoologists, if they use the concept of race at all, apply it to sub-species.

That Knox subscribed to the first of these tenets is apparent at the opening of his book, where he asserts that 'Human character, individual and national, is traceable solely to the nature of that race to which the individual or nation belongs', and he goes on to explain that while there is a process of biological development, 'organic forms seem not to have changed' for a few centuries at least. The second tenet is illustrated in claims such as 'the proper field of action for the Saxon is the ocean'; the third by 'there must be a physical and, consequently, a psychological inferiority in the dark races generally'; and the fourth by such statements as 'The various species of Men constitute one great natural family. Each species or race has a certain degree of antagonism to the others, some more, some less. They never mingle; and should accident cause a commingling, they ultimately separate into their primitive elements'. A sharper passage on this topic, which includes an echo of Knox's political radicalism, occurs in a later passage about racial antagonism in South Africa, where the Anglo-Saxon and Dutch Saxon

> 'so debase the coloured races as to deprive them for ever of all chance of recovering that inestimable treasure beyond all price or value, freedom of speech, thought, and action; in a word, the rights of man. How has this antagonism arisen? The truth is, it has always existed, but it never appeared in its terrible form until the Saxon race began to migrate over the earth, to establish free colonies, as they are called – free to the white man and their own race – dens of horror and cruelty to the coloured.' (1860: v, 6, 36, 224, 254, 546)

Knox's racial theory taught that colonization was evil as well as useless. Though it stressed the powerful qualities of the Saxon race it also represented its members as cordially hating good government, outrageously boasting, arrogant, and self-sufficient beyond endurance. The Celtic population of Ireland he insisted, contained 'the elements of a great race, were she not politically enslaved'. His writing fell far short of being a justification of the prevailing social order.

Knox remarks in his book that 'in 1846 I had the great question of race . . . wholly to myself' whereas by 1850 'the word *race* is of daily use' especially with reference to continental Europe and Ireland. He saw the struggles of 1848–9 on the continent as a war of races and a confirmation of his theories that had brought them a wider audience (1860: 7, 16–17, 20–1). His testimony about the increased use of the word in popular speech deserves respect but other remarks suggest a restricted circle of acquaintance, such as 'I was, I think, the first, or amongst the first, to point out to the reading world the antagonism of the present Norman government of England to her presumed Saxon population' (1860: 370, cf. 54, 135).

The diverse population of the United States with its Indians, Negroes, and varied assortment of Europeans, tended as William Stanton observes, to make every citizen, if not an ethnologist, at least a speculator on matters of race (1960: 10). Here, surely, was fertile soil for the seed of racial typology? Yet the new doctrine was opposed from the outset by the conviction that the book of *Genesis* proved the original unity of mankind. Any suggestion that racial differences might be permanent was attacked as betraying the infidelity of the author. The first American formulations of racial typology were advanced very tentatively by Samuel George Morton, a Philadelphia physician who had taken a particular interest in geology and anatomy. His book *Crania Americana*, published in 1839, provides little suggestion of Cuvier's influence and in its racial classification relies on the fivefold division of Blumenbach, the monogenist. Morton begins with the claim 'From remote ages the inhabitants of every extended locality have been marked by certain physical and moral peculiarities, common among themselves, and serving to distinguish them from all other people. The Arabians are, at this time precisely what they were in the days of the patriarchs . . .'. The concept of type does not appear (though he uses it in 1841) and he presents races as sub-specific classes. Morton introduces some doubts about the orthodox view, as when he refers to calculations that Noah and his family left the Ark 4,179 years previously whereas Ethiopians were known to exist 3,445 years ago; recent discoveries, he adds, make it clear that only by a miracle, could the Negro race have developed out of the Caucasian in the course of 734 years (1839: 1, 88). But the general effect is very restrained. Having obtained a collection of Egyptian skulls, he is willing to go a little further five years later, and in *Crania Aegyptica* (1844: 66) reaches the conclusion that 'Negroes were numerous in Egypt, but their social position in ancient times was the same as it now is, that of servants and slaves'. Negroes have a natural social position as well as a geographical position and give evidence of being a permanent type.

In later publications Morton's attack on orthodoxy became more explicit. He criticized the view that infertility of hybrids was the best test of separate species for creatures that had become domesticated, and emphasized 'the repugnance of some human races to mix with others'. The story of how the orthodox replied, and of the allies who came to Morton's aid, has been admirably told by William Stanton and does not need repeating. Two of those who campaigned most vigorously for the doctrine of the original distinctiveness of human races were J. C. Nott, an Alabama physician, and George R. Gliddon, a popular lecturer on ancient Egyptian culture. In 1846 they were joined by Louis Agassiz, one of Europe's most celebrated natural historians of whom it was said 'after Cuvier, Morton was the only zoologist who had any influence on Agassiz' mind and scientific opinions'.

Assisted by Agassiz, Nott and Gliddon published in 1854 a substantial volume with the significant title *Types of Mankind*. The anthropological chapters were written by Nott who cautions his readers that classifications of races must inevitably be arbitrary 'because no reason has yet been assigned why, if two original pairs of human beings be admitted, we should not accept an infinite number'. They did not define 'race' but used the word in a way that conformed with Prichard's recommendation, and could be contrasted with 'type'. 'Every race, at the present time, is more or less mixed', but 'there is abundant evidence to show that the principal physical characters of a people may be preserved throughout a long series of ages, in a great part of the population, despite of climate, mixture of races, invasion of foreigners, progress of civilization, or other known influences; and that a *type can long outlive its language, history, religion, customs, and recollections*'. Types were 'those primitive or original forms which are independent of Climatic or other Physical influences'. The argument concludes with a set of twelve propositions set out opposite (1854: 80, 83, 95, 96, 465).

One important proposition is missing from this list, for the authors make very clear their belief in the inequality of types and races. They quote with approval Knox's protest 'Human history cannot be a mere chapter of accidents'. To the 'higher castes of what are termed Caucasian races' have been assigned 'the mission of extending and perfecting climes, regardless of difficulties'. Caucasians 'have in all ages been the reckless of danger — impelled by an irresistible instinct, they visit all climes, regardless of difficulties'. Caucasians 'have in all ages been the rulers'. Thomas Jefferson had written 'Never could I find that a Black had uttered a thought above the level of plain narrative; never saw even an elementary trait of painting or of sculpture'. Nott adds 'I have looked in vain, during twenty years, for a solitary exception to these characteristic deficiencies among the Negro race. Every Negro is gifted with an ear for music; some are excellent musicians; all *imitate* well in most things . . .' and he remarks that Negro blood usually makes mulattoes immune to yellow fever, but it is certain that they are included in the author's questions about the future in which 'the inferior types of mankind shall have fulfilled their destinies and passed away' (1854: 67, 68, 79, 80, 456).

The volume brought out by the same authors three years later adds nothing to these arguments save in one particular. If each race has its

Table 1 *Nott and Gliddon's 'Conclusions'*

'1. That the surface of our globe is naturally divided into several zoological provinces, each of which is a distinct centre of creation, possessing a peculiar fauna and flora; and that every species of animal and plant was originally assigned to its appropriate province.

2. That the human family offers no exception to this general law, but fully conforms to it: Mankind being divided into several groups of Races, each of which constitutes a primitive element in the fauna of its peculiar province.

3. That history affords no evidence of the transformation of one Type into another, nor of the origination of a new and PERMANENT Type.

4. That certain Types have been PERMANENT through all recorded time, and despite the most opposite moral and physical influences.

5. That PERMANENCE of Type is accepted by science as the surest test of SPECIFIC character.

6. That certain Types have existed (the same as now) in and around the Valley of the Nile, from ages anterior to 3500 years B.C., and consequently long prior to any alphabetic chronicles, sacred or profane.

7. That the ancient Egyptians had already classified Mankind, as known to them, into FOUR RACES, previously to any date assignable to Moses.

8. That high antiquity for distinct Races is amply sustained by linguistic researches, by psychological history, and by anatomical characteristics.

9. That the primeval existence of Man, in widely separate portions of the globe, is proven by the discovery of his osseous and industrial remains in alluvial deposits and in diluvial drifts; and more especially of his fossil bones, imbedded in various rocky strata along with the vestiges of extinct species of animals.

10. That PROLIFICACY of distinct species, *inter se*, is now proved to be no test of COMMON ORIGIN.

11. That those Races of men most separated in physical organization — such as the BLACKS and the WHITES — do not amalgamate perfectly, but obey the Laws of Hybridity. Hence

12. It follows, as a corollary, that there exists a GENUS HOMO, embracing many primordial Types or "Species".'

(Nott and Gliddon, 1854: 465).

province, its members will be at a disadvantage if they migrate to another province to which they are not suited. In *Indigenous Races of the Earth* Nott therefore takes up the question of whether a type can become habituated to another climate. This was clearly a matter of considerable interest to Europeans settling in the United States. Knox had stated flatly that acclimatization was impossible in the long run. Nott was more restrained, but after reviewing the statistics of mortality and morbidity he inclined in the same direction: 'races . . . have their appropriate geographical ranges, beyond which they cannot go with impunity'. He commented sardonically on man that 'although boasting of *reason*, as the prerogative that distinguishes him, he is, in many respects, the most unreasonable of animals'. One respect was that 'he forsakes the land of his birth, with all its associations, and all the comforts which earth can give, to colonize foreign lands — where he knows full well that a thousand hardships must await him, and with the certainty of risking his life *in climates that nature never intended him for*' (1857: 399–400).

Though Nott and Gliddon (1854: 79) state that 'no two distinctly-marked races can dwell together on equal terms', they do not, like Knox, identify what later came to be called race prejudice and claim that it is an inbred characteristic of some or all types. This seems not to have been something which they regarded as requiring explanation. Nevertheless their doctrine of race includes a theory of race relations, for they assert that the natural order determines what kinds of social relations will be harmonious. If the permanent types have distinctive attributes then any social relationship which did not permit these attributes to obtain natural expression would eventually fail.

Like Knox, Nott and Gliddon inclined to the view that each race had its own habitat and they therefore saw little future for black slavery in the United States. One of Knox's followers, however, was prepared to go further in this direction. Dr James Hunt broke away from the Ethnological Society to found the Anthropological Society of London (the story is admirably told in Stocking, 1971). In his presidential address of 1865, which attracted much attention, Hunt declared 'the Negro belongs to a distinct type. The term species, in the present state of science, is not satisfactory'. He ended with six conclusions much like Nott's, but including

'4. That the Negro becomes more humanized when in his natural subordination to the European than in any other circumstances.
5. That the Negro race can only be humanized and civilized by Europeans.'

Hunt made no original contribution to anthropology but he was the most effective publicist of racial typology in Britain, confidently relating anthropological speculations to current affairs without any of Knox's reservations. The Paris Anthropological Society, though it discussed the question of racial equality at the same time and with equal fervour, was much more temperate in its proceedings and its conclusions (see *Bulletins de la Société d'Anthropologie de Paris*, 1, 1860: 187–218, 255–68, 276–302, 327–86, 419–37, 479–94).

The big threat to typology was Darwin's evidence for the impermanence of species. Knox and Hunt were quite unpersuaded by the new arguments. A more interesting reaction came from Germany's most ebullient typologist, Karl Vogt (1817–1895) or 'monkey Vogt' as he was called when he began to preach the new gospel. Vogt was a professor of anatomy at Giessen, a radical and a militant materialist, who also occupied a parliamentary seat and participated in the revolutionary movements of his time. Dismissed from his chair, he obtained another in geology at Geneva. Vogt was first a follower of Cuvier who translated *The Vestiges of Creation* into German while standing aside from its evolutionary speculations. His materialism is evident in his *Lectures on Man* (1863) which deny the fertility of hybrids and put anatomical explanations to the fore. He asserts that 'the differences in the human genus which we may designate either races or species . . . are original'. Negro intellectual development is arrested at puberty. He quotes 'the general rule of the slaveholder' that Negro slaves 'must be treated like neglected and badly brought up children' (1863: 440, 191–3 and on typology, 214–21). Yet in contradiction of his own arguments he draws attention to measurements reporting a lower cranial capacity for Negroes in the United States than in Africa and asks 'is this the effect of that cursed institution which degrades men to the condition of chattel?'. His radical spirit rising, he remarks that as slavery exercises an equally injurious influence on the master it would be worth collecting the skulls of the Civil War dead to test the hypothesis that the cranial capacity of white Southerners has been reduced below that of Northerners. At the end of the book he has grasped the significance of Darwin's message about the mutability of types and is speculating about man evolving from multiple origins to interbreed: 'the innumerable mongrel races gradually fill up the spaces between originally so distinct types, and, notwithstanding the constancy of characters, in spite of the tenacity with which the primitive races resist alteration, they are by fusion slowly led towards unity' (1863: 92, 448, 468).

It is also worth noting a passage in which Vogt bade his hearers look westwards:

'the Anglo-Saxon race is itself a mongrel race, produced by Celts, Saxons, Normans and Danes, a raceless chaos without any fixed type; and the descendants of this raceless multitude have in America so much intermixed with Frenchmen, Germans, Dutch, and Irish, as to have given rise to another raceless chaos, which is kept up by continued immigration. We can readily believe that from this chaos a new race is gradually forming.' (Vogt, 1864: 433)

This notion of a 'raceless chaos' was later perverted and popularized by his one-time pupil Houston Stewart Chamberlain. But Vogt's book is more interesting as an example of a scientist's inconsistencies as he comes to accept a new theory; the author's combination of political radicalism with the assertion of racial inferiority is also worth some attention as a pointer to the differences in the intellectual scene of his day and our own.

Chapter Two gave reasons for concluding that Europeans first developed the race concept as an interpretation of their own history. Having racialized the West, their successors proceeded to racialize the rest of the world. Gobineau advanced a theory of Aryan superiority couched in very general terms. Morton, Knox, Nott, Vogt, Broca, and others elaborated upon anatomical evidence pointing in a similar direction. Hunt took the process a stage further in the very specific way he asserted the inferiority of the Negro and the case for keeping him subordinate to Europeans.

Earlier in this chapter the question was asked: where did the theory of racial types come from? Evidence has been presented to suggest that the principal source lay in the complex of ideas about the prehistory of the world and the origin of species, but it was influenced by the current state of very partial knowledge about peoples living outside Europe, by the contemporary feeling almost of intoxication about the rate of material progress in Europe and the context of racial contacts overseas in which most of the 'authorities' had made their observations of non-European peoples. There are grounds for believing that the criticism of the slave trade stimulated West Indian planters to develop doctrines of the racial inferiority of blacks in the closing years of the eighteenth century. The works of the egregious Edward Long are regularly quoted in support of such an interpretation. But the evidence is still far from satisfactory and it appears as if the theory of racial typology may well have been more important to the spread of beliefs about natural inferiority. James Cowles Prichard, who was a very sober observer indeed, commented in 1826 that in England black men from the West Indies were able to find English wives 'which is a proof, not only of their own good taste in this respect, but also that our countrywomen, the lower orders of them at least, have no invincible repugnance to the negro race'. Yet it is more interesting to note that when he went on to ask 'whether the faculties of the mind . . . are less perfect in the Negro' he should have written

'as far as I have had opportunities of collecting information on the subject, from the most judicious observers, the result has been a most decided assurance that Negroes are not by any means inferior in intellect to Europeans; at least that, in the sphere of action in which they are placed, no such inferiority is displayed. This has been the almost uniform testimony of many intelligent planters and medical practitioners from the West Indies, with whom I have conversed. Among the former, though this class of men has often been accused of a sinister bias, their prejudices and interest leading them, as it is said, to undervalue the Africans, I have not met with an individual out of a great number, who has not given a most positive testimony as to the natural equality of the African Negro and the European.' (Prichard, 1826: 129, 177–78)

It would seem, therefore, that controversies about the slave trade may have had only a limited effect upon the growth of racial doctrines in England and that the more powerful developments came later in the nineteenth century.

The theory of racial typology which gathered together some of the speculations of the earlier part of that century contained what can now be seen as rather obvious mistakes. The mistaken theories in the field of embryology were fairly quickly rectified, as was the doctrine of the permanence of types in its biological context and certain of the theories about hybridity. But theories claiming that Negroes had a more limited brain capacity than whites, and that the progress of civilizations was determined by underlying racial types, have lasted longer and cause many readers to ask: who were these scholars? Was there anything in their personal backgrounds which has a place in an explanation of their errors?

The personal background to the theory of Joseph Arthur de Gobineau (1816–1882) is certainly relevant. He was born into a bourgeois family with aristocratic pretensions that had been devoted to the Bourbon dynasty and completely opposed to the aspirations of the French Revolution. His experiences of family life, with both his mother and his wife, included much that was unhappy. Gobineau attracted attention in a Parisian salon and earned a living from journalism until the Revolution of 1848, after which he obtained a succession of diplomatic appointments up to 1877. The writer who has most carefully examined his racial theory, Michael Biddiss, believes that the dominant theme in his work is that of pessimism. He human world was degenerating and its decline could no longer be halted. The events of 1848 were compelling evidence of the lengths to which the process had gone. The blood of the creative races had lost its purity and therefore its power. Colonial expansion would only hasten the self-destruction. Personal relations with non-Europeans seem not to have played any important part in the theme of the *Essay* which he wrote without ever having left Europe. In 1855, when he first came in contact with a black people, he wrote home about the Somalis saying that never before had he seen 'creatures so beautiful and perfect'. Gobineau's own philosophy implied the negation of meaningful political action and during his lifetime it was without influence (Biddiss, 1970). The reader who takes up Gobineau's four volumes expecting to find there a doctrine suited to the claims of either the aristocracy or the bourgeoisie of his generation must be struck by its utter uselessness for such purposes.

Robert Knox (1791–1862) was the son of an Edinburgh school teacher who for some years pursued a promising medical career. He served as an army surgeon in Belgium and for three years in South Africa, afterwards establishing himself as a very successful lecturer on anatomy in Edinburgh. His ideas about race may well have been formed during the early 1820s but in 1828 there was a mishap which cast a blight upon the remainder of his life. Medical teachers had to obtain cadavers from some disreputable sources. Two men, Burke and Hare, who were convicted of murder, had sold the body of one of the deceased to an agent acting on behalf of Dr Knox and though he was formally cleared of liability his position in Edinburgh became untenable. Thereafter he held only occasional medical appointments and maintained himself for some periods by writing and lecturing. The unhappiness he must have experienced may well explain the disjointed and dogmatic nature of his pronunciations upon race when they appeared in book form. Though the opposite of a romantic, Knox was politically a radical who implies that had the revolutionaries of 1848 – 9 possessed his insight, they could have moulded these events to their greater advantage. But his book is muddled and certainly expounds no philosophy of political action. He warns his readers that the future is not theirs to control 'ask yourselves what climatic changes destroyed the mammoth, the aneplotherium, the dinotherium, the sivatherium? the fishes of the ancient world? the sourians? Man destroyed them not; yet their race is run. Why dies out, almost before our eyes, the apteryx? . . . The destroying angel walks abroad unseen, striking even at the races of men.' He

pours scorn on the delusions that beset races when formed into powerful nations, in which hubris is so prominent, sarcastically quoting a London sermon as evidence that Condorcet's theory of the advance of mankind towards perfection must be inapplicable to the English since they
are already perfect (1860: 467, 574). The only sensible policy it seems,
in Knox's eyes, was for each race to keep to itself within its natural bor-
ders.

Knox's disciple James Hunt (1833–69) inherited from his father
the ownership of an establishment for the cure of stammering, on
which he wrote an authoritative textbook. Hunt graduated D.Phil.
from the University of Giessen (with which he had a family connection) in 1856 and was awarded an honorary M.D. from the same university in 1867. He was a man of great energy who led a breakaway from
the Ethnological Society to found the Anthropological Society of London (Stocking, 1971). In his short and relatively spectacular career he
seems to have had no experience or connections outside Europe and appears to have been motivated primarily by his enthusiasm for a theory
which he believed of the greatest relevance to the problems of the age.

Josiah Clark Nott (1804–73) an Alabama physician, and George
Robbins Gliddon (1809–57) were an odd pair. The younger man was an
agent for an insurance company, and United States vice-consul in
Cairo, when, in 1837, he was asked to collect Egyptian skulls for Samuel
George Morton the leading American anthropologist. Gliddon has
been described as 'a name-dropper, a sponger, a swinger on the shirt-
tails of the great, a braggart, pretender, and scatologist' as well as
'courageous, generous, warm-hearted and loyal' (Standon, 1960: 46).
He became a lecturer and show-man, putting on displays of Egyptian
culture for American audiences. The skulls he collected were used to
demonstrate that Negroes and whites had been separate in Egypt from
the very earliest times. Nott was a southern gentleman and frequent
contributor to the leading medical journals. An article of his on
hybridity brought him Morton's congratulations and another request
for skulls. Drawn into the discussion of race he published two lectures
with the object (so he told a former governor of South Carolina) of
giving people a weapon with which to oppose abolition. Gliddon drew
him into partnership for their publishing ventures but Nott had
pungent reservations about his collaborator. Gliddon had difficulty
making a living, and when Nott heard that he had taken a post with the
Honduras Railway he was relieved that Gliddon should have been
'transported to a country where there are no printer types'.

Neither Gobineau or Knox benefitted financially to any significant extent from their work in the development of racial theories. Gliddon attracted popular notice but by no means all of it was favourable and he seems to have been motivated more strongly by his dislike of clergymen (skunks, he usually called them) and his enjoyment of 'parson-skinning'. Nott's career was much more successful but he seems to have been a very competent physician and a particularly hard worker. Moreover, he was constantly astonished that the infidelity of his anthropological writing did not damage his medical practice. At the same time it should be recognized that Morton, Nott, and Gliddon all encouraged pro-slavery applications of their theories. It might be expected that these would have been taken up with enthusiasm in the South and used as a justification of slavery, but the response was more complicated.

On the one hand, the more orthodox rejected the suggestion that whites and blacks were separately created, for it appeared to conflict with the Bible. They preferred to rest their defence upon Saint Paul's remarks on the duty of the slave Onesimus to return to his master (*Philemon*, 12–16). The most striking defence of the Southern pattern of society came from George Fitzhugh, who deplored the doctrine of *Types of Mankind* not only because it was at war with scripture, but because 'it encourages and incites brutal masters to treat negroes, not as weak, ignorant and dependent brethren, but as wicked beasts without the pale of humanity'. Fitzhugh insisted that the South must defend slavery in general and not just slavery for blacks. He attacked Northern pretensions, maintaining that the patriarchal slavery of the South was less dehumanizing than the wage slavery of the capitalist North (cf. Genovese, 1969: 118–94). On the other hand, writers and speakers less closely associated with the Southern ruling class tended increasingly to justify black subordination in racial terms. When pointing up the contrast between the two philosophies, George M. Fredrickson describes this latter school as advocates of what van den Berghe has called *Herrenvolk* democracy — democracy for the ruling people and subjection for the others. This outlook challenged the aristocratic or seigneurial social ideal and commanded a wider electoral appeal. The politicians gradually came into line, typological theories were further vulgarized, and *Herrenvolk* egalitarianism became the dominant public ideology of the South at a time when romantic conceptions of racial character, and even complementarity, were gaining ground in Northern opinion (Fredrickson, 1971: 58–129). Popular opinion in the North had, from the 1830s, displayed bitterly anti-Negro and at times anti-abolitionist features. Some of these were well reflected in the

Negro Minstrel shows which, more effectively than any book, catered to popular prejudices and amplified them (Toll, 1974). In discussing what seem to be vices in Southern justifications of slavery, it is mistaken to assume that the men of the North were virtuous.

Racial typology was taken up much more quickly in the United States than in Europe, and the study of how it was developed leads on to questions quite different from that of how it came to be formulated in the first place. In so far as the personal background of the authors influenced the formulation, it is the background in its entirety that must be considered. At times in the *Essay* and in his subsequent writings Gobineau praises other peoples as a way of exhorting his fellow Frenchmen to lead more noble lives, just as Tacitus praised the Germans in order to shame his fellow Romans. Important elements in the work of Gobineau, Kingsley, Knox, and Vogt, as well as of Fitzhugh, can be seen as reactions to contemporary capitalism and as having, in this as in much else, an intra-European orientation. The genesis of racialization was less simple than might be suggested by the course it subsequently followed south of the Mason-Dixon line.

Available evidence about the personal background of these authors may, however, be insufficient to determine how far contemporary circumstances may have influenced the development of new theories and beliefs about racial categories. For example, from the seventeen to the nineteenth centuries there were political advantages in the belief that the English and the Germans were branches of the same race, but these were weakened after 1871 when Germany rose to become England's rival. This may well have influenced the reception in England of the Aryan theory. The contemporary circumstances most closely associated with the first statement of racial typology were political tensions within Europe. These writers' theories were as brutal in their interpretation of differences between European races as between them and non-Europeans. To take but one example, Gobineau propagated a most unflattering image of the Finns as 'always weak, unintelligent and oppressed'. England's first university teacher of sociology, Edvard Westermarck observed that in the 1880s very many educated English people believed that Finland was populated by chubby little Lapps or Eskimos (Westermarck, 1927: 78). As other writers took up the racial theme their targets were often national groups or classes within Europe, and in the English writing of the last three decades of the nineteenth century there is more racial abuse of the Irish than of the blacks. In much the same sense, a recent historical study finds evidence of increasingly arrogant behaviour towards black people within England from the

1860s and interprets this in terms of changes in the social and political temper of English society itself (Lorimer, 1972).

These changes were, of course, related to overseas developments and there is good reason to believe that the reception of typological doctrines and the increase in racial prejudice were stimulated by overseas events: the China war, the Crimean, the Indian 'Mutiny', the American Civil War, the Jamaican uprising, and other colonial involvements. But in view of the currency of assumptions about a connection between imperialism and racial doctrine, it is important to remember that the 1850s and 1860s were not a colonial age in the same sense as the last decades of the century. In 1865 a parliamentary select committee recommended that Britain withdraw from her West African territories, except, perhaps, the then small settlement of Sierra Leone. The composition and policies of Gladstone's cabinet of 1868 are sometimes considered to represent the high point of *anti*-imperial sentiment. The conclusions of another scholar lead him to doubt if imperialism was in any sense a popular political idea before Disraeli's second premiership of 1874–80 and to state there is no clear evidence that British imperialism and Victorian doctrines of race are linked in any causal way' (Watson, 1973: 213, 215). The contemporary history of France and other European powers conformed to a similar pattern in this respect. Moreover, when imperialist sentiment did gather strength in the 1890s it was as a movement for the support of white colonies in countries such as Australia, New Zealand, and South Africa, and not for the rule of black men by white. A comparison between East Africa and Nigeria in the period 1880–1914 suggests that the stereotype of African racial inferiority which emerged in Kenya was a European creation deriving from the social and political needs of white settlers and not from either genuine observation or racial theories (Perraton, 1967: 242).

Nor were racial theories used only to disparage coloured peoples. In India the Aryan theory pointed to common ties between the British and the native population rather than to a division between them, yet neither the British nor the Indians responded to it in any uniform manner. When Max Muller, the Oxford professor of Sanskrit, used the Aryan theory to praise the culture of ancient India and to emphasize the common descent of Englishman and Bengali, this probably evoked no hesitations in Chelsea drawing rooms, for it seemed to prove the providential nature of British rule in India. Englishmen in India were less attracted to it, though Sir Henry Maine, who was at one time Law Member of the Government of India (and himself a scholar who made little use of racial ideas), remarked 'I myself believe that the government of

India by the English has been rendered appreciably easier by the discoveries which have brought home to the educated of both races the common Aryan parentage of Englishman and Hindoo'.

The message that the Englishman was an .elder brother who had been separated from some other members of his family and had now returned to help them learn the skills he had acquired in his more extensive travels, was welcomed by some Indians, but the Brahmins had reason to fear its implications for ther claims to privilege within Hindu culture. Many Indian nationalists stressed the superior political organization and spirituality of the Aryans. They used the expression 'Aryan' in a moral rather than a geographical sense, and without much historical content. Some employed it as a rallying cry. In such ways its significance was diluted, probably on account of its unacceptable presuppositions. The Aryan theory would have denied equality to Indian non-Aryans, including out-caste Dravidians, tribal people, Muslims and Jews. Though some nationalists were not averse from this, the reformers may have been more impressed by the desirability of claiming equal rights for all Asians and have opposed the Aryan theory because it distracted attention from the true obstacles to unity (Leopold, 1970). Nor did the British find that the racial aspect of the theory suited their political ends very closely. To insist on the primacy of racial heredity was to imply that British attempts at reform in India would be useless unless the racial character of the population was changed. The myth of the Aryan past was more serviceable, for it fitted with the mid-Victorian belief in progress and could represent the British as the most progressive branch of the most progressive race. That same myth also validated the claim that British rule in India was merely a family reunion, justifying it to Hindu audiences. But it is just as important to note that, for one reason or another, British officialdom made almost no use of the Aryan theory with respect to India in the period 1850–70 and that thereafter it attracted relatively little official attention (Leopold, 1974).

The study of the processes by which racial categories were developed and applied should also comprehend the intellectual response of black people which is early evident in works such as James Africanus Beale Horton's *West African Peoples and Countries* of 1868. In this volume by an Edinburgh-trained doctor from Sierra Leone (Fyfe, 1972), one chapter is devoted to the 'false theories of modern anthropologists'. It presents evidence in conflict with the theories of Knox, Vogt, and contemporary typologists. Soon afterwards a West Indian-born scholar who entered the diplomatic service of Liberia, Edward Wilmot Blyden, brought together some of his essays in *Christianity, Islam and the Ne-*

gro Race (1887), an impressive volume expounding arguments which can best be seen as reactions to racial typology. Blyden wrote 'each of the races of mankind has a specific character and a specific work. The science of Sociology is the science of race.' Nations were forming along racial lines, and Negroes, though equal to whites, would never resemble them (1887: 94, 122, 277). Across the Atlantic a similar response can be seen in *Froudacity*, the book in which a black Trinidadian, J. J. Thomas, attacked J. A. Froude's account of the English in the West Indies. He asked 'What is it in the nature of things that will oust the African race from the right to participate, in times to come, in the high destinies that have been assigned in times past to so many races that have not been in anywise superior to us in the qualifications, physical, moral and intellectual, that mark out a race for prominence amongst other races?' (1889: 180–81).

Replies such as these did not challenge the assumption that every man possessed racial attributes. They accepted it, but maintained that Europeans had been in error in their application of the theory. Nor did they draw upon the ideas that went into racial theories in order to build a political programme. In Sierra Leone and Trinidad this was scarcely necessary, for political change could easily take place within the structures fashioned under colonialism. Africans could respond to their political subordination by creating movements that brought together into nations congeries of peoples which might previously have been distant but were already conscious of their separately belonging together as peoples. As nationalism was so respectable an ideology in European political philosophy, there was rarely anything to be gained by appealing to race. In the United States, as the previous chapter has suggested, the picture was more complex; but from the 1880s the theme of 'race pride' was increasingly stressed by black leaders and the belief that Negroes like every other race, had distinctive but complementary qualities was voiced by them and by some of their white sympathizers (Meier, 1963: 50–56, 194–96, 270; Fredrickson, 1971: 327–29).

In moving on to consider the relation of the typological theory to beliefs about race in the later years of the century we have, however, been unble to take account of the momentous changes in the scientific understanding of race that were necessitated by the work of Charles Darwin. It may be helpful to turn first to a case study of a writer of the period who was particularly exercised by the implications of those changes.

4

A nineteenth-century racial philosophy: Charles Kingsley

This chapter was written as a self-contained essay for the Kingsley centenary in 1975 but is published here for the first time. It complements the argument of both the preceding and the succeeding chapters by showing how one influential man responded to the ideas of race current in the 1850s and to the challenge of Darwin's teaching. It may also assist by demonstrating that statements about race at the time are not always easily pigeonholed in the classifications of a later generation, and that it can be useful to interpret such statements in terms of the author's racial philosophy. Being of a somewhat different character, this chapter requires a large number of footnotes; as few of the references are shared with other chapters both notes and references have been gathered at the end of the chapter.

The two decades from 1850 to 1870 were a critical period in the history of the race concept.[1] They saw the acceptance of race as a key mode of classification in comparative morphology, and the widening of the breach that had been made in the Christian belief in the brotherhood of man. Prior to the nineteenth century scholars believed that all peoples could progress, but in the middle years of the century support increased for a theory of racial types which held that, because of innate differences, some peoples could never advance as far as others. Europeans were coming to believe that the divisions among themselves were small by comparison with the gulf between white people and other races. Much remains to be uncovered about movements of thought during this period and their relation to Britons' ideas about their country's place in world affairs. Until some of the blank parts of the picture have been filled in by historians, there is much to be said for exploring these movements by considering the life and ideas of particular men. Among the figures who particularly merit attention is that of Charles Kingsley, who was born on June 12, 1819, and died on January 23, 1875. The centenary of his death should attract some notice from students of race relations.

One measure of Charles Kingsley's energy is that his collected works run to twenty-eight volumes. Several of them are collections of sermons, but some are poems, literary criticism, historical essays, popular science, and, in particular, a clutch of novels which were sold in torrential numbers. Kingsley was a man of great vigour and moral earnestness, a prominent figure in the Christian Socialist group who dramatized the plight of the rural poor and of the clothing workers of the East End. He dabbled in marine biology; he spoke for sanitary reform, the co-operative movement, adult education, women's suffrage, and for a theology that would learn from what science had to teach about the processes of nature. Kingsley wrote fluent and at times moving verse, and he had a great gift for friendship. His influence was important in persuading church people to accept Darwin's theory and its implications. But Kingsley also showed some striking weaknesses — rash judgement, sentimentality, a continuing inclination to social snobbery, and a spasmodic one to racial pride. Canon C. E. Raven's conclusion 'if he has earned a high place as a primary advocate of social revolution, he bears a share of responsibility for the jingoism and British arrogance of the end of the century' balances the contrasting aspects of his life, though many would contest this conception of historical responsibility.[2]

Charles Kingsley's father was a clergyman from a family of soldiers and country gentry. His mother was the daughter of Judge Lucas of Barbados 'and in old age the tales which he could tell of the old war days on the Spanish main, and his stories of the wonders of tropical nature, became the delight of his grandson's boyhood'.[3] Brought up in Devon, Charles was sent to school in Clifton; while a pupil he witnessed the Bristol riots of 1831. Later he described to a friend the miserable part played by the mayor; the savage, brutal, hideous mob of inhuman wretches plundering, destroying, burning; casks of spirits broken open and set flowing in the streets, the wretched creatures drinking the liquor on their knees from the gutter, till the flame from a burning house caught the stream, ran down it with a horrible rushing sound, and, in one dreadful moment, the prostrate drunkards had become a row of blackened corpses. 'That sight', he said, 'made me a Radical'. But to someone else he said that the same sight made him 'for years the veriest aristocrat, full of hatred and contempt of those dangerous classes, whose existence I had for the first time discovered'. Far from being contradictory, this reveals the political philosophy behind the first phase of Kingsley's public life. Within his social sphere he was both a radical and a friend of aristocracy. He condemned the exhortations 'Get on' and 'Rise in Life' as the Devil's advice. 'The working man who tries to get on, to desert his class and rise above it, enters into a lie.' Yet this was not simply a condemnation of social mobility. It was also — and Kingsley's actions testify to this — an expression of the belief that the working man's condition should be such that he felt no need to escape from it. In 1852 he wrote about 'my one idea of the last seven years, that the real battle of the time is. . . the Church, the gentlemen, and the workman, against the shop-keepers and the Manchester School'. Kingsley's association with Chartism arose from a desire to put relations between classes onto a better basis, not to remove class distinction.

In 1836 he became a student at Kings College, Cambridge, where among other things he learned boxing under a Negro prize-fighter. Though not strong physically he threw himself into every kind of sport. In 1842 he graduated in the first class of the classical tripos, having been a senior optime in the previous mathematics tripos. After graduation he was ordained and appointed first curate and later rector of Eversley, Hampshire. He married, became acquainted with the group led by F. D. Maurice who were trying to give a Christian direction to the nascent socialist movement, and worked on his morbid poetic drama of the life of St. Elizabeth of Hungary. Published in 1848, this makes occasional reference to its characters as members of racial groups, as in expressions such as 'Out upon these Saxons!' and the injunction '. . . wipe out / By mighty deeds our race's guilt and shame'. The poem was directed against the ascetic and Roman Catholic tendencies of the tractarian movement in the Church of England.

In the winter of 1847 and the spring of 1848, England was in crisis. There were riots in London and major cities. In April the Government had to fill London with troops, barricade the bridges, and garrison many public buildings. In the memoir that prefaces *Alton Locke* Thomas Hughes testifies that Kingsley was more deeply impressed with the gravity of the crisis than almost any of his friends, because as a country parson he was directly in touch with the rural poor. In May 1848 some of Maurice's group published the first issue of a magazine entitled *Politics for the People*. It contained the first of 'Parson Lot's Letters to the Chartists'. In this letter Kingsley wrote 'my only quarrel with the Charter is that it does not go far enough in reform. I want to see you free but I do not see that what you ask for will give you what you want . . . The French cry "organization of labour" is worth a thousand of it' (i.e., constitution-mongering), 'but yet that does not go to the bottom of the matter . . . God will only reform society on the condition of our reforming every man his own self . . .' Kingsley's energetic enthusiasm coupled with his flamboyant style caused him to be regarded as one of the chief figures of the Christian Socialist group. In June the Christian Socialists arranged a meeting with a large number of working men. Maurice's opening address was followed by bitter speeches mounting a vehement attack on the Church and the clergy. Kingsley rose, folded his arms across his chest, and stammered out: 'My f-friends, I am a p-p-parson and a Ch-Ch-Chartist', adding almost *sotto voce*, 'Ch-Church of England, I mean'. He explained how earnestly he sympathized with the Chartists' sense of injustice, and went on to win the respect of his audience. The meetings continued, as did Parson Lot's letters in the magazine.Hughes states that while Kingsley was rapidly gaining the confidence of the working classes, he was raising up a host of hostile critics elsewhere. *Politics for the People* was discontinued and *The Christian Socialist* started in its place. This was identified with 'the cause of Association' (the embryonic co-operative movement) and Kingsley wrote one of its first tracts.

It is interesting to note the use of race in Kingsley's exhortations. In April 1848 he wrote a placard entitled 'Workmen of England' which began 'You say that you are wronged. Many of you are wronged; and many besides yourselves know it' and continued with the exhortation 'Englishmen! Saxons! Workers of the great, cool-headed, strong-handed nation of England, the workshop of the world, the leader of freedom for 700 years . . .' Advising on policy for *The Christian Socialist*, he wrote 'We must touch the workman at all his points of interest. First and foremost at association — but also at political rights, as grounded both on the Christian ideal of the Church, and on the historic facts of the Anglo-Saxon race. Then national education, sanitary and dwelling house reform, the free sale of land, and corresponding reform of the land laws . . .', etc.

The tract which Kingsley wrote for *The Christian Socialist* was entitled 'Cheap Clothes and Nasty'. It contained a vivid account of what unrestricted competition was doing to drive down the wages of East End tailors, forcing them to live in insanitary conditions. He warned that infectious diseases would be spread, via the clothing, to the members of the upper classes who ordered their clothes from the contractors who offered the lowest prices. Drawing a comparison that was not unusual, he wrote:

'We have, thank God, emancipated the black slaves; it would seem a not inconsistent sequel to that act to set about emancipating these white ones. Oh! we forgot; there is an infinite difference between the two cases — the black slaves worked for our colonies; the white slaves work for *us*. But, indeed, if, as some preach, self-interest is the mainspring of all human action, it is difficult to see who will step forward to emancipate the said white slaves; for all classes seem to consider it equally their interest to keep them as they are; all classes, though by their own confession they are ashamed, are yet not afraid to profit by the system which keeps them down.'

The pamphlet was expanded into the book *Alton Locke, tailor and poet: an autobiography* published in 1850, which states Kingsley's criticisms of contemporary capitalism in sharp terms, as when one character explains 'No! No! John, the question don't lie between workman and contractor, but between workman and contractor-plus-grape-and bayonets' and another observes 'everyone fancies the laws which fill his pockets to be God's laws'. There is a scarcely noticeable reference to the Aryan origin myth but little use of the word 'race'.[4] One of the few examples comes from a character who in referring to America is surely expounding what Kingsley then believed to be the most important consideration:

'The black is more like an ape than the white man — he is — the fact is there; and no notions of an abstract right will put that down: nothing but another fact — a mightier, more universal fact — Jesus of Nazareth died for the negro as well as for the white. Looked at apart from Him, each race, each individual of mankind, stands separate and alone, owing no more brotherhood to each other than wolf to wolf, or pike to pike — himself a mightier beast of prey — even as he has proven himself in every age'.

Men and races are unequal in nature but equal in Christ. Only by recognizing this can man realize himself.

1848 also saw the first publication in serial form of *Yeast*. This novel developed in a rural setting Kingsley's concern with sanitary reform and included a bitter criticism of landowners:

> 'There's blood on your new foreign shrubs, squire,
> There's blood on your pointer's feet;
> There's blood on the game you sell, squire,
> And there's blood on the game you eat.'

At this time Kingsley was a notorious and controversial figure. In connection with the Great Exhibition he was invited to preach on the 'Message of the Church to the Labouring Man' as one of a special series of sermons in a London church. He declared that a priest's business was to preach freedom, equality, and brotherhood in the fullest meaning of these words. One of the wisest of Moses' institutions was the year of the Jubilee when at the end of forty-nine years, all debtors and bond-servants were released and land returned to its original owner. Kingsley praised this 'unparalleled contrivance for preventing the accumulation of large estates, and the reduction of the people into the state of serfs and day-labourers. And this acceptable year, the Lord said He was come to preach . . . all systems of society which favour the accumulation of capital in a few hands — which oust the masses . . . or in anywise degrade or enslave them . . . are contrary to the Kingdom of God which Jesus proclaimed . . .' The incumbent of the church rose at the end of the sermon to announce that he believed that the greater part of this doctrine was false, and Kingsley for a time was banned by the bishop.[5]

The Christian Socialist group of 1848 to 1854 was a small one in which the leading organizer was J. M. Ludlow, a layman inspired by French political philosophers, who stepped forward as a spokesman for the engineering workers during the strike of 1851–2. The group regarded Maurice as their master and their source of inspiration, but he was uneasy about political involvement and allowed the group to dissolve after the Industrial and Provident Societies Act became law in 1852. For all his criticisms of contemporary abuses, Kingsley, like Maurice, was respectful of the traditional social pattern. Answering the question 'Who are the friends of order?' Kingsley in this year wrote that the Christian Socialists simply wanted to tell the people 'to do their duty in that state of life to which God has called them' and took pains to argue that the Christian Socialists' work was 'most eminently conservative of order, property, and all else which makes human life pleasant to its possessor or useful to the state. . . .'.[6] As the Christian Socialists lost their impetus and Kingsley's family responsibilities increased, he turned to larger philosophical and theological topics and his racial philosophy became more explicit and prominent. It can be argued that anyone who regards race as a significant element in human affairs must hold to a racial philosophy just as he may subscribe to an economic and a social philosophy. Often a racial philosophy is part of a philosophy of history, as was the case with Kingsley. In his political philosophy, the relations of the social classes seem to have been unalterable, but in his philosophy of history particular races were chosen by God to lead others onwards.

When Kingsley began to write the dominant anthropological view that all men were descended from Adam and Eve was coming under attack. It was becoming increasingly difficult to explain scientifically how if the Creation had occurred only some six thousand years ago, the various races of man could have become so strikingly differentiated. There was also a burgeoning literary romanticism which popularized the doctrine that nations were defined by inherited racial characteristics and their conflicts were racial struggles. Its chief exponents were Walter Scott, Edward Bulwer-Lytton, and the French historian Augustin Thierry whose *History of the Conquest of England by the Normans* appeared in English in 1825. Kingsley was acquainted with their works, but his concern was not with struggle so much as with synthesis. He took from his predecessors the idea that the key groups were races and used it in constructing a Christian philosophy of history. A revealing glimpse of his approach is contained in his advice to a woman who was thinking of becoming a Catholic.

'God . . . has chosen to teach Rome one way and England another. He has chosen to make you an English woman, a member of the Church of England, English in education, character, brain, feelings, duties: you cannot unmake yourself. You are already a member of that Spiritual One body, called the English nation . . . consider whether you know what the Church of England is, what God's education of England has been, and whether the one or the other are consistent with each other. I say they are. I say that the Church of England is wonderfully and mysteriously fitted for the souls of a free Norse-Saxon race; for men whose ancestors fought by the side of Odin, over whom a descendant of Odin now rules.'[7]

Kingsley took the Old Testament record seriously. He believed that 'the human race sprang from a single pair' but that the infantile innocence of the primary race faded away as quickly as it does in the individual child. The story of man's expulsion from the Garden of Eden was the charter for a belief in the degeneration of mankind. Throughout his life Kingsley used the word 'race' to refer indifferently to all mankind and to particular sections of it. In one of his last lectures he posed the question which lay behind the advice he gave to the woman in 1851: 'What if individuals, if peoples, have been chosen out from time to time for a special illumination, that they might be the lights of the earth, and the salt of the world? What if they have, each in their turn, abused that divine teaching to make themselves the tyrants instead of the ministers of the enlightened?'[8] A succession of races had been called by God to accomplish particular tasks in his plan for the world. Each race had its youth, its time of greatness and its decline. On one occasion he claims that there have been four scientific races to whom the credit is due for inductive physical science. First, he mentions the Jews, for the prophets denounced superstition and dread of nature. They taught that the universe was orderly and obeyed laws. Second, the Chaldean astronomers discovered the motions of the heavenly bodies, but they were crushed by their own discoveries and stopped short. Third, the Greeks and Romans (one race, apparently) proved that science was possible. Yet 'It remained for our race to bring science into act and fact'. Our ancestors were a personally courageous race. 'This earth has seen no braver men than the forefathers of Christian Europe, whether Scandinavian or Teuton, Angle or Frank. They were a practical hard-headed race, with a strong appreciation of facts, and a strong determination to act on them.' Providence had put them in a situation that enabled them to deploy their talents. 'Nature was to them not so inhospitable as to starve their brains and limbs, as it had done for the Esquimaux or Fuegian; and not so bountiful as to crush them by its very luxuriance, as it has crushed the savages of the tropics'.[9]

Kingsley's concern with sanitary reform relates to his racial philosophy in two ways. First, he believed that poor sanitation and poor health contributed to the degradation of races. There is a passage in *Yeast* that illustrates both this and the author's belief (shared with many contemporaries, for this was the era of phrenology) that inward nature was reflected in outward appearance. The hero of the book looks round at the men in a drinking booth at a country fair.

'He began examining the faces and foreheads of the company, and was astonished at the first glance by the lofty and ample development of brain in at least one half. There were intellects there — or rather capacities of intellect, capable, surely, of anything, had not the promise of the brow been almost always belied by the loose and sensual lower features. They were evidently rather a degraded than an undeveloped race.'

The hero concludes that they need an infusion of new blood and takes a more friendly view of the Celt than Kingsley was to do a few years later, for he reflects 'Perhaps this Irish immigration may do some good after all'. The plot of *Yeast* concludes unsatisfactorily with the appearance of a strange character decidedly reminiscent of Bulwer Lytton's Zanoni and Disraeli's Sidonia who has mysteriously appeared from a part of Asia where 'her bosom still heaves with the creative energy of youth, around the primaeval cradle of the most ancient race of men'. He assures his protégé 'the day of the Chamitic race is past; you will not say the same of our Caucasian empire. To our race the present belongs — to England, France, Germany, America — to us'.[10]

Another passage is worth quoting at some length, because it develops the themes of physical health and divine mission with respect to England's overseas connections. It is from an address in 1859 to the Ladies Sanitary Association.

'Of all the races upon earth now, the English race is probably the finest, and that it gives not the slightest sign whatsoever of exhaustion; and that it seems to be on the whole a young race, and to have very great capabilities in it which have not yet been developed, and above all, the most marvellous capability of adapting itself to every sort of climate and every form of life, which any race, except the old Roman, ever has had in this world; if they consider with me that it is worth the while of political economists and social philosophers to look at the map, and see that about four-fifths of the globe cannot be said as yet to be in any wise inhabited or cultivated, or in the state into which men could put it by a fair supply of population, and industry, and human intellect: then, perhaps, they may think with me that it is a duty, one of the noblest of duties, to help the increase of the English race as much as possible, and to see that every child that is born into this great nation of England be developed to the highest pitch to which we can develop him in physical strength and in beauty, as well as in intellect and in virtue.'[11]

The second way in which Kingsley's concern with sanitary reform relates to his racial philosophy is to be seen in his preoccupation with the explanation of epidemics and natural disasters. In 1854 he wrote

'as a clergyman, I feel bound to express my gratitude to Lord Palmerston for having refused to allow a National Fast-day on the occasion of the present reappearance of pestilence [cholera], and so having prevented fresh scandal to Christianity, fresh excuses for the selfishness, laziness and ignorance which produce pestilence, fresh turning men's minds away from the real causes of the present judgement, to fanciful and superstitious ones.'

Kingsley's answer was that cholera 'comes by natural causes . . . but that does not prevent its being a visitation of God'. On another occasion he explained 'if you or I caught cholera or fever by no fault of our own, we are bound to say, God sent me this sickness. It has some private lesson for me. It is part of my education.' Behind all events, even the fall of a sparrow to the ground, there are two causes, one physical, one moral. Of the eruption of the volcano on St. Vincent in 1872 he wrote: 'I know well that behind that How there was a Why for its happening, and happening, too, about that very time, which all who know the history of negro slavery in the West Indies can guess for themselves, and confess, I hope that in this case, as in all others, when Lady Why seems most severe she is often most just and kind.'[12] The eruption was God's warning that slavery could not be justified.

In Kingsley's philosophy, races were part of God's purpose for the world. They combined shared physical attributes with shared moral attributes associated with their voluntary response to God's teaching. The events of which human history is composed are to be studied so that men can learn from them God's intentions. When Kingsley in 1848 referred to 'the historic facts of the Anglo-Saxon race' it must have been this which he had in mind. Why the black man should be 'more like an ape than the white man' he does not know; this perhaps he regarded as something which science had to discover. Such knowledge was vital to natural theology, for 'science and religion are twin sisters meant to aid each other and mankind in the battle with the brute forces of this universe'.[13] Kingsley recognized gaps in contemporary understanding, but surely there can be seen in his outlook a racial philosophy that was important to his faith and thought? Previous writers seem not to have discerned it — perhaps because some of these notions have been taken for granted — and this suggests that the work of other Victorian writers needs to be reexamined from this new standpoint.

Kingsley's novel *Hypatia, or new foes with an old face* of 1853, provides further support for such an interpretation. It is based upon the story, mentioned in Chapter 47 of Gibbon's *Decline and Fall*, of the sorry state of the Christian Church in fifth-century Alexandria and the slaughter of the Neo-Platonist heroine named Hypatia. Kingsley presents it as an object lesson in the way vices and virtues manifest themselves side by side, among both the Church's supporters and her rivals. The novel is at the same time a hymn to the strength and valour of the

Goths. Yet 'every attempt of the Gothic races to establish themselves beyond the sea . . . ended only in the corruption and disappearance of the colonists'. Climate, bad example, and the luxury of power degraded them and prevented them exercising on the Eastern world the same stern yet wholesome discipline under which the West had been returned to life. 'Some great Providence forbade to our race, triumphant in every other quarter, a footing beyond the Mediterranean.'

The doctrine of man's voluntary response to God's teaching is set out in some of the earlier sermons:

'when God has given a nation freedom, then, unless there be a free heart in the people and true independence, which is dependence on God and not on man . . . they will fall back into slavery. So it was with the great Spanish colonies in South America a few years ago. God gave them freedom from the tyranny of Spain . . . but . . . there was no righteousness in them; because they were a cowardly, false and cruel people, therefore they only became the slaves of their own lusts . . . Look at the French people, too. Three times in the last sixty years has God delivered them from evil rulers, and given them a chance of freedom; and three times they have fallen back into fresh slavery' . . . 'Civilized nations like England thrive and prosper because they have laws and obey them' but their laws must be in harmony with God's: 'We are in God's Kingdom . . . and our business is, therefore, simply to find out what are the laws of that Kingdom, and obey those laws' . . . Degeneration is a continual possibility, 'the great nations of savages . . . become more and more children of wrath . . . forgetting more and more the laws of right and wrong, becoming stupid and ignorant, until they lose the very knowledge of how to provide themselves with houses, clothes, fire, or even to till the ground, and end in feeding on roots and garbage, like beasts which perish . . . they die out . . . the negroes of Africa and the West Indies, though they have fallen low, have not fallen too low for the gospel . . . thousands of them do embrace it . . . and lead such lives as would shame many a white Englishman . . . But the black people in Australia, who are exactly of the same race as the African negroes, cannot take in the gospel. They seem to have become too stupid to understand it.'[14]

Environment limited the possibilities open for the development of a race and influenced its character. Kingsley expresses the arguments of an unnamed friend and asks for a fair hearing:

'Don't talk to me of the moral and physical superiority of mountain races, for I tell you it is a dream. Civilization, art, poetry, belong to the lowlands . . . the stronger and cunninger races instinctively seize the lowlands, because they half know (and Providence knows altogether) that there alone they can become nations . . .'[15]

Races have their special characteristics, as in the claim 'The conception of a love match belongs to our Teutonic race'[16] but Kingsley's philosophy is not deterministic. The Goths perished because they broke one of the laws in becoming a slave-holding aristocracy.[17]

After *Hypatia*, Kingsley read Hakluyt's *Voyages* and other works about West Country seamen in the Elizabethan era.[18] The result was the most popular of his novels, *Westward Ho!* Hughes said that the Crimean War had literally wrung this book out of him and Kingsley remarked 'It is a sanguinary book, but perhaps containing doctrine profitable for these times'. To many it has seemed an anti-Catholic, anti-Spanish work, though it also expresses anti-slave trade sentiments. It is dedicated to Rajah Sir James Brooke and Bishop Selwyn of New Zealand for they had expressed even more heroically 'that type of English virtue, at once manful and godly, practical and enthusiastic, prudent and self-sacrificing, which he has tried to depict in these pages'. Kingsley describes Sir Walter Raleigh in Ireland condemning seven hundred Spaniards to slaughter as something necessary, but sees Spanish actions in very different terms. A theme that runs through the book is that one English man or ship is equal to a dozen Spaniards — as a sailor calls to a Spanish officer who seems unwilling to yield 'In the name of common sense, ye dogs, do you not see that you are but fifty strong to our twenty?'. There is little reference to race but much to the freedom-loving spirit of the English people, loyal to their queen, who never mutinied because of the fellow feeling between men and officers; the latter, like Homer's heroes or the old Norse Vikings, used their rank to lead and be followed. This was the time when Kingsley's admiration for Carlyle (who had figured in *Alton Locke*) and his emphasis upon the role of force was at its height, though towards the end of his life he still quoted as his favourite motto: 'be strong'.[19]

Sir James Brooke, the white rajah of Sarawak, in 1849 fought a successful battle against a Dyak pirate fleet. His right to prize money was queried in the House of Commons on charges, later investigated and dismissed, of his having needlessly taken the lives of many Dyaks.[20] Kingsley's love of adventure had been stirred by tales of Brooke's exploits and he bitterly resented the attacks upon him in certain London newspapers. In a letter to a friend, extracts from which have often been quoted against him, Kingsley revealed the vehemence he wished to bring to the cleansing of the temple.

'The truest benevolence is occasional severity . . . "Sacrifice of human life?" Prove that it is *human* life. It is beast-life. These Dyaks have put on the image of the beast, and they must take the consequence . . . Because Christ's kingdom is a kingdom of peace; because the meek alone shall inherit the earth, therefore, you Malays and Dyaks of Sarawak, you also are enemies to peace . . . you are beasts, all the more dangerous, because you have a semi-human cunning. I will, like David, "hate you with a perfect hatred" . . . I think the preserving that great line of coast from horrible outrage, by destroying the pirate fleet, *was* loving his neighbour as himself.'[21]

The Crimean War was one of the stimuli which moved Kingsley's attention from 'sanitary and social' questions to national issues and military matters. At the end of 1854 he told Hughes 'As to the War, I am getting more of a Government man every day'. The China War and the Indian Mutiny further excited his nervous temperament but whether they also sharpened his perceptions of racial conflict it is difficult to ascertain. Certainly they troubled his faith. Did God really intend that men should massacre women and children? 'I can hardly bear to look at a woman or child — even at my own sometimes. They raise such horrible images, from which I can't escape. What does it all mean? Christ is King, nevertheless! I tell my people so.' Perhaps it was because of these doubts that Kingsley was drawn to the idea of being a member of a disciplined force and enjoyed visiting the Staff College at Sandhurst and preaching to the troops at Aldershot and Woolwich. 'Even after he took holy orders it was a constant occupation to him, in all his walks and rides, to be planning fortifications. There is scarcely a hill-side within twenty miles of Eversley, the strong and weak points of which in attack and defence during a possible invasion, he has not gone over with as great an intensity of thought and interest as if the enemy were really at hand.'[22] Kingsley's writings had an appeal to soldiers and sailors, many of whom wrote to him for advice. It is small wonder that Kingsley came to be identified as the proponent of muscular Christianity, though he found this expression offensive.

The next topic to engage Kingsley's attention was the abolition of slavery in the United States. He had been very impressed by *Uncle Tom's Cabin* and wrote a novel *Two Years Ago* (1857) which centred on the injustice of racial discrimination as experienced by the heroine of the book, a quadroon. Martin's judgement that 'he felt a natural antipathy towards the coloured races'; that he showed 'contempt for the coloured races' and thought 'the subjects of the Queen were divinely inspired in their task of keeping order among inferior races' does not, I believe, faithfully represent Kingsley's outlook.[23] There is little or no evidence of attitudes specially associated with a dark skin colour or of any personal animus. Kingsley makes general statements about races, suggesting that some are better than others, but his concern is with God's purpose for humanity, and, with proper discretion, he keeps silence on problems he cannot elucidate. It has also to be remembered that he often uses the word 'race' very loosely. He could write that 'there is no more beautiful race in Europe than the wives and daughters of our London shopkeepers'. The serpent in the Garden of Eden is described as 'of lower race'.[24] This habit seems even to have spread to his Cambridge students, one of whom, saying how they liked his lectures, explained 'for undergraduates are an affectionate race'.[25]

One of the best clues to Kingsley's changing opinions is a private letter written in 1866 in which he says he earlier believed that all men were born into the world equals and that inequality, being a product of circumstances, was a wrong done by society to the less favoured. But 'nearly a quarter of a century spent in educating my parishioners, and experience with my own and others' children . . . have taught me that there are congenital differences and hereditary tendencies which defy all education from circumstances . . . I have seen, also, that certain races, e.g. the Irish Celts, seem quite unfit for self-government'.[26] Against de Tocqueville he asserts that circumstance is insufficient to alter the hearts and souls of men. Men act by theories and principles. Free institutions will not succeed without the prior education of men in self-government. The Roman Catholic philosophy of education cannot provide this, so that countries dominated by that Church can never be fit for free constitutional government. This is not a racial theory of backwardness. When in 1867 Kingsley spoke of the Negro race as 'mastered by circumstances' and 'not yet emerged' it seems to have been these moral or cultural causes of backwardness he had in mind.[27]

Kingsley was consistently opposed to slavery but maintained that freed slaves would need a long period of tutelage, 'A system of feudalism, gradually dying out and leaving the negro quite free, would be, to judge from history, the most prudent and practical method'. His personal position was demonstrably relevant for, when asked for a subscription to help the freed slaves after the war, he refused: 'The negro has had all I ever possessed; for emancipation ruined me . . . I am no slave-holder at heart. But I have paid my share of the great bill, in Barbados and Demerara, with a vengeance: and don't see myself called on to pay other men's!' (Kingsley's father's father had made a fortune from dealings in East and West Indian produce but as most of it was dissipated by trustees before Kingsley's father could inherit the grandson may have exaggerated these losses.) His testimony against slavery is the more significant if he believed he had suffered as a result of emancipation.

It would be interesting to learn how Kingsley's views about race were influenced by his relations with England's brashest exponent of the theory of permanent racial types. For worries about his stammering took him to the leading authority on its treatment, none other than Dr James Hunt, a young man of great energy who was soon to be founder of the Anthropological Society of London. Kingsley seems to have consulted him in the mid-fifties. We are told that in January 1857 he spent ten days in London visiting 'Hunt the stammering man' and that he passed a fortnight at Hunt's house in Swanage. Hunt became notorious for his views on Negro inferiority. It was doubtless he who persuaded Kingsley to become an honorary fellow of the Society, but Kingsley appears not to have taken any part in its activities and may well have reacted against the theories of its founder.

In 1859 Kingsley was appointed chaplain to the Queen. His ability to lecture on a wide range of subjects seems to have convinced the Prince Consort that he would be the best man to fill the chair of Regius Professor of Modern History at Cambridge. He took up this appointment in 1860, delivering an uncharacteristically feeble inaugural lecture on 'the limits of exact science as applied to history', which re-stated his belief that history is the story of God educating man and that supernatural causes, as well as natural agencies underly the record. The history of nations is affected by moral laws, such as that which declares that the fruit of unrighteousness is poverty and anarchy, weakness, and shame. His regular lecture course was unusually popular among the undergraduates. Kingsley knew his limitations: he aimed to encourage his students, rather than to instruct them, but he also emphasized the moral implications of the stories he told. Modern history was not necessarily very modern, for in the first year he stipulated that Gibbon was to be the text book. Later he lectured on the History of America because the Civil War was then a burning topic and he felt an obligation to consider how history was enacting itself around his own generation.

Earlier, Kingsley had written of a Norse-Saxon race, of 'our Caucasian empire' and of the Goths as representatives of 'our race'. He had romantically claimed that 'our forefathers were mystics for generations; they were mystics in the forests of Germany and in the dales of Norway . . .'.[28] In his Cambridge lectures Kingsley brought all these elements together in a new racial classification. Right at the beginning he advanced the remarkable statement 'I wish in this first lecture to give you some general conception of the causes which urged our Teutonic race to attack and destroy Rome'. It was a story compounded of Tacitus and forest children in a Troll-garden, misty as well as mystic. 'What circumstances', he later enquired, 'enabled our race to conquer in the most vast and important campaign the world has ever seen?'. He described it as a series of battles, imagined like the tactics for attacking a hill-side at Eversley and executed by captains of genius. The balance swung from side to side. For example 'the years from A.D. 550 to A.D. 750 and the rise of the Carlovingian dynasty, were a period of exhaustion for our race, such as follows on great victories, and the consequent slaughter and collapse'. But we won. Was this just the reward of our 'admirable military position'? Kingsley thought not. 'Shall I not believe that though this great war had no general upon earth, it may have had a general in Heaven? and that in spite of all their sins, the hosts of our forefathers were the hosts of God?'.[29] This celebration of the Teutonic ancestor myth reminds us that the myths of Teuton and Anglo-Saxon identity were fashioned in a context of European nationalism. The English population was expanding fast. A new social structure was in the making. A doctrine which told the people of all classes that they had a racial identity which was the key to glorious history, was of the greatest significance for the internal affairs of the country. Theories asserting the inferiority of coloured peoples could co-exist easily with such an outlook.

The mid 1860's were a time of intense activity for Kingsley. He was increasingly interested in the implications of Darwin's *Origin* and the controversies it occasioned, for he had himself a scientific inclination and was elected a Fellow of both the Linnean Society and the Geological Society.[30] In 1863 he published *The Water Babies*, which has links with his 1855 book *Glaucus, or The Wonders of the Shore*. In the following year he was involved in the controversy with John Henry Newman which resulted in the latter's *Apologia Pro Vita Sua*. In 1866 the snobbery flowered when the Kingsleys briefly entertained at Eversley rectory Queen Emma of the Sandwich Islands. As far as can be discerned, the Kingsleys regarded her as a Queen and not as a woman of inferior race. Queen Emma was received with fulsome obsequiousness. The same year also saw the publication of Kingsley's historical romance *Hereward the Wake: Last of the English*, in which he makes more use of the word 'race' than in any other of his novels. Hereward and William are presented as representatives of races in conflict; one character is able to see 'that his appeal to the antipathies of race had told'. But there were more than two races, for Kingsley speaks of the valiant peasants between Halifax and Cheshire as 'still the finest race of men in all England' as if there were then several English races. He stressed the independence of the English but remarks that land ownership was concentrated in an inbred aristocracy 'a state of affairs sufficient in itself to account for the easy victory of the French'. In Kingsley's story an earl can be recognized outwardly by his superior appearance even when disguised as a beggar. This is a heroic conflict set 'in times in which all English folk are one, and all old English feuds are wiped away' but 'the Anglo-Saxon race was wearing out' so it ends in defeat and English men see 'their race enslaved'.

The distinction between 'earl and churl' — the noble and the non-noble freeman — was crushed out in England, Kingsley thought, by the conquests of Sweyn, Canute, and William of Normandy. They created a community of suffering and a homogeneous people. Caste, or rather the wicked pride that perpetuates caste, was never permitted to develop. So Drake's officers would work alongside their seamen and there 'sprang up that respect, and even fondness for, severe, bodily labour, which the educated class of no nation save our own has ever felt; and which has stood them in such good stead, whether at home or abroad'. And in the same way it was possible for the squire's son to marry a bailiff's daughter and, later on, for the masses to share in political power.[31] In a preface to a Cambridge lecture, Kingsley asserted 'in England now the lower classes are ethnologically identical with the upper'.

In 1866 there was a bitter controversy over Governor Edward Eyre's repressive actions in putting down the Jamaican rebellion the previous October. Kingsley played an undistinguished part in the furore. Eyre was relieved of his post and ordered home. A committee had been formed in England whose intention it was to prosecute him for murder. On his arrival at Southampton he was received by a committee who proposed a banquet in his honour and organized an address of welcome. The dignitaries who welcomed Eyre at the banquet included some of the local nobility together with Charles Kingsley who happened to be staying with one of them. Kingsley gave a speech remarkable as much for its ignorance of Eyre's actions as for its adulation of 'the English spirit' and unctuous flattery of his company:

'Mr Eyre [said Kingsley] is so noble, brave and chivalric a man, so undaunted a servant of the Crown, so illustrious as an explorer in

Australia and a saviour of society in the West Indies, that Peers — actually Peers — my soul sinks with awe as I repeat *Peers* — members of the "sacred" order, which represents chivalry, which adopts into its ranks all genius, all talents, all virtue, and all beauty, condescend not indeed to give him a dinner — that would be too much — but to dine in the same room with him.'

Perhaps Kingsley's inclinations had been encouraged by the refreshment!

Friends of the ex-Governor organized the Eyre Defence Committee. Carlyle, Ruskin, Tennyson, and Dickens contributed. Henry Kingsley was an active member but not his brother Charles, who in Carlyle's words was 'hanging back afraid' after the criticism which his Southampton speech attracted, especially from the radicals who sensed betrayal. One who in days past had defended the working man had now turned his coat, and they excoriated him. Nor could Carlyle and Ruskin forgive Kingsley's 'cowardice'.[32] His old Christian Socialist friend Ludlow believed that Kingsley supported the Eyre Fund. Kingsley's abolitionist views counted for less than his weakness for the aristocratic ideology and he became an avowed pro-Southerner in the controversies over the Civil War. Ludlow therefore brought their friendship to an end. Like Kingsley's other old friend, Thomas Hughes, Ludlow supported the rival Jamaica Committee, together with J. S. Mill, Charles Darwin, Herbert Spencer, and T. H. Huxley. Eyre's case dragged on to 1872 when he was eventually vindicated.

The remainder of Charles Kingsley's chronology can be summarized briefly. In 1869 he resigned his chair and it was given to a more whole-hearted imperialist, J. R. Seeley. Kingsley became a Canon of Chester and gave there scientific lectures and excursions that were so popular that special trains had to be arranged. He presided over the educational section of the Social Science Congress at Bristol. In 1869–70 he visited the West Indies and wrote a book, *At Last! A Christmas in the West Indies*, about his journey. In 1873 he became a Canon of Westminster and undertook a journey through the United States. Then two years later he died at the age of fifty-five years.

Kingsley's tour in the West Indies would have brought to the forefront any ideas he might have entertained about Negro racial attributes, but there is little mention of them in the book. It is noteworthy that the book capitalizes the N when referring to Negroes, which was unusual at that time. He remarks that the Negro is probably one of the most ancient varieties of the human race, a variety which — to the Negro's great misfortune — has remained isolated 'on that vast island of

Central Africa' until three hundred years ago. Referring to an encounter with a Trinidad-born black man of great stature, beauty, and strength, Kingsley observes 'one could not look at him without hopeful surmises as to the possible rise of the Negro . . . by the appearance among them of sudden sports of nature; individuals of an altogether higher type'. Referring to instances of self-assertion and rudeness he counsels 'Let it be. We white people bullied these black people quite enough for three hundred years, to be able to allow them to play (for it is no more) at bullying us'. On the other hand, he did write home, 'I am afraid I don't like the negroes, especially the women . . .'. Black women departed further from Victorian standards of propriety than Hindu women in the West Indies, and Kingsley could not approve of their demeanour.[33]

To students of racial thought, the chief interest in Kingsley's later years lies in his attempts to come to terms with Darwin's revolution. Kingsley was torn in several directions. He gloried in the thought of force used to do God's work and believed his nation had an important mission in an expanding world. Much in demand as a speaker, he was drawn to the facile rhetoric of his racial philosophy of history. Having moved to a less optimistic view of individual human potentialities, he had to revise his ideas, spell out that philosophy in more specific terms, and work out the implications of the new scientific knowledge. His interest in science, and commitment to this way of finding truth, was genuine and deep. Darwin's book on the fertilization of orchids (1862) opened up a new world to Kingsley. He wrote to the author 'Your work helps mine at every turn'. But what was he to do about race? Darwin's vision of continual change conflicted with that of the permanence of types, lending support to the earlier view that races shaded into one another by continuous gradation. It also introduced the bogey of chance instead of design in the scheme of the universe.

Kingsley's first inclination was to see biological change as something that could either raise or lower a species in the evolutionary scale. *The Water Babies* (1863), though a children's story, is also a commentary on the contemporary disputes about evolution. He has the fairy remark 'Folks say now that I can make beasts into men, by circumstance, and selection, and competition, and so forth'. Arguing against anyone who says that things cannot degrade Kingsley refers ominously but unilluminatingly to 'the strange degradation of the common goose-barnacles, which one finds sticking on ship's bottoms; or the still stronger degradation of some cousins of theirs, of which one hardly likes to talk, so shocking and ugly it is'.[34] At the same time he writes to a scientific acquaintance about 'my belief, which I hardly dare state in these days . . .

that the soul of each living being down to the lowest, secretes the body thereof' and asks him to consider the possibility that the gorilla and the baboon may be degraded human beings.[35] Kingsley's faith in the Old Testament doubtless underlay his predisposition towards the theory of degradation which is an important theme in Victorian thought.[36] *The Water Babies* contains a tale intended to exemplify this. It concerns the Doasyoulikes who live at the foot of the Happy-go-lucky Mountains where Flapdoodle grows wild. Among the mountains is a volcano (volcanoes fascinated Kingsley) and an eruption reduces the population to one-third. A series of snapshots over a three-thousand year span show the Doasyoulikes degrading. They take to the trees where natural selection favours those with feet that can best grip the branches. The less well adapted are eaten by lions. They grow hair. Finally all that is left is one big gorilla 'and Mr Du Chaillu came up to him and shot him'.[37] The passage was received with glee in the *Anthropological Review* which stressed the permanence of types and resisted Darwinian interpretation. 'According to our interpretation, when the Doasyoulikes had once ascended the trees, and the weaker individuals had all been eaten up by the lions, the felines would have had nothing to eat . . . unless their structure was modified to catch something else . . . they must have died. Then, when the lions were all dead, the Doasyoulikes might have safely descended the trees.' Or the lions best able to climb would have been favoured by natural selection; they would have climbed trees after the men who would have reverted to living on the ground. The selective process would come back to the point of departure.[38] However, Kingsley did not pursue his degeneration theory. It was too speculative.

A more serious reassessment came in 1871 with a lecture entitled 'The Natural Theology of the Future' which he read at Sion College, London, early in 1871. The author regarded this as one of his most important statements for it is printed not only in his *Scientific Lectures and Essays* but as a preface to his *Westminster Sermons*, because these sermons, he says, develop the idea pervading the lecture, 'namely that facts, whether of physical nature, or of the human heart and reason, do not contradict, but coincide with, the doctrines and formulas of the Church of England, as by law established'. In one of the scientific lectures delivered in Chester in the same year, Kingsley set out the reasoning for the unity of the human race and the belief that the Negro is a man and a brother.

'If the only two types of man in the world were an extreme white type, like the Norwegians, and an extreme black type, like the Negroes, then there would be fair grounds for saying "These two types have been always distinct: they are different races, who have no common origin". But if you found, as you will find, many types of man showing endless gradations between them both and a third type, whose extreme perhaps is a Chinese . . . then you are justified in saying "All these are mere varieties of one kind . . .".'

In the Sion College lecture Kingsley pleaded for a natural theology which would set forth a God whose character is consistent with all the facts of nature. Physical science would demand that theologians were aware of important issues, especially those of Embryology and Race. Some people had a nervous fear of the word race and of allowing any importance to differences between races. Some thought it endangered democratic principles. Kingsley claimed that science had proven whites and Negroes to be of the same race. 'I should have thought, as a humble student of such questions, that the one fact of the unique distribution of the hair in all races of human beings, was full moral proof that they had all had one common ancestor.' 'Physical science is proving more and more the immense importance of Race . . .'. She is proving, said Kingsley, that natural selection operates as Darwin claimed, as a daily and hourly scrutiny of every variation, rejecting that which is bad, preserving and adding up that which is good. Did not this reveal God's care and God's providence as even more magnificent than had been supposed?

Kingsley argued that natural theologians must learn from the lessons of science, but tell the scientific men 'Your duty is to find out the How of things; ours to find out the Why. If you rejoin that we shall never find out the Why, unless we first learn something of the How, we shall not deny that.' He asked his audience 'What is the central fact, save One, of the New Testament, but the conquest of Jerusalem — the dispersion, all but destruction of a race, not by miracle, but by invasion, because found wanting when weighed in the stern balances of natural and social law?'.[39] Thus he wishes to represent the Jews as a race while maintaining that all mankind is of one race. He wants the literary flourish at the same time as he acknowledges, and publishes, the scientific truth.

The lectures he gave on his American tour two years later show how difficult it was for him to revise his view of human history to acknowledge that different people were indeed but 'mere varieties of one kind'. It could have been done, for the South African Calvinist theologians have pictured nations as the agents of God's purpose. But Kingsley could not discard the rhetoric of race and he could not bring himself to accept an evolutionary anthropology that left no room for moral laws.

The savage might derive from an ape-like creature, but there was no good evidence for civilized man's having done so. 'In history there is no record, absolutely no record, as far as I am aware, of any savage tribe civilizing itself.' Our line did not come from 'the savages who chipped flints and fed on mammoth and reindeer in North-Western Europe, shortly after the age of ice, a few hundred thousand years ago'. It must have come from the 'true mass of mankind — spreading northward from the Tropics into climes becoming, after the long catastrophe of the age of ice, once more genial enough to support men who knew what decent comfort was, and were strong enough to get the same, by all means fair or foul'. In Kingsley's view the theory of organic evolution was not so much wrong as by itself insufficient, for 'what we see at the beginning of all known and half-known history, is not savagery, but high civilization'. His dream was that the origin of civilization might lie in the 'education of a man, or a family by beings of some higher race than man'.

In another lecture Kingsley made Cyrus the Great the founding ancestor of a racial succession which had reached an even higher pinnacle in late eighteenth century Anglo-Saxon Englishmen and Americans. This is the only other occasion I have noticed on which he uses the expression Aryan race, in saying that in Cyrus and his hardy Persians 'first does our race, the Aryan race, appear in authentic history. In them first did our race give promise of being the conquering and civilizing race of the future world.' After telling the story of Cyrus and his successors, Kingsley concludes 'that we are now the last link in a chain of causes and effects which reaches as far back as the emigration of the Persians southward from the plateau of Pamir'. On another occasion he refers to the effects on France and Spain of British actions in the American War of Independence which 'made certain, as I believe, the coming day when the Anglo-Saxon race shall be the real masters of the whole New World'.[40] Perhaps the dais of an American lecture hall was not the best place to expect a considered statement of a late Victorian Englishman's views on such topics. Kingsley's judgement, like that of other visiting Englishmen, seems to have been impaired by the vision of a transatlantic unity.

In his day Kingsley was a grand public figure. In religious discussions his name was well known for his opposition to Catholicism and high church tendencies within the Church of England. He preached a direct, manly, middle-of-the-road Christianity and his moral earnestness won him the respect of the dissenters. It was they who first adopted 'Kingsley' as a Christian name and it may have been their missionaries who took this practice to the West Indies where the name is popular. There is a special irony in the popularity of *Westward Ho!* and others of Kingsley's works for school reading in Jamaica. But it was probably Kingsley's literary popularity that had the greatest influence. His works sold widely (*Westward Ho!* sold 8,000 in two years, later rising to 500,000; in 1889 Macmillan brought out a million copy edition of his works at 6d. per volume; thousands were ordered for Mudie's lending libraries, while the Education League printed 10,000 copies of the 1869 Bristol lecture).

What part Kingsley's teaching may have played in the swelling European racial thinking of the next decades is not easy to estimate. In a loose and unphilosophical way his novels must have encouraged English people to think in racial categories and to believe that this was a key to the understanding of history. Ironically, the word 'race' suggested that the clue lay in the inherited physical characteristics of the people so classified, whereas Kingsley's continued endeavour was to persuade his audiences that physical causes were only part of an explanation. Climatic changes might impel a race to move to a new and more favourable environment, but men regularly fail to take advantage of their opportunities, 'increasing the inequalities of nature by their own selfishness, instead of decreasing them, into the equality of grace, by their own self-sacrifice'. Kingsley's message was that moral causes were also essential in any philosophy of history and he summed up his doctrine in the proclamation 'As a people behaves, so it thrives; as it believes, so it behaves'.[41] It would have been surprising had any writer of this generation with Kingsley's interests not made some use of the notion of race in expounding such a philosophy.

Notes and References

1. The title of this essay is intended as a tribute to Cedric Dover, the Eurasian poet and writer on race relations who was born in Calcutta in 1904 and died in London in 1962. (See *inter alia* the obituary notice in *Man* vol. 62, 1962, article 85.) In the later years of his life Dover embarked upon a series of studies of the racial philosophies of crucial cultural figures: Ibn Khaldun, Jehuda Halevi, Johann Herder, and Antarah, the Arab poet (see *Phylon* vol. 13, 1952; 107–19, 312–22; vol. 15, 1954: 41–57, 177–89, and *Br. J. Sociol.* vol. 3, 1952: 124–33). Dover's essays were presented with grace and sensitivity; his programme displayed an originality of far more than antiquarian interest, so it is sad that his work inspires little emulation today.

86   The Idea of Race

2. *Encyclopaedia Britannica*, 1970 edition. To reduce the number of notes I have not always given page references for information available in *Charles Kingsley: his letters and memories of his life*, edited by his wife, of which there have been thirty-one editions or reprintings. The first edition appeared in 1877, an abridged two volume edition in 1890 contains some new material. There are also differences in arrangement so I have referred to both editions.

3. C. W. Stubbs, *Charles Kingsley and the Christian Social Movement*, London: Blackie, 1899, p. 32. It is worth noting a reference to contemporary beliefs about factors other than race which influenced an individual's temperament. Mrs Kingsley believed that all impressions made on her own mind during pregnancy would be transmitted to the infant, and in this faith gave herself up to the enjoyment of Devonshire scenery. Cf. Veronica Pearson's unpublished Bristol M.Sc. thesis on Telegony, of 1972.

4. The thirty-sixth chapter contains a dream sequence which reflects the contemporary biological theory that a human embryo became fully human only by passing through less evolved living forms. After having been a baby ape the dreamer believes himself a child on a woman's bosom. 'Was she . . . some ideal of the great Arian tribe, containing in herself all future types of European woman?' A similar female figure later declares 'in the Asgard of the Hindoo-Koh, in the cup of the four rivers, in the womb of the mother of nations, in brotherhood, equality and freedom the sons of men were begotten . . .'. In 1848, according to Susan Chitty, *The Beast and the Monk: A Life of Charles Kingsley*, London: Hodder & Stoughton, 1974, p. 115, when lecturing on English literature, Kingsley advanced the theories that the Anglo-Saxon, a 'female' race, required impregnation by the great male race, the Norse, before it could produce the famous ballads of the border. The notion of male and female races is not, however, made explicit in his published writing.

5. Margaret Farrand Thorp, *Charles Kingsley, 1819-1875*, Princeton: Princeton University Press, 1937, pp. 83–4. It is noteworthy that this was not among the sermons which were reprinted and copies of it are now rare.

6. Torben Christensen, *Origin and History of Christian Socialism 1848-54*, Aahus: Universitets förlag, 1962, *passim*, esp. pp. 140n, 256, and 297n. See also R. B. Martin, *The Dust of Combat, a life of Charles Kingsley*, London: Faber, 1959, pp. 154—5.

7. *Letters and Memories* 1877, i 252-53; 1890, i 203.

8. *Historical Lectures and Essays*, p. 297. Unless otherwise indicated, references to Kingsley's works are to the collected edition published by Macmillan.

9. *Scientific Lectures and Essays*, pp. 232-6.

10. *Yeast*, pp. 249 and 250.

11. *Sanitary and Social Essays*, pp. 258-59.

12. *Letters and Memories*, 1877, i 414-15; 1890, i 317. *Good News of God*, p. 163; *Madam How and Lady Why*, p. 97.

13. *Discipline*, p. 37.

14. *National Sermons*, pp. 245–46, 266, 483, 415–16.
15. *Prose Idylls*, pp. 36–8.
16. *Letters and Memories*, 1877, ii 94; 1890, ii 103.
17. *The Roman and the Teuton*, p. 151.
18. Charles Kingsley's niece, Mary Henrietta Kingsley, ascribed the rumbustious style that characterizes her writing on West Africa to her reading of the early navigators and books like Johnson's *The Robberies and Murders of the Most Notorious Pirates*, which she believed her father and uncle read in their father's library, stocked with ancestral books and records relating to the Spanish Main, to Barbados, and Demerara.
19. For a contemporaneous suggestion of Kingsley's that a general war might elevate England's spirit, see *Literary and General Essays*, p. 98.
20. Sir Steven Runciman, *The white Rajahs: a history of Sarawak from 1841 to 1946*, Cambridge: Cambridge University Press, 1960.
21. *Letters and Memories*, 1877, i 222–23; 1890, i 340–42.
22. *Letters and Memories*, 1877, ii 34, 48; 1890, ii 61, 70.
23. Martin. *op. cit.*, pp. 213, 257–8, 172.
24. *Sanitary and Social Essays*, pp. 264 and 170.
25. *Letters and Memories*, 1890, ii 118.
26. *Letters and Memories* 1877, ii 242–43; 1890, ii 199–201. On a visit to Ireland in 1860 he wrote of being 'haunted by the human chimpanzees I saw along that hundred miles . . . if they were black one would not feel it so much, but their skins, except where tanned by exposure, are as white as ours'. *Ibid.* 1877, ii 107; 1890, ii 111–12. On anti-Irish prejudice in Victorian England, see L. P. Curtis, Jr., *Anglo-Saxons and Celts*, Bridgeport, Conn: Conference on British Studies, 1968.
27. *Historical Lectures*, pp. 204–205, 209.
28. *Literary and General Essays*, p. 301.
29. *The Roman and the Teuton*, pp. 292–306. According to J. M. Robertson, Charles Kingsley apart from being 'the most flagrantly hysterical type in all modern literature' was 'one of the first prophets of the Teutonic forefather gospel in England', see *The Saxon and the Celt*, London, 1897, p. 9. The second statement at least is definitely wrong and it is puzzling that Kingsley's use of the Teutonic theme should have seemed original to a writer of Robertson's perspicacity.
30. Kingsley confessed great admiration for scientific men, and included in this respect the economists, for he considered economics 'the subject matter for all future social science' (*Letters and Memories*, 1877, ii 36; 1890, ii 66). He told military officers 'Respect scientific men . . . they are fighting their nation's battle, often on even less pay than you' (*Scientific Lectures*, p. 196) and asserted to an audience in the Railway Works, Crewe, 'Power will pass more and more, if all goes healthily and well, into the hands of scientific men . . . and specially those of the Teutonic Race' (cf. *Ibid*, p. 21). Part of the attraction of science for Kingsley seems to have been the power it could bring. The lecture continued by prophesying a sequence in which aristocracies of mere birth give way to aristocracies of mere wealth, then of the noisiest, then to the aristocracy of mere 'order', which means organized

88   The Idea of Race

brute force and military despotism. The only alternative is an aristocracy of sound and rational science which can establish a rule of health, wealth, peace, prudence and justice.

31. Preface to The Ancient Regime, *Historical Essays*.

32. Bernard Semmel, *Democracy versus Empire: the Jamaica Riots of 1865 and the Governor Eyre Controversy*, New York: Anchor Books, 1962 (originally published in England under the title *The Governor Eyre Controversy* and in the United States with the title *Jamaican Blood and Victorian Conscience*), in the Anchor edition, see especially pp. 97–106.

33. Earlier Kingsley had befriended J. A. Froude when he fell into disgrace for writing a supposedly anti-religious book. On his West Indian tour Kingsley was introduced to a black Trinidadian, J. J. Thomas, and probably acted as his patron when the latter came to England. Thomas is now celebrated as the author of *Froudacity*, a criticism of Froude's book on the West Indies (see p. 15 of the 1969 edition, London and Port of Spain: New Beacon Books).

34. *The Water Babies*, pp. 276 and 85.

35. *Letters and Memories*, p. 247.

36. A literal view of the Biblical record is evident in a relatively early sermon when referring to Noah's generation, 'Their enormous length of life (six, seven, and eight hundred years commonly) . . .' *Village, Town and Country Sermons*, p. 77, but by 1867 he is writing to Darwin ('my dear and honoured master') about an article which pleases him because the writer is 'forced to allow some great duration of the earth', *Letters and Memories* 1877 ed. ii 248–49.

37. *Ibid*, pp. 266–75. The explorer Paul B. Du Chaillu had reported on the gorilla species in *Explorations and Adventures in Equatorial Africa*, 1861.

38. *Anthropological Review* vol. 6, 1868, pp. 472–76. For a valuable commentary on the scientific background to Kingsley's fiction, see Arthur Johnston, 'The Water Babies: Kingsley's debt to Darwin', *English* XII, 1959: 215–19

39. *Scientific Lectures and Essays*, pp. 92, 321–24, 329, 325.

40. *Lectures delivered in America in 1874*, London: Longmans, 1875, pp. 132–35, 101, 120–23, 30. The first two lectures are reprinted in *Historical Lectures and Essays*, see pp. 295–97, 267, 283–86.

41. Richard D. Altick, *The English Common Reader: a Social History of the Mass Reading Public 1800-1900*. Chicago: University of Chicago Press, 1957, pp. 313–14, 385. *Lectures delivered in America*, p. 135, *Historical Lectures*, p. 297, *The Roman and the Teuton*, p. 337.

The author is indebted to Michael Biddiss, Kenneth Grayston, Colin Holmes, Mrs Joan Leopold, Delroy Loudon, Christopher Ricks, George Stocking, and Norman Vance for comments on topics in this essay.

5

Social Darwinism

By social Darwinism is meant the application to society of principles believed to have been established by Charles Darwin. For the present discussion its chief features are those that entailed a modification or outright reversal of the propositions of racial typology. The theory of types in its purest form stated that underlying the superficial variations in human constitutions there was a limited number of permanent types of distinct origin. Interbreeding had no effect as hybrid stocks were ultimately sterile. The diversity of human forms made this a difficult doctrine to defend, and most exponents admitted some possibilities of change. Their statements usually implied that there had been pure races in the past and that interbreeding was leading to degeneration. Several versions of the theory presented inter-racial antagonism as something bred into the nature of races, or at least of the successful races. Social Darwinism also saw relations between peoples of different races as biologically determined, but in a less mechanical way. In contrast to the pessimism of men like Gobineau, Darwinists thought that the operation of natural selection would create pure races out of the prevailing diversity; while many of them held that if eugenic measures were adopted biological change could be on the side of human progress.

Like its predecessor, social Darwinism denied the split between body and spirit crucial to Christian theology. Evolution offered, or appeared to offer, a physical cause explanation of everything in the human realm, including morals. The theory of natural selection exerted an immeasureable influence upon most aspects of early twentieth century thought. The basic concepts of social Darwinism, as seen by one of its expositors (Chatterton-Hill, 1907: 3) were four. First, variability: no two living beings were alike. Species changed over time, so there were no permanent types. Second, heredity: an individual's characters were not acquired by adaptation but inherited from his ancestor. This principle was regarded as limiting the power of an individual to achieve certain ends and as weakening the significance of moral causes in human affairs. Third, excessive fecundity: the demonstration that so many more organisms were generated than were necessary for the maintenance or even the expansion of the species damaged earlier notions of a divine economy in nature. Fourth, selection: the proposition that certain individuals because of accidental variation would be favoured by the selective process appeared to base evolution upon chance instead of supernatural design and was disturbing to those who thought in the old terms. Biological fitness was not judged in terms of merit but simply of success in leaving the most numerous progeny.

In England and the United States the development of social Darwinism was overlaid by the fame accorded Herbert Spencer (1820–1903). Spencer was a prophet of evolution and an exponent of the recommendation that societies be regarded as organisms well before the days of Darwin's fame. He believed that acquired characters could be inherited. His work is not characterized by any acceptance of Darwin's outlook so much as by political individualism and the attempt to synthesize contemporary knowledge within an evolutionary framework. Spencer's writing was often on a high plane of generalization. He defined evolution as 'an integration of matter and a concommitant dissipation of motion; during which the matter passes from an indefinite, incoherent homogeneity to a definite coherent heterogeneity, and during which the retained motion undergoes a parallel transformation'. This was promptly satirized as 'Evolution is a change from a nohowish, untalkaboutable, all-alikeness, to a somehowish and in general talkaboutable, all-alikeness, by continuous somethingelseifications and sticktogetherations'. The general tendency of social Darwinism was to stress the society as the unit of competition and selection; many contemporaries defined Spencer's doctrine as 'individualist' and saw the core of Darwinist applications as pointing to attempts to improve the inherited stock by eugenic measures (cf. Halliday, 1971). There are good reasons (cf. Peel, 1971: 234) for regarding Spencer as standing a little outside social Darwinism and for concentrating upon other elements in this movement which stood closer to concepts of race.

The response to Darwin's work in France was slower than in England, the United States, or Germany. Partly this was because the French word *évolution* was applied to the development of individual creatures and the proper equivalent to Darwin's notion was *transformisme*. Be that as it may, there are advantages in starting an exposition of social Darwinism with Germany, for there the intellectual scene was more straightforward, and in Haeckel and Gumplowicz may be found two accomplished and influential expositors. For a time sociology was in some quarters identified with biology, as may be seen in P. Lilienfeld's motto 'sociologus nemo, nisi biologus' and in the remark of a character in Chekhov's *The Duel* 'I am a zoologist or a sociologist, which is the same thing'.

Ernst Haeckel (1834–1919) was a famous zoologist in his own right, but much of his fame came from his popular science writing. The first edition of his *History of Creation* (1867) proved very successful and he followed it later with *The Riddle of the Universe* (1899) which sold 100,000 copies in its first year and under the Nazis reached the half-million mark. In the *History* and in a similar volume, *Wonders of Life*, Haeckel maintained that racial differences were fundamental. The lower races were nearer to the animal creation: 'woolly haired Negroes' were 'incapable of higher mental development'. Papuans and Hottentots were 'fast approaching their complete extinction' because 'in the struggle for life, the more highly developed, the more favoured and larger groups and forms, possess the positive inclination and the certain tendency to spread more at the expense of the lower, more backward, and smallest groups'. Haeckel went on to make a secular religion out of evolutionary ideas, developing a philosophy he called Monism which insisted on the unity of organic and inorganic nature.

Another enthusiast was the Polish-born sociologist Ludwig Gumplowicz (1838–1909) who lectured at Austrian universities on sociological and political theory. Though he afterwards moved away from social Darwinism, Gumplowicz' early work is interesting as a systematic development of a naturalistic theory of political evolution in which all institutions are to be explained in terms of their contribution to a grand evolutionary sequence. In *Race and State* Umplowicz argues that every where the organism of the state grows out of contact between two different races, one having better blood and ruling the other, but for the state to be properly established a middle estate of traders and manufacturers has to be inserted between the others. The relation between the constituent races is one of physical and economic struggle, the form of the state being the means used by the element then in power to advance its interests. But culture flourishes and citizens benefit if the internal oppositions can be reconciled, and education fill the gaps between the separate elements. 'The secret of political and culture-historical evolution lies in the variety of population elements, in the struggle of races and their eventual amalgamation . . . in the shared consciousness of the state arise burning patriotic and national sentiments; out of the agglomerate of races arises — the nation' (1875: 30–34, 56).

Six years later Gumplowicz introduced the expression 'ethnocentrism' in a clumsy passage which shows how his evolutionary theory contained a sociology of knowledge.

'As man sees himself as the centre of the earth (anthropocentrism), as every people sees itself as the foremost (ethnocentrism), so has the biblical myth, and so likewise have the myths of other peoples only one purpose, which is to invent a first pair, created by God so that their own people are always represented as the direct descendants of this first pair — as those whom God as Lord of creation expressly in this fashion called into existence.' (1881: 71)

In the comprehensive statement of Gumplowicz' theory of racial struggle which followed shortly afterwards ethnocentrism reappears as 'a limited and self-satisfied approach to the social world' but now its evolutionary function is identified 'Short and to the point, ethnocentrism in all its forms produced the prospect of advance, because every people and every time considers itself better than every other people and every previous time'. Reviewing the history of Europe, he concluded 'the means by which all this was accomplished, by which tribes became peoples, peoples nations, nations grew into races and developed themselves, is something we know already; it is the perpetual struggle between races for dominance, the soul and spirit of all history' (1885: 353, 342). This theory represented race relations as relations of conflict, and conflict as something biologically determined; it was not something to be avoided, for out of conflict and prejudice came progress, and when conflict was eventually subdued by amalgamation this came about because a dominant group used the apparatus of the state to regulate the struggles of races.
struggles of races.

A quite different expression of social Darwinism can be seen in what was known as the school of anthropo-sociology. This was an international school represented in Germany by Otto Ammon, in France by Georges Vacher de Lapouge, in England by John Beddoe, and in the United States by G. C. Closson. While more detailed studies of the work of these writers in relation to their milieux would probably prove of interest, their main contentions have been adequately summarized and discussed elsewhere in several readily accessible sources (see Sorokin, 1928: 233–51; Stark, 1961; Barzun, 1965). They approached the study of race from physical anthropology, devoting much energy to the measurement of head shape, counting the incidence of different eye and hair colours, and so on. This produced little of value. In so far as the anthropo-sociologists advanced any explanation of patterns of race relations it was in terms of the migration of races, differential fertility, and the theory that the conditions of urban living led to physical degeneration. Racial antagonism was often seen as innate.

In many of the writings about racial superiority the author interprets the evidence as suggesting that it is his own race that is superior, but this was not always so as the case of de Lapouge illustrates. He devoted many years to the collection of cranial measurements and, believing that the superior Aryan element could be recognized by their long-headedness, he acknowledged that the population of England was racially superior to that of his own. He hastened to point out that he did not mean that every Englishman was superior to every Frenchman. One of his countrymen, Edmond Demolins, had published a volume which went through many editions in French and was entitled in translation *Anglo-Saxon superiority: to what it is due.* In it he argued, among other things, for the adoption in France of an educational system along English lines. Lapouge maintained that this would be useless for racial character determined educational practice and not the reverse. He testified to his love for political demonstrations in Anglo-Saxon countries but was confident that broad-headed peoples' minds could not comprehend the spirit behind the political liberties of the long-headed (Lapouge, 1889: 375–6, 392, 402). Thus racial theories could create self-doubt and pessimism in European countries. Within the terms of such theories it was possible to counter-attack by disparaging the unimaginativeness of 'the creeping Saxon' and stressing the superior spirit and creativity of the Celts. In this way those who disliked particular applications of racial typology could pick up threads from the earlier themes of racial romanticism, but in so doing they only strengthened the assumption that temperament was determined by race.

In Germany Haeckel's influence did not fall away when he retired from teaching at Jena. In 1906 the Monist League was established to propagate his doctrines and formulate programmes for their application. Otto Ammon stood close to Haeckel and so did Ludwig Woltman, Gumplowicz's favourite pupil and winner of a Krupp-sponsored prize for an essay on 'What we can learn from the principles of Darwinism for application to inner political development and the laws of the state'. The Monist League stressed the importance of the nation as an evolutionary entity, aggressively denying the political and social assumptions of bourgeois liberalism (such as conceptions of civil rights, the importance of observing constitutional principles, and separating the spheres of the individual and the state). Haeckel and the Monists were the first to formulate a programme of racial imperialism and the acquisition of *lebensraum* for Germany. The League had its own social Darwinist penal philosophy which entailed the establishment of asylums for the feeble-minded where they would be prevented from breeding and kept strictly isolated. Haeckel supported one of German's most militant, imperialistic, nationalistic, and anti-Semitic organizations, the Pan-German League, helping to fashion the social Darwinist and racialist features of its programme. David Gasman (1971) has maintained that Germans saw Darwin and Darwinism through the distorted lenses of Ernst Haeckel and that parallels to his ideas can be seen in the writing of Adolf Hitler (cf. also Poliakov, 1974: 283–325). Nazism assimilated the fundamental ideas of Haeckel and the Monists, defining itself as 'political biology'. Nevertheless, Haeckel never achieved the status of a major Nazi prophet like Houston Stewart Chamberlain, the Englishman turned German citizen who wrote *The Foundations of the Twentieth Century* in which he proclaimed 'a noble race . . . becomes noble gradually, and, this gradual process can begin anew at any moment'. Probably Haeckel's doctrines were regarded with some suspicion by the Nazis because they wished to play down the animal origin of man. Their chief ideologist, Alfred Rosenberg, did not use as he might have done earlier writing on the anthropology of race, preferring to write in empty but high-sounding phrases. As the Nazis assigned a heroic and eternally superior character and racial constitution to the Aryans, they were closer to the theory of permanent types than to social Darwinism.

In Britain the chief expositors of social Darwinism were Walter Bagehot in *Physics and Politics* (1872), Benjamin Kidd, and the energetic propagandist for eugenics, Karl Pearson. I have little to add to what I have written elsewhere about these authors (Banton, 1967: 37–50) and their relation to contemporary movements has been discussed in some other works (e.g. Semmel, 1960: 29–52). They also attracted contemporary critics like Prince Peter Kropotkin whose stress on mutual aid was just as legitimate an application of Darwin's social message as that of the authors who saw in it the thesis of unavoidable and continuous competition.

This raises the question whether Charles Darwin himself was a social Darwinist. There is little in the *Origin* to support such a conclusion, but by the time he came to write *The Descent of Man* (1871), Darwin was willing to follow Francis Galton and W. R. Greg in underlining the importance of natural selection as a process affecting the civilized nations and calling for eugenic measures. He wrote 'the wonderful progress of the United States, as well as the character of the people, are the results of natural selection; for the more energetic, restless, and courageous men from all parts of Europe have emigrated . . . and have there succeeded best'. A few pages later there is an implicit comparison as he writes about the declining fertility and likely extinction of savage races — with their smaller brains — unable to change their habits when brought into contact with civilized races. At the same time it would be misguided to attribute Darwin's over-emphasis upon the importance of selection in social change to the temper of his times. Darwin's theory does not depend on any analogy with the kind of social competition supposed to be responsible for nineteenth century progress; it can be subjected to testing just like any other scientific theory. In any case struggle is not a basic element in natural selection, but a metaphorical description of the conditions in which it occurs. The essential element in natural selection is differential reproduction (cf. Ghiselin, 1969: 59–77). To understand why Darwin emphasized selection so much in this section of the *Descent* it is more instructive to appreciate the error in his conception of variation. Darwin subscribed to a 'blending' theory of inheritance according to which an inherited character appears as a compromise between parental attributes (to over-simplify, a black-haired man and a blonde woman will have brown-haired children). He did not know, with Mendel, that inheritance was particulate. According to a blending theory, if a clever person married someone stupid, the capacities of the former would all be lost in the next generation (a stimulus to eugenic proposals). As the beneficent effects of new variants would so soon be lost, selection would have to be drastic to be effective. The cause of variation was not central to Darwin's problem and his mistaken presentation of it may have given the social Darwinist recommendations an added urgency.

By the end of the nineteenth century there are clear signs in England of much greater hostility towards and contempt for, black people. This was doubtless related to changes in the social structure as well as to purely intellectual currents. Philip Mason relates it to class differences and the fear of equality. He suggests that in the early eighteenth century men took it for granted that they were not equal and behaved as though they were. By the end of the nineteenth century, however, it would have been unusual to hold that there were innate differences between Englishmen and yet it would have been eccentric to behave in practice as though there were not. There was a growing aloofness evident in the way the lower classes were believed to smell and the servants were kept firmly below stairs. Economic growth enabled the rich to lead a more separate existence and to resist challenge by erecting physical barriers that prevented others from seeing how little different they really were (Mason, 1962: 12–38).

However it came about, the expression of racial superiority could be quite unequivocal. Joseph Chamberlain, sometime Secretary of State for the Colonies, declared: 'I believe in this race, the greatest governing race the world has ever seen; in this Anglo-Saxon race, so proud, so tenacious, self-confident and determined, this race which neither climate nor change can degenerate, which will infallibly be the predominant force of future history and universal civilization' (quoted in Laver, 1966: 230). Such a profession of faith from Chamberlain is perhaps less surprising than evidence of the hold that racial thinking had on Gilbert Murray, the classical scholar, humanitarian, and devoted supporter of the League of Nations. After having written of the murderous brutality of white men towards aborigines in Australia in terms which would not suggest much claim to moral superiority on the part of white races, Murray continues 'There is in the world a hierarchy of races . . . those nations which eat more, claim more, and get higher wages, will direct and rule the others, and the lower work of the world will tend in the long-run to be done by the lower breeds of men. This much we of the ruling colour will no doubt accept as obvious' (1900: 156). James Bryce, who would never have accepted the complete Darwinist doctrine, displayed its pervasiveness when lecturing at much the same time. He described 'race-antagonism' as 'an evil more dangerous, because rooted in nature', and went on to advise 'for the future of mankind nothing is more vital than that some races should be maintained at the highest level of efficiency . . . it may therefore be doubted whether any further mixture of Advanced and Backward races is to be desired' (Bryce, 1902: 27, 36).

At the end of the nineteenth and in the early twentieth century the British saw race relations in an imperial context as involving them with backward races overseas. Social Darwinism flourished both in this context and in discussions of the relations between social classes at home. Similar patterns were present in the United States. The Spanish-American war and Theodore Roosevelt's warnings that 'we cannot avoid the responsibilities that confront us in Hawaii, Cuba, Porto Rico, and the Philippines' provide examples of the one, and the National Conference on Race Betterment at Battle Creek in 1914 of the other (Hofstadter, 1955: 161–200). But the situation in the United States was different in two important respects: the internal race 'problem' and the earlier development of academic sociology.

The most recent studies emphasize the continuing white hostility towards black Americans in the South in the years following the Civil War (Friedman, 1970). Darwinism contributed to the general belief that Negroes were so much less well endowed than whites, that in a natural struggle they would die out (Haller, 1971: 209; Fredrickson, 1972). The conflicts in American society and the different expectations of groups within it stimulated the growth of sociology. Its harbinger was George Fitzhugh's pro-slavery attack on the 'free society' of Northern capitalism, entitled *Society for the South* (1854). The first college course described as 'sociology' was one taught at Yale by William Graham Sumner (1840–1910), who after pursuing theological studies at Geneva, Göttingen, and Oxford became Professor of Political and Social Science at Yale in 1872. Just at this time he came upon Spencer's work and, plunging into Darwin, Haeckel, and Huxley as well, he saturated himself with evolutionism (Hofstadter, 1955; 51–66). As a social critic, Sumner's position was that of 'the forgotten man' — the middle-class citizen who went quietly about his business, providing for himself and his family without making demands upon the state. Society was a superorganism changing at a geological tempo in accordance with natural laws. Socialists and other social meddlers who ignored those laws and engaged in 'the absurd effort to make the world over' were foolish romantics unwilling to learn the lessons of history.

As his teaching became more systematic Sumner regretted the lack of a suitable textbook; he sat down to write one of his own, which became *Folkways*, one of the most influential works of early twentieth-century sociology. Apart from his own ideas, his inspiration came from Herbert Spencer and two Europeans, Julius Lippert and Gustav Ratzenhofer, though he also borrowed the concept of ethnocentrism without acknowledgement from Gumplowicz and has been credited with its invention by generations of American sociologists who do not read the classics. In *Folkways* Sumner presented a panorama of human customs, interpreting them as instinctive responses to the stimuli of hunger, sex, vanity, and fear, selectively guided by pain and pleasure. His emphasis was upon the limited ability of 'stateways' and legislation to change behaviour which had such deep physical and emotional roots. This shifted the stress from the efficacy of competition to the stability of social forms. It is evident in the book's most influential innovation, the concept of *mores* (the plural form of the Latin *mos*, meaning custom).

Folkways is subtitled 'a Study of the Sociological Importance of Usages, Manners, Customs, Mores and Morals'. It brings together reports from different times and different parts of the world concerning such topics as slavery, abortion, infanticide, cannibalism, marriage, incest, kinship, primitive justice, sacral harlotry, and so forth. Sumner begins with the remark that 'the first task of life is to live. Men begin with acts, not with thoughts.' From man's solutions of problems arise customs. From customs and instincts arise folkways which gradually become arbitrary, positive, and imperative. They are seen as 'right' and 'true'. When they are developed into doctrines of welfare they become mores; this leads to the definition 'The mores are the folkways, including the philosophical and ethical generalizations as to societal welfare which are suggested by them, and inherent in them, as they grow'. Later comes a chapter entitled 'The Mores Can Make Anything Right and Prevent Condemnation of Anything'. This proposition was demonstrated by examples of modes of punishment and courting customs formerly acceptable in Europe which an American of Sumner's generation would have thought contrary to human feeling.

When he came to discuss blacks and whites in Southern society Sumner maintained that prior to the Civil War relations were based on legal rights and the races lived in peace and concord. The war 'was due to a great divergence in the mores of the North and the South' and afterwards blacks and whites were left to find a new basis for living together. Because the white had never been converted from the old mores they and the blacks had not at that time made new mores.

> 'Legislation cannot make mores. We see also that mores do not form under social convulsion and discord . . . The two races are separating more than ever before . . . It is evidently impossible for anyone to interfere. We are like spectators at a great natural convulsion. The results will be such as the facts and forces call for. We cannot foresee them. They do not depend on ethical views any more than the volcanic eruption on Martinique contained an ethical element.' (1906: 81–2)

There were powerful forces in the United States in favour of a do-nothing policy with respect to Southern race relations. Sumner's presentation of the problem and his use of the concepts of folkways and mores were, as Myrdal wrote, widely followed by social scientists, particularly in the approach to race relations (Myrdal, 1944: 1031–32; for a relevant example of their use see Weatherford and Johnson, 1934: 71–6). It is possible to find in Sumner's work a conception of the relations between law and social change that could be called realistic rather than ultraconservative (Ball, Simpson and Ikeda, 1962). Nevertheless, to follow Myrdal, the concept of mores was almost invariably used to imply that legislation on inter-racial behaviour would be in vain. If he accepted the mores as a homogeneous, unproblematic, and fairly static social entity, the observer was likely to underestimate the differences between individuals and groups and the changes in time. In the present connection, however, it is important to note that Sumner's conceptions of the 'struggle for existence' and social selection, though inspired by Spencer and Darwin, were not really Darwinist, and that his concepts of folkways and mores bore little relation to the elements of social Darwinism in his earlier essays.

It is, indeed, an unrewarding exercise to try to work with a sharp definition of social Darwinism (Halliday, 1971). The impulses generated by the *Origin* travelled down many channels and were modified in many ways. At the beginning they are politically neutral, capable of being used to support opposite ideologies. American society saw its own image in the tooth-and-claw version of natural selection, but by 1918 social Darwinism as a conscious philosophy had largely disappeared from America (Hofstadter, 1955: 201–204). Its influence lingered in sociology for the lack of any paradigm that could offer a persuasive conception of the determining influences upon society as a whole. In anthropology the social Darwinist impress had never been so strong. From the clash between the older conception of ethnology and the doctrine of permanent types emerged a conception of cultural evolution which drew impetus from Darwin but directed research workers towards the study of continuities in evolution rather than towards the prospect of group conflict, individual competition, and the selective control of fertility.

Nevertheless there were certain elements in social Darwinism that will persist since they embody a particular mode of interpreting social patterns. Talcott Parsons observed that 'one of the outstanding characteristics of the Darwinian movement in its application to social problems is its complete abandonment of the subjective for the objective point of view' (1937: 115). The state of mind of individuals matters little for the determinants of success and failure lie elsewhere. Perhaps the most distinctive element in the social Darwinist conception of race relations was the claim that these relations were characterized by an antagonism that was to be understood in terms of its evolutionary function. The view of prejudice as innate was not new; to cite a further example, one American ethnologist, inclined to the theory of permanent types, had written 'the immeasurable contempt and prejudice against the inferior race which characterize all branches of the English race . . . is an unfortunate but legitimate inheritance from Teutonic ancestors' (Brace, 1869: 308). What the Darwinists added to this was the proposition that prejudice assisted evolution by keeping inter-breeding populations separate and enabling emergent races to develop their special capacities. The clearest statement of this view came relatively late in Sir Arthur Keith's rectorial address to the students of Aberdeen, in which he likened racial prejudice to the team spirit of successful football teams (Keith, 1931: 34–5, quoted Banton, 1967: 43). He also pointed to the evolutionary value of warfare: 'Nature keeps her human orchard healthy by pruning; war is her pruning hook.'

This kind of argument is one that occurs again and again (for a recent example see Gregor, 1967). Some biologists seem to be attracted to it as moths to a candle. Its weakness is summarized in the Latin expression *qui nimium probat, nihil probat* (who proves too much, proves nothing), for anything at all can be represented as having a place in evolution and therefore as being justified. There is no way of determining whether evolution proceeds better under conditions of high or low racial prejudice or warfare. There is no evidence of the genetic transmission of attitudes of this kind, and much evidence to indicate that prejudice varies in association with factors of a quite different order. Even if it were established that prejudice assisted evolution this would not mean that men should not resist it. The doctrine that 'good is what the future will bring', which Popper (1957: 105–19) calls moral historicism, is open to grave objections from a philosophical standpoint.

The application of social Darwinist ideas in the field of race relations inspired a claim that moral, psychological, and sociological aspects of this field were ultimately of little account. The determining influence was biological and operated on the race as a unit. The actions of individuals and their subjective perceptions were to be interpreted in terms of the objective forces working inexorably but slowly on a more general level. Until the hold of such a doctrine was weakened it would be difficult to represent race relations as consisting of social relations between men.

6

Social interaction

Any approach to race relations based on social Darwinism was bound to have major weaknesses. It had to emphasize organic evolution, to deal in speculative terms with long-term trends, and could cast little light upon superorganic or socio-cultural evolution within which the major historical events would have to be located. A historical explanation of the prevailing pattern of relations in terms of the expansion of economically progressive European powers had more to offer. Darwinist theories could not explain the variations between individuals or situations in the expression of 'race antagonism'. They could not be used to formulate falsifiable hypotheses applicable to particular circumstances, but remained at a generalized level of justifying European pretensions.

   A viable sociological alternative to such an approach first begins to appear in the work of Robert Park (1863–1944). Born in Pennsylvania, Park studied in the United States, and then in Germany, being deeply influenced by the teaching of Georg Simmel at Berlin and later writing a doctoral thesis entitled *Masse und Publikum* under Windelband's direction at Heidelberg. In between his studies, Park worked as a journalist on several American daily newspapers and afterwards served as an informal secretary to Booker T. Washington. While observing race relations in the South, Park wrote for a popular magazine a series of exposures of Belgian colonial atrocities in the Congo. Then at the age of fifty he returned to university teaching (Coser, 1971: 366–72; Park, 1973) publishing in 1921 with E. W. Burgess an influential textbook *Introduction to the Science of Society* which included many readings selected from other authors. A distinctively sociological approach to the study of race relations begins in the United States because sociology was established earlier and more centrally in their universities. Americans had long believed that their country had a 'race problem'. The imperial nations of Europe perceived their relations with people of other race more in political terms. The kind of sociology that had obtained a limited academic recognition in Europe was not directed towards domestic social problems and there was scarcely any attempt to analyze the new social relations created by imperialism. In discussing race relations as a field of study this chapter and the one that follows therefore have to concentrate almost exclusively upon developments in the American academic world. They select for examination the books that did most to rise above national concerns and contribute to the establishment of a potentially international sociology of race relations.

Park was responsible for the sections of the book that dealt with questions of race. He rejected the theories of those who, like Gobineau, defined culture as a racial trait. His sympathies lay with Ratzenhofer, with Boas, and those who held that the differences were due to the geographical and cultural isolation of the less advanced races. A clear departure from the social Darwinist emphasis upon organic evolution is evident in his statement

'The individual man is the bearer of a double inheritance. As a member of a race, he transmits by interbreeding a biological inheritance. As a member of society or a social group, on the other hand, he transmits by communication a social inheritance. The particular complex of inheritable characters which characterizes the individuals of a racial group constitutes the racial temperament. The particular group of habits, accommodations, sentiments, attitudes, and ideals transmitted by communication and education constitutes a social tradition.' (1921: 140–141)

Park rejected equally some contemporary psychological views, maintaining 'the thing that distinguishes a mere collection of individuals from a society is not like-mindedness, but corporate action . . . sociology . . . may be described as the science of collective behaviour' (1921: 42).

How were sociologists to study corporate action? Borrowing from Simmel and Gumplowicz, Park attributed central significance to the concept of interaction. This was not clearly defined, but society was said to be in some respects reducible to interaction, communication was a medium of interaction, while imitation and suggestion were presented as mechanistic forms of it. There were 'four great types of interaction' — competition, conflict, accommodation, and assimilation. Concepts of this kind came straight from the fashion of describing the living natural world in terms of the inter-relations of organisms, but it is important to note that Park was seeking to transcend this heritage in a way found in few of his contemporaries. A comparison with the influential and also impressive study by Pitirim Sorokin, *Contemporary Sociological Theories* (1928), is illuminating. Apart from Park himself, the author from whom Park and Burgess reprint the largest number of selections is Simmel with ten. Next come Darwin, Small and Sumner with four selections each. There are two extracts from Durkheim but there is little to suggest that at this time the authors appreciated the significance of the work of Marx or Max Weber. Yet neither in Sorokin's review is there any suggestion that Marx, Weber, and Durkheim stood head and shoulders above their contemporaries — as later generations have concluded — and Sorokin never questioned many of the major assumptions of the social Darwinist approach. He finished his chapter on the 'Anthropo-Racial, Selectionist, and Hereditarist School' by saying that it 'has been one of the most important and valuable schools in sociology' (1928: 308). The focus is on race and there is no conception of race *relations* as a social phenomenon.

The most distinctive feature of the Park and Burgess selections is the prominent place given to ecological concepts. The chief novelty lies in the way Park seeks to utilize the passages concerning inter-relations between plants, ants, pigs, and so on, as a means not only of appreciating what is distinctively human, but as a way of uncovering patterns of unconscious relations. The modern sociologist will recognize concepts of adaptation, colonization, commensalism, dominance, invasion, isolation, migration, parasitism, segregation, succession, and symbiosis, even if he does not use all of them himself. He may forget that all of them are ecological concepts that can be applied to plants as well as humans. Plant life, says Park, offers the simplest examples of communities that are not societies. Anyone who has tended a rock garden has seen how some species spread at the expense of others, acquiring a monopoly over a territory. Some plants live together in peace. Others migrate or invade and establish their dominance. Sometimes one species gives way to a series of others, establishing a natural succession. Such concepts the Chicago school of sociology afterwards used in their study of the natural areas of the city. Here it is necessary to note that Park was interested in human ecology as early as 1913. He saw ecology as a way of looking at the whole world and when about 1925 he first gave a course entitled 'Human Ecology' the emphasis was on large scale human geography: the development of navigation, or world-wide insur-

ance, and news-gathering; such changes had made it possible to colonize and establish economic enterprises at a great distance.

Park wrote 'of the four great types of interaction — competition, conflict, accommodation, and assimilation — competition is the elementary, universal and fundamental form . . . The ecological conception of
society is that of a society created by competitive cooperation.' What he
meant by its being fundamental becomes clear in the following passage:

> 'Competion is the process through which the distributive and
> ecological organization of society is created. Competition deter-
> mines the distribution of population territorially and vocationally.
> The division of labor and all the vast organized economic interde-
> pendence of individuals and groups of individuals characteristic of
> modern life are a product of competition. On the other hand, the
> moral and political order, which imposes itself upon this competi-
> tive organization, is a product of conflict, accommodation and
> assimilation.'

The political process is a means of dealing with crises. The process of
competition is continuous and unobserved (1921: 506, 559, 508–509).
There is a resemblance to social Darwinism in that when dealing with
competition (though not when dealing with the other types of interaction) Park is concerned with objective processes operating over long periods of time and independent of subjective states of mind.

This may help explain why the Park and Burgess book gives space to
many matters foreign to modern textbooks and neglects some topics
that now feature prominently. The chapter on competition includes a
famous passage from Adam Smith on the natural harmony of individual interests, explaining how by pursuing his own interest a man is led
as by an invisible hand to promote the common good in the most
effectual manner. Park did not regard this proposition as necessarily
applying outside the economic sphere, yet it is striking that the chapter
on conflict includes no discussion on conflicts of interest (indeed the
notion of interest appears chiefly in a psychological sense, 'an
unsatisfied capacity, corresponding to an unrealized condition').
Conflict is presented only as a feature of collective behaviour without
mention of the way conflicts are structured or individuals coerced. It is
said that 'the psychological bond of the class is community of interests'
but there is no discussion or proper definition of class. The unity of the
social group among humans is described in terms of shared social

tradition without mention of external oppositions. 'All social problems turn out finally to be problems of social control' (1921: 785), yet there seems to be no place for a conception of power in the elucidation of these problems! Nowhere in the book is there reference to such matters as the inheritance of social inequality. Valuable as was Park's use of the ecological metaphor it may have contributed to some blind spots in his analysis of types of interaction forming the superstructure of social patterns. The study of collective behaviour needs to be complemented by the study of social structure.

The direction of Park's personal interests may explain his description of Sumner's *Folkways* as 'the most subtle analysis and suggestive statement about human nature and social relations that has yet been written in English'. Park not only included selections concerning folkways, mores, and the in group-out group distinction, but adopted in his commentary some of Sumner's basic assumptions. 'As members of society, men act as they do elsewhere from motives that they do not fully comprehend, in order to fulfil aims of which they are but dimly or not at all conscious . . . Under the influence of the mores men act typically, and so representatively, not as individuals but as members of a group'. Park distinguished the political from the cultural process. Politics was concerned with matters in regard to which there was division and difference, but 'the political process, by which a society or social group formulates its wishes and enforces them, goes on within the limits of the mores' (1921: 30, 52-3). This meant that every time a Negro appeared in an unaccustomed situation it provoked comment as something contrary to the mores. Though Park might himself have acknowledged that this was a facet of the relations of power between black and white he did not say so and his writing, like that of most of his contemporaries, neglects this dimension in a fashion that must astonish a later generation.

The chapters in *Introduction to the Science of Sociology*, dealing with race relations, like those reflecting the ecological approach, were mostly Park's work. Ecology is rarely absent from Park's view of race relations; it underlay his conception of prejudice which he defined as 'a spontaneous, more or less instinctive, defence-reaction, the practical effect of which is to restrict free competition between races'. Prejudice was an attempt to restrain competition, to establish a monopolistic hold over a particular social territory (1921: 623). On another, later, occasion, Park asked why anyone should expect racial peace before there was racial justice (Hughes, 1969: 169) but the difficulty with his early formulation was that it left no place for such considerations. Park observed that caste, by relegating the subject race to an inferior status gave it a monopoly over the unattractive roles at the same time as it gave the other category its monopoly. He went on 'when this status is accepted by the subject people, as is the case where the caste or slavery systems become fully established, racial competition ceases and racial animosity tends to disappear. This is the explanation of the intimate and friendly relations which so often existed in slavery between master and servant'. Slavery was discussed in the chapter on accommodation, not in that on conflict. There was no mention, for example, of slave revolts, suicides, or escapes. If conflict, accommodation, and assimilation were types of interaction which were acted out on a basis of the more fundamental phenomenon of competition some means had to be found for analyzing monopoly power and the processes by which part of the population was reduced to inferior statuses. This Park did not achieve. He saw the process of competition as resulting in economic equilibrium on which a political order was built, and did not consider the ways in which political considerations dictated the terms on which individuals could compete (1921: 510). Racial conflicts sprang from the unwillingness of those of superior status to compete on equal terms with those of inferior status (1921: 578). The aggressive aspects of prejudice are not mentioned; nor were ways in which unwillingness to compete is translated into political action and that action intensifies the original unwillingness.

Park wrote of prejudice as a 'phenomenon of the group mind', presenting prejudice against the Japanese as a reaction to their having the wrong skin colour and not as a consequence of white prejudgements which themselves require analysis (1921: 623–25, 760–61). It is important not to pillory an author by picking out passages that convey an untruthful impression. Park's statements about prejudice are all of them defensible and many of them draw attention to aspects of these phenomena previously neglected. Most of the criticism must be about the inadequacies of his presentation arising from what he failed to say. His pioneering interest in collective behaviour proved valuable for the development of American sociology, but collective behaviour cannot be understood in any depth if it is isolated from the structures that can mould it just as much as the instincts and other qualities of human nature to which Park and Burgess devoted so many pages.

After the publication of the textbook some signs appear of Park's broadening his approach to these questions. Offering suggestions as to the material needed for a survey of race relations on America's Pacific

coast, Park in 1923 opened his remarks with the statement 'Race conflicts have their biological and economic aspects but it is the attitudes
they express and provoke which are of first importance'. He went on to
develop an alternative to the earlier view of attitudes as biologically determined, taking from W. I. Thomas and F. Znaniecki the notion that
'personality is the subjective aspect of culture' and that cultures develop
their own patterns. The book which these two authors wrote on *The*
Polish Peasant was the first, or almost the first, to call attention to the
way the situation of the European immigrant in the United States could
be defined in terms that implied its logical relation to that of the Negro,
although the Negro had been settled in the New World for three centuries (Park, 1950: 159, 358, 198–99). The recognition of this 'logical relation', obvious though it may now seem, was of fundamental significance for establishing a sociology of race relations.

The most mature statement of Park's views in this field is the essay
'The Nature of Race Relations' published in 1939. This puts forward a
more complex scheme for examining interaction. In one sense, says
Park, race relations are not so much the relations that exist between individuals of different races as between individuals conscious of these differences. From such a standpoint it would appear that there are no race
relations in Brazil because race consciousness is absent from there.
From another standpoint, however, race relations includes relations
that are not at that time conscious or personal though they have been in
the past. This means that 'one may think of race relations as existing
not only on different levels, that is (1) ecological, (2) economic,
(3) political, (4) personal and cultural, but one may think of these different levels as constituting a hierarchy of relations of such a nature
that change upon any one level will invariably have repercussions, not
immediately, but finally, upon every other' (1950: 81–3, 107). Race
problems, he said, have invariably arisen in response to the expansion
of European peoples; this could be seen as a historical extension of European domination accompanied by an increasing integration of, and in-
timacy with, the races and peoples affected. But he preferred to regard
it as a succession of changes connected with, and incidental to, the expansion and integration of a vast and new social organism. The succession ran from trade to political domination, missionary activity, and
then, 'the final stage' when 'Europe begins to export not goods but capital' to finance mines, rubber plantations, and eventually factories 'to employ native laborers in the manufacture of commodities which are then
sold not only in the colonies, but, as in the case of Japan, in Europe and
in competition with European products'. Other features of the succes-

sion were the appearance of hybrid peoples, port cities to service world trade, and then the growth of nationalism among both majorities and minorities. This last development was evidence that 'we are at the end of one epoch in human and racial relations and at the beginning of another'. Contradicting the social Darwinists, he predicted that race conflicts 'will be more and more in the future confused with, and eventually superceded by, the conflicts of classes'. Returning to his opening problem of what precisely distinguishes race relations from other fundamental forms of human relations, he offered a further formulation:

> 'it is the essence of race relations that they are the relations of strangers; of peoples who are associated primarily for secular and practical purposes; for the exchange of goods and services. They are otherwise the relations of people of diverse races and cultures who have been thrown together by the fortunes of war, and who, for any reason, have not been sufficiently knit together by inter-marriage and interbreeding to constitute a single ethnic community, with all that it implies.' (1950: 100, 107–16)

Park's ecology of race relations as the product of European expansion inspired the study *Race and Culture Contacts in the Modern World* by his pupil E. Franklin Frazier, but Frazier dissented from Park's interpretation of relations in the Southern states, preferring to stress the unresolved class conflicts among Southern whites (Edwards, 1968: 5–7). A much sharper criticism came from Oliver C. Cox who deplored the 'ring of fatality and mysticism in Park's discussion of the stability of race relations in the South' deriving from his reliance upon the interpretation of behaviour as conforming with folkways and mores. Cox also disputed his inference that there was a fundamental antagonism between Negroes and poor whites. Cox states 'probably the crucial fallacy in Park's thinking is his belief that the beginnings of modern race prejudice may be traced back to the immemorial periods of human associations'. This reflects Cox's belief that race prejudice appeared only with the establishment of a capitalist economic and social order. His criticism is probably better expressed a few pages earlier when he accuses Park of confounding racial differences and cultural differences, observing 'Park states neither the characteristics of racial conflicts nor those of culture-group conflicts'. To state them, in Cox's view, it is necessary to differentiate between the types of social systems which may or may not produce the variation in human nature necessary for an expression of racial antagonism' (Cox, 1948: 463–77). The assumptions behind Cox's approach will be discussed in the next chapter.

A more recent criticism of Park comes from a sociologist who regards his conception of a race relations cycle as central to his conception of the field. This judgement is difficult to sustain since Park wrote on the topic primarily in the later 1920s and subsequently began to have doubts about it. Stanford M. Lyman contends that Park was in thrall to Aristotle's doctrine that science must deal with the slow and orderly development of immanent qualities and not with accidents or the real history of events. The only supporting evidence is the critic's view that all the principles of Aristotle's theory of change are reproduced in Park's race relations cycle (Lyman, 1972: 30). This is circumstantial evidence, and very unpersuasive considering how much else there is in Park's writing to indicate that this was not his philosophy of science. The motive behind this criticism seems rather to lie in the author's objection to a deterministic theory of the black man's place in American society which he reads into Park's work. As an exponent of classical sociology, Lyman charges, Park 'systematically presented the stages through which the black would pass on the way to his eventual assimilation in a racially homogeneous world' (1972: 121). This needs to be seen in the context of Park's general theoretical problem.

Any assessment of Park's contribution to race relations study must give a high place to his leadership in formulating an alternative to social Darwinism. While acknowledging and even emphasizing man's biological natuture, Park maintained that human society differed from a community of plants because the organization of human individuals is based on a moral consensus embodied in tradition and sentiment and manifested in the spirit of belonging, collective will, and what Durkheim called collective representations. Though starting with notions of racial temperament and innate dispositions, his teaching came to concentrate on racial hostility as the product of the norms of social distance and prejudice which individuals learned when they were socialized into their communities. The view of prejudice as a learned attitude was an achievement of the 1920s, and though Park was not involved with the psychological studies his teaching can be seen as part of the same general reassessment of inter-group relations. His influence as a teacher has properly been celebrated by all who have written about him (cf. Coser, 1971: 372, 382–83). Much of his writing consists of occasional essays and prefaces, some of them developing seminal notions like those of social distance, etiquette, and the marginal man; to get an estimate of Park's contribution it is well to follow the careers of these innovations and not concentrate too much on the differences in his formulations as Park continually found new ways of examining familiar phenomena. He was distinguished for his talent in discovering good questions to ask, more than by his ability in answering others' questions. Park's own career as a journalist also left its mark. He had a much better sense than his contemporaries of the way graduate students could advance sociological theory by leaving the university to undertake firsthand studies of the life that was going on around them. Indeed he may be most honoured for his work in the development of urban sociology. Where the Darwinists had seen race relations as governed by inbred behaviour patterns distinctive to races, Park moved the emphasis in the expression 'race relations' from the first word to the second. The effect of his teaching was to put race relations in the context of developing urban patterns and the developing power relations stemming from the expansion of the capitalist economy. This too was a crucial advance.

Yet the issue raised by Cox and Lyman remains. What are the characteristics of racial conflicts that Park failed to identify? What might a more mature sociology have said about the future of the black man in the society of the United States? When Park moved to the view that race relations are defined by present or past consciousness of racial differences what did this imply for his theoretical framework? When men were conscious of such differences, what form did that consciousness take? Many of the beliefs white Southerners held in 1921 about racial differences are now known to have been false. If what distinguished these relations was a false consciousness and the falsity was eliminated, then unless there was some intervening variable, nothing substantial would remain to divide blacks from whites. Assimilation was the implicit outcome. An author who criticizes this in 1972 has the advantage of more hindsight than one writing in 1948 or in 1939. It is easy now to observe that there was an intervening variable of a kind having something to do with nationalism. Park worked in an intuitive manner and did not reason in terms of independent and dependent variables. If he had done so, he would have been no more likely to predict this. It is striking how many of his contemporaries and even most later critics failed to forsee the kinds of change that occurred in American race relations around 1960. When he criticized Park, Cox was no more prescient, for he testified that the solidarity of Negro Americans was not nationalistic (1948: 545). It is fairly clear that Park did not regard racial conflicts as a special kind of conflict, but tended to emphasize what they had in common with other sorts of conflict. He wrote that growth of nationalism was changing the consciousness of peoples in the colonial world and therefore changing the character of the conflicts. Race conflicts were giving way to class conflicts, and though Park would not have accepted Cox's conception of class, his view that racial conflicts do not have any special characteristics that distinguishes them in the historical dimension was of great importance in his generation and can easily be defended against criticism today.

7

Structure and function

This chapter will concern itself with some of the major contributions to the study of race relations in the United States between 1930 and 1950. If the early years of these decades are seen as re-orientating the line of work sketched out by Park in the previous period, it is well to remember two of the chief weaknesses in Park's approach. First, Park's interests, though broad, were still selective; he concentrated on race relations as a phenomenon of collective behaviour and did not warn his readers about the aspects of the field that were neglected when such an approach was employed. Second, though Park was interested in the ecological aspects of social life he made little progress with methods for the study of local situations as social systems, which meant that the explanatory adequacy of his various concepts were not assessed. Had this been done it would have become more quickly apparent that Park neglected the part played by political and economic power in social interaction and lacked a conception of social structure that would have facilitated the fitting together of the relevant influences.

The studies that inaugurated the new period were those carried out in Indianola, a town of a little over 3,000 persons in Mississippi, by John Dollard and Hortense Powdermaker. Dollard's book, *Caste and Class in a Southern Town* was published in 1937; Powdermaker's *After Freedom* appeared two years later. Neither of them seems to have taken any direct inspiration either from Park or from Robert and Helen Lynd's *Middletown* (1929) which was then regarded by sociologists as the best example of a community study. Dollard's training was in psychology, Powdermaker's in anthropology. They took a lead from the Yale Institute of Human Relations and from the blending of ideas from psychoanalysis with others from cultural anthropology developed by Edward Sapir, but followed this lead in different directions.

Dollard had undergone psycho-analysis in Berlin. He was the first writer to apply Freudian interpretations to American race relations in a persuasive full-length study that could be appreciated by the general reader. He transformed the significance of the concept of prejudice and the study of race relations could never be the same again. Dollard opened his discussion of prejudice with a reference to the view that it was a defensive attitude intended to preserve white prerogatives: he acknowledged that this might be one of its functions but regretted that though these accounted for events well enough in their own terms such explanations were not really satisfying.

'Persons with little need to prop self-esteem through the pain and humiliation of others may participate in formal prejudice patterns, but they will participate without much affect and as a mere convention . . . Race prejudice is an emotional fact and must be connected with the rest of the emotional life of each individual who experiences it.' (Dollard, 1937: 442)

To ask why do people need prejudice? was to ask a new and important question. His answer was the frustration and aggression hypothesis. When a child is brought up all sorts of limitations are placed upon its freedom. Social living and human culture require a degree of orderliness and discipline to which children have to be trained. The character of the adult person is therefore a record of frustrations and of reactions to them. According to Freudian theory the basic reaction is the aggressive response designed to reassert mastery, but a child frequently cannot react in this way because the person limiting his freedom is a parent or someone whom he finds it unprofitable to attack. He must either turn the aggression in on himself or store it up, waiting for a suitable opportunity to discharge it. This was Dollard's first key concept, that of a generalized or 'free-floating' aggression held in store. The second one was social permission to attack a particular target group. Society prohibits many kinds of aggression because it can be disruptive, but certain relatively defenseless groups may be made to serve as scapegoats open to legitimate attack. The third key proposition was that scapegoats must be uniformly identifiable so that other persons run no risk of being mistaken for them. This was where Negro 'visibility' came in. The badge of colour was the sign that told the prejudiced person whom to hate and made easy and consistent discrimination possible. 'In our sense' wrote

Dollard, 'race prejudice is always irrational' (1937: 443–46). In a later article he improved on this formulation by distinguishing two kinds of aggression. When someone attacked the person or group responsible for his frustration, like a striker attacking black leg labour or an agent of his employer, this was direct aggression. When, however, the person frustrated could not or did not dare attack those responsible but instead took it out on a substitute, he was displacing his aggression. Because there would also be some free-floating aggression seeking an outlet this would latch on to the expression of direct aggression adding to it an extra and more emotional element which might be responsible for the irrational features often observable in situations of rational conflict (Dollard, 1938).

To judge from his book, Dollard's stay in Indianola consisted of a visit in 1933 and a spell of five months during 1935–6. He conducted intensive interviews with nine Negro people, three women and six men; these lasted over a hundred hours each, entailed the collection of life histories, and had a psycho-analytical orientation such as in the recording of dreams. He had more superficial contacts with another two hundred or so individuals. By comparison with what has come from much larger and more expensive studies it is astonishing how much Dollard achieved with his. Particularly striking is the way he used his understanding of the psychological dimension to interpret the social structure. When he started his work it was quite common to regard the social system as a machine with its members interacting with one another in historically defined ways. 'This machine has inertia and goes on working according to its traditionally prescribed pattern. The societal unit continues to function until it is in some manner disorganized; it then goes through a cycle from disorganization to reorganization, and orderly life continues.' This explanation did not satisfy Dollard who thought it plain that powerful pressure was constantly exerted on Negro people to make them display submissive attitudes. The system was maintained not by intertia but by active pressures, social and physical. To identify these pressures it was necessary to discover the differential advantages of membership in particular classes and colour-castes and find out how these advantages were translated into personal, ultimately organic, gratifications (1937: 97, 178).

Dollard's answer to this problem was to describe three kinds of gain which middle-class whites derived from their social position at the expense of blacks and to some extent of lower-class whites. There were economic, sexual, and prestige gains. The first of them he documents by reference to occupational rewards. The backbreaking and ill-rewarded nature of some jobs was epitomized in cotton-picking, but middle-class whites picked very little cotton. Relatively, middle-class whites got much higher returns for their work than did the lower-class groups who performed the more laborious tasks. This might well have been the case, but it is not an easy matter to prove. In effect, Dollard asserts that whites used their political power to get greater rewards than would otherwise have come to them. The difficulties in this argument have been displayed in the sociological controversy about the so-called functional theory of stratification. By what criteria can it be decided how much more one occupation should be paid than another? Only when this problem is resolved can one decide how much particular rewards are above the norm that would be established in a perfect market. Dollard's claim is that the social position of middle-class whites entailed certain costs and that they were imprisoned within an inhospitable socio-economic situation as much as any other category, but he asserts that they gained more than they lost by it, and that they therefore had a vested interest in maintaining that system (1937: 98–115). He describes the poverty of most Negroes and the incidence of pellagra, a disease caused by dietary deficiency. He also provides plenty of examples of the ways in which white power was used to prevent black workers getting their just reward, or forming labour organizations, and in controlling the jobs that were available to them (on the exploitation of tenant farmers see Dollard 1937: 120–24; Powdermaker, 1939: 86–94). The distribution of rewards in the labour market was clearly determined by the mobilization of white power as well as by the market value of individual's skills. To this extent at least it may be agreed that one factor in the maintenance of the social system wsa the economic gain that whites derived from it.

The second kind of gain was sexual, and in its simplest terms consisted in the way white men had access to Negro women as well as white women. It will not escape notice that this was a gain for white men only. Dollard remarks that Negro women also had an advantage in that they might receive the attentions of men from both racial categories. In so far as this was a gain for Negro women it was balanced by a loss, in that this situation meant the degradation of the Negro male and that in turn reduced in many ways the satisfactions that Negro women could obtain from married life. The same situation reduced the satisfaction of the white woman. Dollard conjectured that they were idealized in such a way that white men felt it unbecoming to regard them as sexual objects, feeling guilty and restrained in sexual relations and finding black women better sexual partners. White women unconsciously envied the greater sexual freedom of black women (1937: 135 – 168). In such circumstances the calculation of sexual gain seems a dubious exercise, but one can go along with Dollard in accepting that the patterning of sexual attitudes was a factor important to the motivations which maintained the social system.

The third kind of gain was what Dollard called prestige but would now be called deference. He had in mind the features of Negro behaviour which in inter-personal relations tended to increase the white man's self-esteem. It was illuminating for the traveller to compare the experience of having his bag carried at the Grand Central Terminal in New York and at a railway station in the Deep South. In the former, 'the Negro is a mechanism for moving weight from one point to another . . . in the South he is this, and something more. The Southern porter is extremely nice about it to boot and does various things that are flattering and exhilarating.' Dollard was clear that, first, deference behaviour was something used by Negroes to manipulate whites, and, second, that it had functions in respect of social control. Deference was demanded by whites and any Negro who would not accord it was defined as 'uppity', threatening, and in need of correction. But nevertheless deference was psychologically rewarding to the recipient: it seemed to prove that the Negro was not hostile and to allay the anxiety among white people provoked by the fear that the racial situation engendered in them. The crucial feature for the white man was that he was receiving deference in advance of demand; it appeared as a submissive affection freely yielded, suggesting that his aggressive demands were being passively received and giving him a gratifying sense of mastery over others (1937: 173–87). In non-Western cultures it often appears from the studies of anthropologists that the highest category of economic values is that which brings command over people while the disparagement of the role of personal servant in industrial societies suggests that deference is a service commanding a high price in the eyes of the one who pays it and the one who receives. The very substantial white deference gain in the South was therefore an index of how much white power affected the bargaining relations of the two racial categories.

The gains were not exclusively on the white side of the colour line. There were many ways in which blacks were able to gratify their impulses, though, as Dollard points out, this was often at an appreciable long term cost. Negroes had greater sexual freedom among their own number; greater freedom of aggression; and the psychological luxury of a dependence relationship in respect of whites. Whites had the satisfaction that went with mastery, superiority, control, maturity, and duty well-fulfilled. They had the pleasure of despising blacks. Negroes were permitted slack work habits, irresponsibility and, within limits, more personal freedom than is possible in a competitive, economically progressive society. This helped explain why they did not try harder to change the system. The 'tolerant' attitude of whites towards crime in the Negro quarter and their acceptance of slack work habits further weakened Negro resources for mobilizing pressure against traditional expectations (1937: 393, 431–33, 282).

The other major influence upon Dollard's work was that of Lloyd Warner, the anthropologist who in 1930 had started his massive study of Newburyport, Massachusetts. Warner soon afterwards directed a study of Natchez, Mississippi (described in the book *Deep South*). This was the work of a team of students (Negro and white) whom Dollard visited while he was carrying out his Indianola research. In the preface to the 1957 edition of *Caste and Class* Dollard remarks that were he to rewrite his book he would follow the caste and class analysis developed by Warner, but this should not distract attention from the extent to which the strengths and weaknesses of Warner's community study method were built into the foundations of Dollard's sociology. He presented Indianola society as constructed round the interlocking categories of caste and class: '. . . they organize local life securely and make social cooperation possible . . . Caste has replaced slavery as a means of maintaining the essence of the old status order in the South. By means of its racial animosity is held at a minimum' (1937: 61–2). This statement is worth notice for its demonstration of the weakness of functionalist explanations. Caste and class were equally responsible for the *in*security of local life and for lack of cooperation. By means of caste racial animosity was evoked and heightened. Any community has a degree of integration, the component parts being to some extent interdependent. Every relation between them is therefore to some degree functional and to some degree dysfunctional. To point to a connection between colour-caste and animosity says nothing about whether animosity would be higher or lower if relations between blacks and whites were regulated in some other way.

The structural interpretations Dollard borrowed from Warner's scheme are much more valuable. He argued that in relations with middle-class blacks, middle-class white people combined class loyalty and caste hostility. Situations of economic position and advantage called forth class-based patterns of behaviour whereas situations of social and ultimately sexual, contact evoked caste-based patterns. The former was not difficult to account for since the middle-class Negro bought more gasoline, better groceries, more insurance, more medical services, engaged a lawyer more frequently, and was in general a good customer, Whites would bid for the custom of such Negroes and found it worth while to keep Negro landowners in line. One such landowner said the whites put pressure on him to treat his tenants as they did theirs'. Another used his influence to dissuade some of the local Negroes from bringing a potentially costly suit for damages and had been given special favours in return. Educated Negroes often found themselves the objects of a more respectful and friendly attention, provided nothing happened to evoke caste differences. These signs of inter-racial class sympathy were to be set alongside the striking evidence of hostility between middle-class whites and lower-class whites. A landlord, for example, deplored the meanness and spitefulness of his white tenant farmers stating that next year he would replace them with Negroes. Poor whites were intractable and undeferential but there were Negroes who 'knew their place'.

In Warner's caste and class analysis a key element is the definition of situations. This is expressed more clearly in *Deep South* (Davis *et al.*, 1941: 477) but it is also presented in a straightforward way in Dollard's book. He describes the situation of a Negro landowner who had five white people picking cotton for him. The risks were the greater because three of them were women. If one of them said that he had 'shined up' to her, it might have cost him his life. If a white woman had charged him with breaching caste norms, the whites would have accepted her testimony without question. In a second instance a Negro storekeeper took a white man who would not pay his bill to court. He was forced to pay. The white man regarded this as an intolerable affront and came to beat up the Negro, but the Negro won the fight and the white man took a beating. Other whites refused to aid him. They would not define the incident in caste terms. In a third instance a Negro man found a white man coming to visit a Negro woman with whom he was 'friendly'. He gave the white man a severe beating but was then obliged to leave town as a posse came out looking for him (Dollard, 1937: 90–5, 165, 292). Apparently the sexual element in this situation resulted in its being regarded as a breach of caste norms. (For a similar incident with similar outcome see Powdermaker, 1937: 192, and for one in which a black man is not punished for shooting a white plantation manager who was living with the black man's sister, see Davis *et al.*, 1941: 337.) To understand how caste and class norms continued side by side it is necessary to appreciate not only the nature of the norms but

the influence of leading figures in interpreting their relevance and the
way in which the socio-economic structure generated particular kinds
of conflict. Such factors as the proportion of Negro landowners and
the competition between tenant farmers obviously made a great
difference.

Powdermaker's book, based on twelve months' field-work in
1932–34, written before the appearance of Dollard's volume though
published afterwards, aimed to present the portrait of Indianola as a
functioning community while providing a closer description of the Negro population. The book's merit lies in the quality of the ethnography
rather than in any explanation of why the community functioned in
this instead of some other manner. In so far as the latter objective was
attempted, the author's answer was to give prime place to 'the attitudes
and strains attendant upon the process of acculturation . . . acculturation, for all its pains and problems, is what the Negro wants'. Powdermaker remarks that among the whites the upper class is the least hostile towards blacks, and the lower class most, whereas among the Negroes it is the other way round. Of the lower-class whites and upper-
class blacks she observes 'each serves as an agent for its race towards
the other, taking actions and expressing sentiments to which the group
as a whole is not ready to commit itself' (1939: 372, 334). But the significance of the 'curious inversion' of typical attitudes and of class-related
hostility is missed. At the very least it needs to be noted that within the
socio-economic structure of Mississippi at that time the interest of upper-class whites lay in playing blacks and lower-class whites against
each other, while that of upper-class blacks lay in creating a separate set
of social institutions. This is turn raises questions about the kind of acculturation the Negroes wanted. Did they want to be acculturated to the
way of life of lower class Mississippi whites (red-necks and pecker-
woods as they were called) or to some ideal of American life that no one
attained? It is an important question, but the concept of acculturation
used by American anthropologists at that time made no allowance for
divisions in a population defined as maintaining a particular culture.

Warner's use of the expression 'colour-caste' has attracted criticism,
most notably from Cox who maintained, very rightly, that race relations in the South were fundamentally different from the relations of
Hindu caste. Given the way in which Warner and his associates used
the concept of colour-caste, and its advantage in identifying a social category by a social instead of a biological term, this quarrel basically concerns the suitability of verbal labels and does not merit the excitement
loosed around it. (Parenthetically it should be noted that the issues

raised in the later debate about caste led by Berreman and Dumont are more fundamental and of considerable significance.) A more important objection to raise in criticism of the works of the Warner group concerns the adequacy of the methods used in community studies. It is presented in more acute form by a subsequent study of a Negro community called Kent (in the Piedmont region of the South) by a black sociologist who writes of his work 'the study was conceived as a comprehensive treatment of culture in a sub-group', going on to remark that while the minority status of blacks in the United States as a whole was very relevant, this was not the prime focus (Lewis, 1955: 5). An author has the right to choose his own focus but he cannot provide a comprehensive treatment of a local community unless he demonstrates any ways in which its life is influenced by events in the wider society. Given what we now know about black social movements in the United States during the last twenty years, it occasions surprise to read the conclusions of the Kent study: this points to an evolving black national subculture and the need for comparative personality studies without mentioning the effects of the civil rights struggle and all the national and even international political and economic policies that had so much effect on local communities. In this sense, the feature of the Warner diagram which deserves closest examination is the box-like framework which assumes that the local community can be isolated as a relatively independent social system. This is in itself not an unreasonable assumption, but it is essential to watch for the respects in which the local system is not independent.

Another question which does not receive the attention it merits, concerns the definition of the racial categories. In Brazil and in the West Indies, interbreeding between persons of European and African descent has produced populations of varying shades of skin colour. Pigmentation attracts every bit as much attention as in the United States, but it is not used to define two mutually exclusive social categories. Differences in the socio-economic structure of these countries during the eighteenth and nineteenth century go some way towards explaining the contrast yet it seems certain that more remains to be discovered about its causes. North American research workers have tended to take for granted a generalized American conception of racial categorization; they have not done much to pursue the variations of place, situation, and circumstance, or to compare the forces making for the change and reinforcement of these definitions.

The Indianola studies were conducted at a time of economic depression (Dollard, 1937: 111, 114, 128). After the Civil War this region was seriously over-populated and living conditions deteriorated. Between 1870 and 1930 the acreage devoted to agriculture diminished, but the labour force on the farms almost doubled. Negro-operated farms produced less cotton. The fecundity of Negro women declined because of pellagra and venereal disease. Fighting to retain their position in a declining economy, the whites pushed the blacks ever further down (on whites taking over previously black jobs, see Davis *et al.*, 1941: 427–28, 464). The recession hit the cotton-producing areas particularly hard. The only escape for the Negro was emigration, but, except for wartime, whenever there were jobs going in the North white immigrant labour came in to seize them. The chief weakness in the accounts of Indianola and Kent — as in most community studies of this period — lie in the authors' failure to show adequately how local patterns were related to national ones, and in particular to political forces generated at the state and federal levels by economic and status interests. This was an immense task but its difficulty should not lead the social scientist to shy away from its significance for understanding racial discrimination. The book *Deep South* represents a conscious, and partially successful, attempt to solve these problems. The study *Black Metropolis* (Drake and Cayton, 1945), on the other hand, shows that the simple model of a local community as divided by class and colour-caste is of much less value in the interpretation of race relations in a large complex urban society like Chicago.

Deep South is divided into two equal parts. The first half describes the social patterns of the town of Natchez, a small city of over 10,000 people which knew grander days when it was a trade centre on the river route from the cotton country to the sea. The second half of the book analyzes its economic system. The authors distinguish three levels of adaptation of man to his natural and human environment. The first is the technical adaptation organized and controlled by an economic system. The second is that of social organization, and the third that of the beliefs and concepts that explain and rationalize the other adaptations. A change at any one level affects the others, but they consider it useless and unscientific to postulate any one level as determining the others (Davis *et al.*, 1941: 266–68). There is therefore no reason of principle for presenting the material in part one before that in part two. The social system is pictured as a self-sustaining whole and most of the explanations of its features are in terms of their functions. This weakness is particularly evident in respect of one of the major problems that such a situation surely presents, namely the explanation of racial prejudice and discrimination. Is discrimination to be seen as the product of economic interest? Or does prejudice distort the economic system so that total output is lower than it might be? It is such questions the authors avoid. They say that a social system cannot be understood in terms of prejudice as an individual attitude. Prejudicial sentiments are expressed in practices that are part of the caste system; this has its origins in the division of labour on the cotton plantation under slavery. The problem of cause is thereby buried.

But the social system had continually to adjust to changing circumstances. In 1936 cotton yields increased and there was a shortage of agricultural workers such that 10–15,000 cotton pickers had to be imported into the Delta region studied by Dollard. Law officers dragged tramps from railroad box cars and hobo colonies, and rounded up vagrants for work in the fields. Landlords had earlier competed with one another for good tenants and had much preferred black tenants to white, but with better yields competition in the area around Natchez became acute. In such circumstances it might have been expected that dissatisfied Negroes would emigrate and that competition between whites would result in a diminution in discrimination. How was the system maintained? Davis and his colleagues reply that by far the most important element was the face-to-face relationship of landlord and tenant. Intimidation and legal subordination had bred in the black man a habit of dependence on the landowner. He had become accustomed to a low standard of living such that he left the system only in periods of destitution or at times, such as during the war, when conditions were generally disturbed. Standards were kept uniformly low by upper- class white pressure on industrial concerns able to pay blacks wages higher than those conventional in other kinds of employment (Davis et al., 1941: 401, 378, 261). To examine properly the hypothesis of black dependence it would have been necessary to study perceptions of emigration opportunities while there is sufficient evidence in the book itself to evoke the reader's doubts about the adequacy of this explanation. Other doubts arise with respect to political relations. The authors describe the antagonism between upper and lower class whites. They state that political power is exercised by a 'ring' which is dependent on the support of rank and file middle and lower-class voters, nearly all of whom are white. Independent organization by lower-class whites is frustrated. Instead of the system's being maintained by inertia and psychological reactions like dependence and habituation to low standards, it seems to rest on the continual use of governmental power to balance lower-class whites and blacks. Deep South very properly emphasizes the importance of white power to the maintenance of the system and its authors recognize that 'since political control is vested in the upper-middle class of the white caste, it is not surprising that there is a close connection between political power and the control of the economic system, which is also in the hands of this class' (1941: 491), but do not relate this as well as they might to the political history of the state or to the explanation of the distinctive features of the social system.

The continuing utility of the very simple model of Southern rural society as split into two mutually exclusive colour-castes, has recently been demonstrated from a different angle by two studies that illuminate the definition of racial status. Both concern anomalous minorities: the Chinese and the Choctaw Indians. The Chinese first came to Mississippi about 1870; they were single men working as contract labourers in groups brought in to help bring the Mississippi-Yazoo delta under cultivation. Wage labourers were then scarce in this region. It seems that some of the Chinese were dissatisfied with their work conditions and broke away to establish small retail stores. They spoke no English. A Negro customer would come in to the store, take up a pointer to show what he wanted to buy; the trader would never sell the last item, as he kept this to use when showing the wholesaler on his monthly visit what items he wished to restock. Some Chinese lived with Negro women and had children by them. Generally Chinese counted socially as blacks though in a few towns where their numbers were sufficient, separate schools were built and they lived as a distinct community.

It was difficult for the Chinese to bring their relatives in from China so long as the whites looked down upon them so much. In the struggle to improve their status they had one social attribute that was to prove of great importance to them and made their prospects very different from the blacks. They had a powerful extended family structure. In the Chinese communities there were a few powerful individuals who could control others by their relations with wholesalers and by their key position in communication with powerful whites. These leaders forced their fellows to cease association with blacks and virtually expelled those who were recalcitrant. When one of their children was turned away from a white school they brought a legal action which eventually went to the US Supreme Court. That body upheld the Mississippi view that white schools were for Caucasians only, but by persuasion, negotiation, and pleading, the Chinese began to make progress. From the late 1930s until 1953 more and more white schools opened their doors. The Chinese found it easiest to be accepted as whites in small towns where they formed only a small part of the population and where the whites were also a minority so that by counting the Chinese as white the Negro majority was somewhat reduced. But their success was also due in large measure to their affluence (which permitted large contributions to causes in which whites were interested, like War Bonds) and their ability to project a favourable image of their community. The Civil Rights movement helped them further; since 1950, 95 per cent of all Chinese high school graduates have gone on to college, usually entering the 'five year' fields, like engineering and pharmacy, which confer professional status and relatively high starting pay. All but a handful have left the state after qualifying. The Chinese population of the Delta, now a little over 1200, has been denuded in the age groups 20–40 years (Loewen, 1971).

The Choctaw Indians were resident in Mississippi prior to the white invasion. While Britain, France, and Spain were struggling for control of the region Indian groups were often accorded legal recognition as Indian 'nations', as equal or semi-equal allies. Their leaders were given European titles and often commissions within the military hierarchy of the colonial power. When Southern state governments were established they terminated Indian sovereignty and in the 1830s the bulk of the remaining Indians of the South-East were forcibly removed to Oklahoma. Some Indians remained, however, as ethnic minorities rather than members of nations. They resisted enslavement, so that during the slave period there was no place for them in Southern society. They were forced to the social and geographical periphery and overlooked so long as nothing happened to draw attention to them. Whereas prior to the 1830s a growing number of Choctaw were becoming converted to Christianity and learning to read and write in English, during slavery this tendency was reversed. After the Civil War this movement was able to reassert itself. The change in agricultural work which resulted in some whites becoming share-croppers, made it possible for Indians also to engage in share-cropping without being treated like blacks or being refused white status. The changes in black-white relations made possible a change in Indian status and a dramatic transformation of Choctaw communities (now including some 3,600 persons) leading first to rapid progress in literacy, ethnic organization, and conversion to Christianity. The later impact of the Civil Rights movement of the 1960s often benefitted Indians as much as Negroes (Peterson, 1971).

Within a social system of two-colour castes there are pressures to prevent the emergence of any third racial category. There are obvious economic objections to any situation requiring the construction of a third set of waiting rooms, schools, drinking fountains, etc., and political hesitations about any system that could come to depend on the formation of a coalition between two out of three categories. But there are also ideological reservations, for the more categories are recognized the more questions will be raised about the definition of the original categories (cf. Banton, 1967: 145–46). In one country of South Carolina the Lumbee Indians (a mixed blood group, cf. Berry, 1972: 202–205) amount to about a third of the population and there three colour-castes are recognized. Elsewhere the size of the Indian minority may decide whether they count as black or white. In the area of Indian concentration in Mississippi, Choctaws are classified as non-white and denied almost all aspects of white status. Where there are few of them they count as whites. Thus by travelling only forty miles an Indian can change from white to non-white. There are not enough Indians in their area of concentration to create a non-white majority in combination with blacks which means that the political risks in assigning them to the lower category are not so great, whereas elsewhere it would seem that their numbers and demeanour are such that it is less inconvenient to allow them white status (Peterson, 1972: 1288).

The study of intermediary groups such as the Chinese and Indians in Mississippi can be valuable out of all relation to their numerical strength (note also Dollard's comparison of the position of lower-class blacks and Italian immigrant workers, 1937: 429–30). The treatment of individuals who are anomalous with respect to major features of the social structure — like the children of mixed unions — can reveal a great deal about that structure and the way in which it is maintained. It can suggest questions about features of the social pattern that might otherwise be taken for granted. It also reinforces the case for viewing the study of race relations as a field of work defined by a tradition of enquiry, for no definition in terms of the objects of study would suggest that the study of groups like the Mississippi Chinese would prove rewarding.

The nineteen-thirties was one of the most notable decades for the study of race relations. The contributions of the authors already mentioned together with those of Charles S. Johnson, Allison Davis, Burleigh Gardner, Kingsley Davis, Robert Merton, and others, culminated in that magisterial judgement of their generation, *An American Dilemma: The Negro Problem and Modern Democracy.* Most of the scholars who had studied race relations in the United States had been either Northerners (some of them inspired by the brash Yankee ideals that Southerners found so tiresome) or Negroes. There were few white Southerners who, like E. T. Thompson, tried to reconcile sociology with a respect for Southern ways. It was perhaps appropriate therefore that their work should be synthesized by a foreigner. For though his massive review was prepared by a team, the central analysis and interpretation was Myrdal's and is epitomized in the title. Myrdal contended that the 'Negro problem' was really a 'white problem', constituted by the

> 'ever-raging conflict between, on the one hand, the valuations preserved on the general plane which we shall call the "American Creed", where the American thinks, talks and acts under the influence of high national and Christian precepts, and, on the other hand, the valuations on specific planes of individual and group living, where personal and local interests: economic, social and sexual jealousies; consideration of community prestige and conformity . . . dominate his outlook.' (Myrdal, 1944: xlvii)

Subsequent consideration suggests that however meritorious the study, this analysis was in error in two central respects.

A pointer to the first mistake is the sub-title with which he introduces part of his argument, 'The Negro Community as a Pathological Form of an American Community' (1944: 927). He assumed not only that the blacks wanted to be assimilated into American society like any other minority group, but that this outcome was the only one worth serious consideration. Like Warner in his treatment of inter-group relations in *Yankee City*, Myrdal thought that any attachment of Negroes to separate institutions delayed their assimilation. They could be assimilated only as individuals. Negro associations which combatted discrimination could ease the acceptance of Negroes as a social category and could negotiate the terms on which Negroes would support other groups or parties in the social structure, but Myrdal neglected this. The mistake lies in approaching such matters under the influence of questions like 'what is the problem?' or, 'is the problem one of type A or type B?'. From the standpoint of, say, the government, there may appear to be one problem, but from the standpoint of the people concerned the nature of their government may appear as the problem. Nor is there any reason for social scientists to take over political definitions of 'the' problem. There are many problems, and human beings have not hitherto been so good at predicting the course of affairs that it is prudent to base reviews of the Myrdal magnitude on the inevitability of any particular outcome.

The second major mistake was Myrdal's failure to distinguish between a dilemma and an inconsistency. A dilemma exists when someone has to choose between two alternatives that are both unfavourable to him. As others have said, the tragedy of race relations in the United States is that there *is* no dilemma. White Americans are upset when their peace is disturbed and their business interrupted but they manage to live fairly amicably with the 'ever-raging conflict'. A critic has observed that besides the 'high national and Christian precepts' there are other value premises which are equally approved by American culture and there are some less idealistic American creeds to which Myrdal does not give due weight. Myrdal should not have assumed that social change will operate so as to reduce inconsistency, for in many respects 'it divides up social domains, increasing discontinuities between them but offering ways of regulating what to an outsider may seem inconsistencies' (Medalia, 1962: 223–27; Campbell, 1961: 228–34).

To understand why Myrdal made these mistakes it is necessary to appreciate that the United States can look different and Americans can seem to share more values, when seen through an outsider's eyes, especially when those eyes are Swedish. In 1890 one out of every ten Swedish-born persons was living in the United States. America was the golden land, and it had a special attraction for Swedish radicals because by emigrating the people were voting with their feet and showing what they thought of the highly stratified Strindbergian Swedish society. Myrdal had visited the United States previously. His eminence as an economist, his wide-ranging talent and his personal background in a country dissociated from the American heritage of slavery and racial prejudice, suggested to the sponsors of the study that he would be the man to give then an independent view of issues which divided the United States. So Myrdal returned, accompanied by his wife Alva — later a noted Swedish politician and ambassador — and bringing as his chief assistant Richard Sterner of the Royal Social Board, Stockholm.

In an earlier book written for the Swedish public Alva and Gunnar Myrdal stated that the American, even the scholar, is not very aware of what is distinctive about his society. 'The secret is that America has a living system of explicit ideals for human association that is more coherent, firm, clearly formulated, and alive in popular consciousness than in any other country, large or small, in all the Western world. . .in America we used to talk about "the American Creed" to identify what we had in mind' (1941: 33). The main roots of this value system were listed as: the philosophy of the Enlightenment, the Anglo-Saxon conception of law, and low-church protestant religiosity. This is recapitulated in *An American Dilemma*, but originally it appeared in more enthusiastic tones: 'America has preserved in almost undamaged form the Enlightenment's morning-clear confidence in reason, its belief in the individual's potentialities, its passion for individuals' rights.' There was also a profound kith-and-kin strain in their outlook: 'for us Swedes America can never be one foreign country among other foreign countries because somewhere between a quarter and a third of the people of Swedish descent live in that country. There they have struggled forward, built their homes, and grafted themselves into the great American democracy . . . in our many and long journeys we have met them in all the states of the Union' (1941: 34, 315–16).

Myrdal's Swedish background also has something to do with the second mistake, for the philosophy of the Enlightenment, which was impatient with what appeared inconsistencies, has exerted a powerful influence on the Swedish radical tradition with which Myrdal identifies himself. He touches on this in the 'personal note' which concludes the text of *An American Dilemma* where he states 'Social study is concerned with explaining why all these potentially good people so often make life a hell for themselves and for each other' (1944: 1023). This philosophy — to invert the title of a famous sociological essay — is grounded in an undersocialized conception of man. People have long presented themselves as moral and put the blame on immoral society: it avoids some nasty questions. People are conditioned also, and their societies make conflicting demands upon them (increasingly so, perhaps) so that some situations have to be defined as different from others (e.g., those in Mississippi to which class norms are applied compared to those evoking caste definitions).It is his eighteenth-century rationalism that explains why Myrdal assumed that moral unease in individuals will be the principal factor causing change at the social level, eliminating the allegedly particularistic value systems that would say that it is no more wrong to treat blacks differently in socially intimate situations than to recognize a sphere of private life distinct from the sphere governed by civic obligations. Myrdal recognized the importance of economic power at the national level to the maintenance and change of the social structure, but he was unable to relate this convincingly to his discussion of the way race relations posed a moral problem at the individual level.

The Myrdal study has been attacked from other directions. Aptheker charged that 'the Negro question is basically a material one, not a moral one', that had to be understood in the terms of class struggle. He repudiated Myrdal's gradualism and castigated his historical writing. Aptheker concluded that 'there is no American dilemma for believers in, and fighters for, democracy and full rights for all people' (1946: 66).

Cox criticized Myrdal for employing a mystical approach. He interpreted Myrdal as explaining white-black relations primarily in terms of caste, which in turn was vaguely conceived as a belief in white superiority that had to be upheld by its own inertia and by the superior caste's interest in maintaining it. This may not seem mystical or vague to everyone, but Cox saw here a suggestion that racial beliefs could be primary social forces whereas he was sure that they had been intentionally built up to facilitate a definite purpose. He was not so much concerned to discover mistakes within Myrdal's approach as to define that approach as motivated by the need of the ruling class to have a rationalization available that distracted attention from the political-class analysis (1948: 509, 519, 531). In a review that was not published until nearly twenty years later, Ralph Ellison advanced criticisms which cover similar ground but in a different way. He objected to Myrdal's statement that 'the Negro's entire life and, consequently, also his opinions on the Negro problem are, in the main, to be considered as secondary reactions to more primary pressures from the side of the dominant white majority'. Instead, he asked 'can a people (its faith in an idealized American creed notwithstanding) live and develop for over three hundred years simply by *reacting?*'. When Ellison wrote of 'the Negro people' he meant more than could be accommodated in Myrdal's vision. Ellison found in the Myrdal study 'the most detailed documentation of the American Negro's humanity yet to appear'. He complained that the Left should have 'failed even to *state* the problem in such broadly human terms' and praised Myrdal's skill. For the Swedish author had to question his hosts' motivation and present his findings in a way that would not offend them; he had to tell the South some unpleasant things about itself, and to present facts unacceptable to certain reactionary sections of the capitalist class. His findings had to be located in the context of a need for a new ideological approach to the Negro problem; they were to be 'the blueprint for a more effective exploitation of the South's natural, industrial and human resources'. The 'profit motive of the Right' had to be considered as well as the intentions and reasoning of the author (Ellison, 1964).

One of the most impressive books on race relations of the 1930s and 1940s was Oliver C. Cox's *Caste, Class and Race*, which was one of the first theoretical works in which the author put his contentions into context by placing beside them critical studies of his predecessors (in this case, Park, Benedict, Warner, and Myrdal). One of the book's chief merits is that it offers a coherent synthesis of the entire field. Two themes run through it. One is the meaning of 'caste'. The other stems from

Cox's conviction that racial problems — and most social problems also — can be explained only in the terms of a political class analysis. The second theme consists of his attempts to explain and expose the intellectual devices of writers who reject this view and seek to put in its place theories less disturbing of the established order. Because this book's approach is so different from those previously discussed and its claims are so important, it needs to be considered at some length.

The concern with the meaning of caste is almost an obsession. In his Preface, Cox remarks that he spent some months observing the partial operation of caste among the thousands of East Indians in Trinidad (where he was born). It looks as if, because of his prior acquaintance with caste, he was intellectually offended when Lloyd Warner began to use the term in writing about race relations in America. There was nothing novel about a recognition of the relative rigidity of status in some social systems. 'What is new, however, is an insistent attempt by many students of social stratification to identify rigidity of social status, in whatever social context it is found, with caste; and to conceive of castes as mere petrified, rigid or endogamous social classes' (1948: 298). So he went to the literature on Hindu caste and analyzed it with a perspicacity that won him praise from Dumont (1966: 295). In the first section of his book Cox held that 'one caste cannot exist in an otherwise casteless society, for castes are interdependent social phenomena. Indeed some question has arisen as to whether a two-caste system is possible.' He refused to add any new definition of caste to the long list of those already available. Instead, he presented Hindu caste as a unique system of relations distinguished by a variety of characteristics (1948: 3, 5). Whereas Cox inclines to economic interpretations of race relations, when discussing caste, he emphasizes instead the distinctiveness of the cultural system.

The concept of system is at the very centre of Cox's conception of society. He sees many phenomena as coming into existence because they are required by the system, and their continuance as explained by the functions they serve in that system. 'Wars are significantly functions of social systems . . .' 'Both the "master race" ideology and fascism are social attributes of a particular social system.' 'Modern slavery may be thought of as developing out of a need for the rapid proletarianization of workers.' 'Morality is a function of the social system, and a better system can change both morality and human nature for the better.' 'Race prejudice and Negro standards . . . are both produced by the calculated economic interests of the Southern oligarchy. Both prejudice and the Negro's status are dependent functions of the latter interests.' 'Exploitation of militarily weaker peoples is inherent in capitalism.' 'There will be no "crackers" or "niggers" after a socialist revolution because the social necessity for these types will have been removed . . . If we attempt to see race relations realistically the meaning of the capitalist function is inescapable' (Cox, 1948: xxix, xxxviii, 357, 537, 530, 477, 537). Even on Cox's own terms the question which these extracts must raise is: are social systems, and particularly capitalist systems, so well integrated that these various developments can be seen as necessary, and functionalist explanations accepted, without better evidence than has so far been furnished? Cox himself sometimes falters on this score. For example, he writes 'from one point of view the masters did not have so great a need for racial antagonism during slavery. Black workers could be exploited in comparative peace' (1948: 525). If the need for rationalizations and divisive tactics varies with the state of the system, discussion of the limits of variation is required and propositions concerning this must feature in the explanation.

According to Cox, the class struggle is the motive power behind the history of our era. 'Racial antagonism is part of this class struggle, *because* it developed within the capitalist system as one of its fundamental traits. It may be demonstrated that racial antagonism, as we know it today, never existed in the world before about 1492; moreover, racial feeling developed concomitantly with the development of our modern social system.' The italics have been added in this quotation for it is my contention that the connection is not as close as Cox claims. The historical sequence is unique; many things contributed to it. There is no way of determining which features of it were necessary and which accidental. At this level of abstraction it is impossible to ascertain causal relationships. It is true that on this very general level racial feeling developed concomitantly with the social system but it is doubtful if there was so marked a change around 1492 or that racial antagonism is a 'fundamental trait' of capitalism. Cox did not wish to be read as stating that the white race was the only one capable of race prejudice. 'It is probable that without capitalism, a chance occurrence among whites, the world might never have experienced race prejudice.' He remarked

'If we had to put our finger upon the year which marked the beginning of modern race relations, we should select 1493–94. This is the time when total disregard for the human rights and physical power of the non-Christian peoples of the world, the coloured peoples, was officially assumed by the first two great colonizing European nations . . . However, the capitalist spirit, the profit-making motive, among the sixteenth century Spaniards and Portuguese, was constantly inhibited by the philosophy and purpose of the Roman Catholic Church.' (Cox, 1948: xxx, 345, 331-33)

Because Cox stresses so strongly the functions that racial prejudice serves within the social system, he represents as a combined entity things that are better distinguished in analysis. Thus he writes 'Colour prejudice, as a psychological phenomenon, is a complex emotion manifested by a positive attitude of distance and reaction; specifically it is an insistent attitude of white superiority and dominance and an accommodating reaction of persons of colour' (1948: 350-51). It is surely unhelpful to include in an account of prejudice a description of others' reaction to it. Emotion, attitude, distance maintenance, and other facets of unequal race relations are best studied in a way that distinguishes causes from functions. Inflation, as an economic phenomenon, can be managed by a privileged class. It can then be said to serve a function in the social system, but inflation can have varied causes and consequences and cannot be properly accounted for in terms of its functions.

A peculiar feature of *Caste, Class and Race* is the way Chapter Sixteen, concerning the history of racial antagonism, suddenly yields place to a chapter describing seven situations of race relations. As the author is chiefly concerned with the qualities of social systems, the reader expects a typology that shows how structures of race relations are associated with particular social systems and phases of their development, but Cox advances his seven situations simply as the major forms in which racial conflicts present themselves in the modern world. A systematic typology would state the criteria of classification and would probably end up with a set of boxes, some of which might well be empty.

Cox defines race relations as 'that behaviour which develops among peoples who are aware of each other's actual or imputed physical differences' (1948: 320) and he has quite a lot to say about the kinds of awareness that characterize the various situations. The most important of these are the ruling class and bipartite situations and it is under these headings that Cox compares the societies of Trinidad and the US South that he knows best. The first three are situations of a different kind: stranger, original contact, and slavery. Stranger and original contact situations can develop later into either ruling class or bipartite

ones. Slavery resembles the latter but has a different legal basis. The
last two situations are also equivocal. Cox counts Brazil as representing
an amalgamation whereas it seems on his criteria to belong in the
ruling class category. It is when describing the amalgamative situation
that he chiefly discusses nationalism as 'an exploitative, socio-
psychological instrument of actual or potential ruling classes'. The
seventh category, the nationalistic situation, is described only briefly
and inadequately; to deploy the theory he states elsewhere Cox would
need to describe the material forces in Haiti in 1792 or India in 1857
which were the basis for the uprisings he mentions. The nationalism of
the underdogs appears as the sort of process by which peoples lift
themselves up, but any suggestion that beliefs can be prime movers is
in Cox's view mysticism and he pushes it out of sight. Relations
necessary to the social system have pride of place. 'Haiti might be taken
as the classic illustration of an exploited racial group which has
achieved nationhood. Negro Americans will probably never become
nationalistic; the numerical balance of the races will not allow the
development of nationalistic antagonism on the part of the coloured
people' (1948: 403). In this scheme the white ruling class is given a
power to rule the minds as well as the bodies of the black citizens to an
extent which was never possible even under slavery.

It may also be justified to examine Cox's typology from a different
perspective and to ask whether there is not here another chain of
reasoning of which the author is not himself fully aware and therefore
fails to develop as he might have done. Elsewhere Cox criticizes Myrdal
for assuming that beliefs about the nature of race are 'primary social
forces'. Myrdal fails to acknowledge that the propagators of the ruling
ideas in the United States know that these beliefs are without objective
justification but deliberately spread them because they serve a purpose
(1948: 531). This is a clear statement of the thesis mentioned in
Chapter One, that race is a political idea. If a sociologist adopts this
viewpoint and defines race relations in terms of an awareness of 'actual
or imputed physical differences', he should attempt to identify the
kinds of political and economic structures which generate a racial
consciousness. Cox does indeed present the bipartite situation as one in
which 'definite racial attitudes are developed' but he does not analyze
his seven situations in terms of the cultivation of racial beliefs or indeed
in terms of exploitative relations. Some of his situations provide
illustrations of neither of these and in this respect his typology is
inconsistent with his own theories.

In his concluding chapter Cox hands down his judgement that the
race problem of the United States 'is primarily the short-run

manifestations of opposition between an abiding urge among Negroes to assimilate and a more or less unmodifiable decision among racially articulate, nationalistic whites that they should not . . . the solidarity of American Negroes is neither nationalistic nor nativistic'. The racial policy of the country is formulated by Southern ruling-class whites and the Negro's political position is one of great weakness. For him to come to full manhood and citizenship the liberation of the Southern poor white will also be necessary. 'A great leader of Negroes will almost certainly be a white man, but he will also be the leader of the white masses of this nation.' Cox seems to have thought that he would need to be someone like Franklin D. Roosevelt (1948: 545, 581–82). Time has not dealt kindly with this diagnosis and it is necessary to ask whether there was anything in Cox's sociology that led him astray. The answer suggested by this examination is that Cox over-estimated the integration of the capitalist system and under-estimated the independence of beliefs in social processes. In this connection his discussion of religious movements is symptomatic. He writes 'In all significant social revolutions, organized religion will necessarily be involved . . . the Church is normally rightist' (1948: 171). There is no recognition of religious belief as an inspiration in slave insurrections or in movements for status change. Religious belief has often been associated with the nationalism of unprivileged groups and it played a crucial part in the process by which black Americans attained a new consciousness of themselves. Oliver Cox's assumptions prevented him from seeing the significance in his own observation 'One is amazed at the strength of the simple faith of the older, unlettered, rural Negroes. Powerless in the hands of their white exploiters, they go beyond them directly to their omnipotent God, almost happy in the assurance that retribution will come' (1948: 566). Here was something that was not determined by the needs of the social system, and it was out of this kind of psychological strength that a new movement emerged.

The sociological writing of the 1930s and 1940s, brought to a head in Myrdal's great synthesis, persuaded social scientists that America's 'Negro problem' was really a 'white problem' and that the major determinant of racial relations was not any inherent Negro incapacity but white prejudice. This movement of thought was given an added impetus by Nazi anti-semitism. Many of the Jewish scholars who fled from Germany brought their preoccupations to American social research. These led to the publication in 1950 by T. W. Adorno and others of the volume *The Authoritarian Personality* which in its scope and impact deserves a place beside *An American Dilemma*. In examining the characteristics of people susceptible to fascist propaganda Adorno and his colleagues discovered a particular personality type. People of this kind, as well as being inclined to fascist doctrines, were likely to be anti-semitic, anti-Negro, very concerned about sexual propriety, and so on. If such people could be given therapy, a major source of tension in social relations could be removed. This possibility inspired much of the American research into race relations during the 1950s, a decade when, thanks to men like Senator Joseph McCarthy, research into the socio-structural origins of prejudice ran the risk of being accounted an un-American activity. But it was not the only reason for concentrating on the white side of the inter-racial equation. Liberal whites, like Myrdal, believed that there was nothing in the nature of race to prevent black men being as good citizens as white. If Poles and Italians and Armenians were being assimilated, Negroes should also look to assimilation. The only obstacle was prejudice. The political left, both black and white, put their emphasis on class formation and denied that in the long run there could be any other basis for solidarity. They too were concerned with white prejudice even if they had a different theory of its source. The 1950s, therefore, was not a good decade for research on the structure of race relations. The central problems appeared to have been solved and academic interest moved to the application of this new understanding.

8

Ethnogenesis

In the 1930s and 1940s social scientists learned a great deal about the nature of race relations from studies of white American society and the position in that society of the black minority. Though much of this new knowledge was particular to the American context, a great deal related to fundamental social processes, such as the psycho-dynamics of prejudice, and the structure of two-category social systems, and could therefore be applied in attempts to explain patterns of inter-group relations in other countries. The new social movements manifested among black Americans in the 1960s surely had some lessons of another kind to teach, but at this distance in time it is unwise to be too confident about their precise character. This chapter will contend that while the emphasis of the earlier studies was on the nature and power of majorities, the 1960s illuminated the power that minorities could mobilize in changed circumstances. It will also argue that the two-sidedness of the relations to be analyzed can be more easily grasped by opposing the concept of ethnicity to that of race, so that the former reflects the positive tendencies of identification and inclusion where the latter reflects the negative tendencies of dissociation and exclusion.

The most searing evidence of white power and the way it was used comes from the data on lynching. Between 1889 and 1940 there were 3,833 recorded lynchings, four-fifths of those lynched being Negroes, with most of the incidents occurring in the South. The number of unrecorded racial murders was probably very much higher. It is also clear that in many instances the victims were falsely accused or had incensed whites by merely breaching the etiquette of race relations — for example, by purchasing an automobile (Myrdal, 1944: 564). Nor was there anything at all judicial about many lynchings; often they involved torture, sexual assault (e.g. castration), and a scramble to obtain fingers or other portions of the body as souvenirs or exhibits. Reports of lynchings were regularly carried in the journal of the National Association for the Advancement of Coloured People and their testimony to the unwillingness of the United States government to protect its citizens burned itself into the memories of more than one black generation. It is a passage in the black experience that must long affect black judgements of American society.

Weighed in the balance against evidence of this kind was the tenacious optimism about American ideals that inspired generations of black leaders and was characteristically expressed in the pulpit language of Martin Luther King's 1963 Washington speech 'I have a dream'. It was a dream of a society in which racial discrimination was no more. Already in 1963 those hopes were tinged with desperation. Expectations had been raised by the 1954 US Supreme Court declaration that school desegregation should proceed 'with deliberate speed'. Black Americans waited, but felt mounting frustration as their hopes were not fulfilled. With the mechanization of Southern agriculture, more and more of them left for the Northern cities. 1960 was the year that saw the admission of so many new African countries to the United Nations and, by no means coincidentally, the forward surge of the civil rights movement among black Americans.

Black leaders of the 1960s were more successful than their predecessors in recruiting support and mobilizing their potential followers. They benefitted from the new social and economic situation which had concentrated many blacks in the cities, improved mass communication, and lessened traditional controls. Previously the terminology of race had been chiefly used by white peoples as a way of defining others. 'Black' had been an adjective of disparagement, a possible insult lying behind gentler adjectives like coloured. The activists transformed it, persuading their followers to display 'black pride' and to elevate 'black culture'. All non-whites were invited to join the struggle. The slogan 'black power', which Stokeley Carmichael launched in Mississippi in 1966, marked the beginning of a process whereby a variety of subordinated groups are coming to a consciousness of their position, defining it in opposition to what they represent as an exploiting white power structure, and reversing the use of race as a principle for ascribing group membership. Their success was unprecedented; it stimulated other groups to follow their example and made the white majority change some of their governmental programmes in ways that offered new opportunities to all minorities. One such group were the Spanish-speaking population of California who illustrate the new tendency to use the terminolgy of race as a means of recruiting minority support, for they call themselves *La Raza* as well as *Chicanos*. But it was not only minorities in the United States that benefited. Black groups in Great Britain have drawn inspiration from American Negro leaders and their strategies, while the American influence on the black consciousness movement in South Africa has also been significant.

An element crucial to the success of the black power movement was the coverage it received from the mass media. The issues lent themselves to dramatic presentation and many people, particularly in the younger generation, were ready to identify with the protesters. Outside the United States, men and women who felt ambivalent about the country's rise to its commanding position in world affairs were the more ready to sympathize with a minority so clearly being ill-treated in what was sometimes called America's backyard. Thus the impression spread of black Americans as a political minority relatively united in the demands it was making upon white America, though the research of social scientists revealed a less straightforward situation. This is illustrated by a survey of conceptions of 'black power' conducted in Detroit in 1967 in those areas of the city where rioting had taken place (Aberbach and Walker , 1970). When asked 'what do the words "black power" mean to you?' over 23 per cent of the black respondents replied 'nothing' (which is generally used as a term of derision); all told, 49.6 per cent of blacks said that for them the expression had unfavourable connotations while 42.2 per cent said it had a favourable meaning. Respondents were also asked what form of race relations they preferred: integration, separation, or something in between. Of the blacks who reported a favourable interpretation of black power, 46 per cent favoured integration, 46 per cent something in between, and the number favouring separation was too small for valid statistical comparison. Those who disliked black power presumably favoured integration to a greater extent. Approval for the slogan came mostly from the younger blacks who had been born or grew up in Detroit, were not members of churches, and had begun to doubt the trustworthiness of the federal and municipal governments. Their chief concerns were with black unity and 'fair shares'. There seemed from this study to be a greater willingness to take part in political campaigns of all kinds, while there is evidence from many sources of a movement towards a more unified, more highly mobilized black community; but differences in political consciousness and orientation remain profound.

It was remarkable that blacks should have been able to achieve so much politically at a time of economic weakness, at a time when some commentators were asking 'who needs the Negro?'.

'The tremendous historical change is taking place in these terms: he is not needed. He is not so much oppressed as unwanted; not so much unwanted as unnecessary; not so much abused as ignored. The dominant whites no longer need to exploit the black minority . . . White America employs the new technology not with thoughts of incorporating but, rather, of doing away with the coloured race.' (Willhelm, 1970: 210–11)

As this author repeatedly asks, why discriminate when by employing objective criteria the Negro candidates will usually fail? The elimination of discrimination would therefore not reduce racial inequalities. It is also important to see the changes amongst the blacks against the pattern of United States pressure groups. Much is achieved in American politics by the process of coalition-building whereby different interest groups are brought behind a particular candidate or party. Ethnic politics has often lent itself to such a process, but no groups wished to be identified with the blacks, and their leaders have had great difficulty entering into coalitions with other groups. To escape from this trap more was needed than a black vote: the blacks had to threaten the existing structure sufficiently to cause elements in other groups (notably the more liberal whites) to form tacit coalitions with them.

Every social system has to offer its participants rewards for their loyalty and commitment. To white immigrants, America promised material advancement and the opportunity to share in the fashioning and government of the society. For the system to function white immigrants had to transfer their allegiance to a new flag, to a new constitution in a new language, and to endorse new rules. It had to be made worth their while to do so, for they had the chance of living in the United States but not being of them, by forming separate communities like some of the self-segregating religious groups, though on a larger scale. Blacks for a long time did not have such a choice, although there were a few self-segregating all-black communities. No one thought it necessary to bid for the allegiance of black citizens because they seemed to have no future other than assimilation, and assimilation was to be on the white man's terms. Blacks were to enter majority society by bidding for white acceptance and as no whites wished to be identified with the social category at the bottom of the hierarchy, it is doubtful whether blacks would ever be accepted in the way that members of less easily distinguishable minorities had been. Therefore blacks had to fight white discrimination on the grounds that it was un-American, and this trapped them in a posture that implied that they wanted acceptance because they preferred the company of whites to that of blacks. To get out of the trap they had to make whites believe that they had a choice and that their commitment to America could not be taken for granted. They could not persuade whites of this unless there was in fact a choice open to blacks; even if ninety nine out of a hundred opted for the majority society, there had to be the possibility that the balance might shift towards an alternative that white Americans disliked.

The history of black politics in the United States since the early years of this century — the period when black fortunes were at their very lowest — can be seen as a testing of alternative strategies and possibilities. Booker T. Washington, it has been said, was a greater leader of white opinion than of black people. Marcus Garvey, with his 'back to Africa' movement, played an important part in cultivating black pride, but his programme had only a restricted appeal. In a similar way some of the unorthodox religious movements, like the Black Jews and Black Muslims, had an importance far greater than their membership might suggest because they sketched alternative conceptions of the place of blacks in the midst of white America. This new element was signalized in the title of E. U. Essien-Udom's study of the 'Nation of Islam', *Black Nationalism*. Social scientists had studied obstacles to assimilation on the white side and had observed none on the black side; but perhaps there was one that could be seen in these movements and perhaps its character was best seized by the sociologically slippery concept of nationalism which was defined as

> 'the belief of a group that it possesses, or ought to possess, a country; that it shares, or ought to share, a common heritage of language, culture and religion; and that its heritage, way of life, and ethnic identity are distinct from those of other groups. Nationalists believe that they ought to rule themselves and shape their own destinies, and that they should therefore be in control of their social, economic, and political institutions.'
>
> (Essien-Udom, 1962: 21–2)

Some of the new nations of Africa are too heterogeneous to qualify in terms of these criteria, but black nationalism in the United States has particular difficulty in fitting itself to such a definition. Essien-Udom picks out a more restrained objective from statements such as that by DuBois who believed it 'the duty of the Americans of Negro descent, as a body, to maintain their race identity until the mission of the Negro people has become a practical possibility'. This doctrine of embryonic nationalism, of preparing for a future when a more positive programme will be possible, he calls cultural nationalism. In recent years it has absorbed many new elements from African culture, supporting Franklin Frazier's 1962 prophecy when, in the course of a bitter criticism of the black intellectual, he averred that 'the American Negro had little to contribute to Africa, but that Africa, in achieving freedom, would probably save the soul of the American Negro in providing him with a new identification, a new self-image, and a new sense of personal dignity' (Edwards, 1968: 279).

The cultural identification with Africa probably affected only a thinking minority. Americans generally were remarkably ill-informed about Africa prior to the entry into international politics of the independent black states. Black Americans in the 1950s thought of Africans as lacking civilization so that when at the end of the decade they saw African statesmen and diplomats on their television screens and learned of the attention they were receiving at the United Nations, they felt that they had been overtaken by runners they had thought far behind them in the race. They looked at their own condition in a new way. This element of changed expectations, of new reference groups, seems to have been a vital one in the new consciousness of identity. Comparison of themselves with African nations and talk of nationhood did not make black Americans into a nation, but it enabled them to achieve a new kind of belonging which is perhaps best expressed by saying that they are now much more conscious of being a distinctive people living within the framework of the United States. This process, of creating a people, has been described by Lester Singer (1962) as one of ethnogenesis. He revived an expression employed in French writing more than a century earlier (Moreau de Jonnès, 1861: Broca, 1874 ii: 508) which in recent years has been increasingly employed — doubtless   independently — by   Soviet   anthropologists (Bromley, 1974: 18).

The relationship between ethnogenesis and nationalism will require further discussion, but, assuming there has been some such development as the one sketched in the previous paragraph, it may be helpful to pause over its relationship to the conceptual schemes that have formed part of the sociological tradition. It has been observed that sociologists failed to predict the result of the mid-1960s, although to talk of prediction in such a connection may be to ask too much of a subject like sociology, and certainly American social scientists for several decades identified race relations as posing problems more serious than politicians and the general public were prepared to acknowledge. A more serious criticism is that the developments of the 1960s could not be satisfactorily interpreted within the conceptual frameworks of either Myrdal or Cox. Neither of these authors paid sufficient attention to the dynamics of the Negro community. They treated it as an involuntary minority, a category created by whites, but if there is a basis for identification, minorities built up mutual aid and solidarity, creating positive ties between their members. Myrdal failed to examine adequately the preconditions for assimilation into American culture. Cox overlooked Max Weber's warning that communal action, based upon a feeling of belonging together, has to be distinguished from societal action, based upon a uniformity of individual calculation; to treat 'class' conceptually as having the same value as community leads to distortion, for class situations only emerge on the basis of communal action (Weber, 1947: 183 – 85 cf. 1968: 928 – 30). The tradition of sociological writing had been to regard blacks as the victims of other groups or classes rather than as groups in their own right. Neither Myrdal nor Cox presented them as people who were making their own history.

Sociologists had greater difficulty enquiring what sort of community the Negro community was because, in the attempt to establish independent foundations for their subject, sociological theorists had neglected the political dimensions of group formation. Most modern textbooks pay even less attention to the concept of nation than they do to the way some peoples define themselves as races. In seeking to rectify this neglect, Elie Kedourie's argument (1960: 9) that nationalism is a doctrine invented by European philosophers at the beginning of the nineteenth century deserves the closest attention. Prior to that century the people of Europe were divided and united along many different lines of language, religion, and region; nation was not predominant. Italy, after all, was unified only in 1870 and Germany in 1871. What the nineteenth century movement achieved was to persuade people that the possession of a nationality was natural to a man; that it was to be expected that he should wish to be ruled as a member of a national unit; and that such sentiments are politically legitimate. As Ernest Gellner (1964: 147–50) explains, these claims involved philosophical-anthropological, psychological, and normative propositions which look much less persuasive when they are subjected to critical examination. Nationalist movements, he says, have invented nations where they did not exist. And why have they done so? Because individuals and groups have agitated for their own ends.

Nineteenth-century economic liberals did not expect that national-ism would become important. The expanding network of world trade would create so many counter-balancing interests. Nor did the Marx-ists. Their philosophy of history told them that the ultimate determi-nants of social patterns lay in the means and relations of production; all else must eventually be subordinated to these. But if the Marxist predic-tion is being fulfilled the process is a slow one. The national conscious-ness of peoples has been having a profound effect upon their produc-tive activities. Nationalism became one of the most potent and most le-gitimate factors in twentieth century politics, encouraged by Woodrow Wilson, the professor who became President of the United States. He brought to international politics the conviction that the only legitimate governments were those of the people. Every people should be enabled to rule itself. One of his four principles for the peace after the war of 1914-18 was 'all well-defined national aspirations shall be accorded the utmost satisfaction'. But what was a people? What was a nation? Wilson did not regard the Irish as one of the nations 'struggling to be free' and the British Foreign Office warned 'It would clearly be inadvis-able to go even the smallest distance in the direction of admitting the claim of the American negroes' (a hit at Wilson!), 'or the Southern Irish, or the Flemings or Catalans, to appeal to an Inter-State Conference over the head of their own Government'. Yet Wilson's political philosophy had such an influence on the diplomatic scene that the war brought what appeared to be the final triumph of nationalism while the peace led to the creation of an international organ, the League of Nations, which made it the most respectable of political principles. Applied to the tangled political geography of Europe it gave diverse minorities new grounds for complaint without providing any satisfactory basis for re-negotiating frontiers. Israel Zangwill, the theorist of the 'melting pot', commented sardonically on the new doctrine's weaknesses, remarking 'national thought is not a cerebration but a contagion, not an activity but an epidemic (1917: 64).

The war of 1939-45 gave further encouragement to nationalism and weakened those political units, like the colonial empires, which were not based upon it. It marked out the path of independence for former colonies as one leading to membership as states (each with its own new minority problems) in a reconstituted body which was international in the sense both of being global and of being an organization of nations, the United Nations. Yet the development of nationalism does not follow the same course in all circumstances. It forms in opposition: so much depends on who are the neighbours or rulers of a territory and upon the issues that bring the masses into conflict with them. There is an important difference between a nationalist movement trying to mobilize its forces and the situation in which it has succeeded, having persuaded others that there is now a new nation, and being faced with the problem of cultivating unity in new circumstances. Bangladesh succeeded and is now accepted. Biafra did not. The difference between the before and after situations is such that one authority reserves the term nationalism for the former alone, preferring to speak of 'national sentiment' in the established nation (Smith, 1971: 68).

Nineteenth-century sociologists like Gumplowicz saw race and nationality as social groupings that resulted from qualities inherent in human nature at a particular stage in its evolution. Contemporary sociologists see political groupings as the outcome of alignments in group encounters. People may cooperate with one another in a community situation without being aware of what is distinctive of their group. When they meet strangers they become aware of things about themselves that previously they had taken for granted, and the kind of consciousness they acquire of their own identity may be influenced by a desire to differentiate themselves from those that happen to be nearest to them. Perhaps the simplest illustration of the process is to be found in descriptions of urban migrants in the mining towns of Zambia. Men have left their ethnically homogeneous homelands and come to the cities where they have met other Africans speaking different languages and following distinctive customs. In these circumstances the men have welcomed as 'brothers' men from groups who might previously have been enemies but with whom they have more in common than with strangers from further away. New groupings have been precipitated: migrants from one region as opposed to those from another, and all Africans as opposed to Europeans. As new groups form, their members acquire a new consciousness of themselves as members of these groups, sharing common interests with other members and recognizing that they stand in opposition to groups of whose existence they had earlier been unaware (Epstein, 1958: 231–40).

In recent years it seems as if there has been a world-wide increase in ethnic consciousness, though it is difficult either to establish this or to be certain about its explanation. There are young Jews in the United States today who have reacted against their parents' unwillingness to meet the ritual requirements of Judaism: the children study Hebrew, visit Israel, join orthodox synagogues, and reinstitute the rituals of the Sabbath and the holidays. Nor is the sudden upsurge in interest among

Soviet Jews in emigration to Israel all that easy to explain. Many of the would-be emigrants enjoy privileged positions and a style of life in the Soviet Union that they may be unable to find in Israel, yet they risk punishment and persecution for themselves and their families by persisting in their wish to emigrate. Soviet Jews have suffered restrictions on their religious practice and other forms of discrimination for many generations. Why then has this apparent change in sentiment come at this time? The Jewish case has some special features because of the relatively recent establishment of the state of Israel (which in turn has stimulated a process of ethnogenesis among the Palestinians) but there are comparable developments all over the world. In Canada and the United States ethnic sentiment seems to revive. In many parts of Europe, like the Basque region of Spain, in Belgium, Scotland, and Wales there can be little question of its significance. In Malaysia, India, and parts of black Africa the outcome of political changes has been a strengthening of ethnic alignment.

To seek to explain variations in the level of ethnic consciousness in terms of a single cause would be to repeat a nineteenth-century kind of mistake. The phenomena that have to be explained are varied and have still to be analyzed and classified, but it may be necessary to make a basic distinction between the sense of ethnic identity at the national level and that within the nation-state. National rivalries increase the sense of national solidarity and strengthen consciousness of ethnic belonging at this level so that in one sense war promotes ethnic consciousness. But the promise of peace may equally promote ethnic consciousness at the lower level because it enables groups within the state to express their feeling of distinctiveness without threatening the larger unit. Economic and social changes in the last twenty years have increased the importance of ethnic identifications within states. The development of world trade has meant that states are no longer sovereign bodies in the old sense. That great numbers of people migrate to take up work in other countries is not particularly new, but it is notable that they are no longer under as much pressure to assimilate to the culture of the receiving society. They can keep in touch with the sending societies in many new ways, not just by sending letters but by telephoning, sending photographs, tape-recordings, and paying personal visits. For an Irish immigrant in Boston to visit his relatives in Killarney may cost less than a month's wages and can be fitted into a two-week holiday. Fifty years ago it would have cost much more and taken much longer. With the improvement in living standards many people seem to wish to cultivate distinctive ethnic origins as a way of making their lives a bit more interesting. The increased importance to people's lives of their choices as consumers has much to do with this. Then the tremendous rise in the coverage and significance of the mass media has given people in many countries a greatly enhanced sense of belonging to an international society and lessened their respect for the slogan 'My country — right or wrong!' Many different kinds of sentiment can affect the level and character of ethnic consciousness and it must be continually compared with other kinds of identification. For example, it has sometimes been suggested that Welsh and Scottish nationalism has to be seen as a reaction to English pressure in which English class distinctions play an important part. Nationalism provides Welshmen and Scotsmen with a basis for relations that cross class lines and for affirming values to which class is irrelevant.

In each particular situation of changing ethnic consciousness a great variety of forces and circumstances interact. With the benefit of hindsight it can now be seen that the influential American sociologist Louis Wirth led his colleagues astray when he persuaded them that it was best to approach this problem area with a composite concept of a minority. He looked round at the groupings which in contemporary Europe and America were called minorities and discussed their common characteristics. What he described was the European and American folk concept of minority, which bears no better relationship to sociological analysis than the popular conception of race bears to the analysis of relations between peoples of different skin colour. For Wirth, a group was a minority only if it was singled out for differential treatment because of its physical or cultural characteristics, and its members therefore regarded themselves as objects of collective discrimination and tended to develop distinctive atttitudes which set them further apart (Wirth, 1945: 347). Wirth classified minorities according to their orientation towards the majority society but did not explore the significance for their social relations of the different kinds of physical and cultural characteristics that set them apart. In insisting that the concept of minority was not statistical, that a group could be more than 50 per cent of the population and still be a minority. Wirth has been followed by other writers equally influential in their generation (e.g. Wagley and Harris, 1958: 10).

Wirth's definition combines many characteristics that can usefully be distinguished. It distracts attention from divisions within minorities and from the nature of the unit within which a group constitutes a minority. It conflicts with the ordinary use of the word, which permits one to say that Catholics are a majority in the city of Boston but a minority in the state of Massachusetts or in the United States of America. If a minority is defined numerically it is easy to refer to minorities within minorities and to apply the term to linguistic groups, religious groups, privileged groups, and so on. According to Wirth's definition, blacks in South Africa are a minority even though they account for well over half the population. If blacks there gain a greater share in political power there could come a time when it would be difficult to reach any agreement as to whether they were, or were not, a minority in Wirth's sense. On the other hand, it is straightforward to hold that they are a numerical majority but a political minority (even if this does make the assumption that power is measurable), and that they are further divided into ethnic minorities (Zulu, Khosa, Venda, etc.).

In most inter-group situations, minorities are defined in two different ways: by themselves, and by the majority. Wirth's classification of minorities, as assimilationist, pluralistic, secessionist, and militant, related to minority policies and took no account of variations in the disposition of the majority population. The approach advocated here assumes that there are two boundaries, one of inclusion, reflecting minority members' recognition of each other as belonging together, and one of exclusion, reflecting the way the more powerful section of the population defines a less powerful social category as consisting of people to be set apart (who could be a numerical majority). When a minority sets itself apart, the majority is likely to respond by forming a boundary that excludes them from certain relationships. When a majority excludes a category of people from participation in any area of social life, they can be expected to come together in their own interest and in this way to build an inclusive boundary. Beliefs about common nationality, common ethnicity, and common religion often form the bases for inclusive boundaries. Beliefs about race have frequently served as a basis for exclusive boundaries. This way of defining racial and ethnic groups is not without its problems, since the racial ideology of white minorities, and that of the Nazis, has served both inclusive and exclusive functions. A complex typology would be necessary to classify the various possible inter-relations between inclusive and exclusive boundaries in different circumstances, but for the purposes of this chapter it is not necessary to embark on a fully comparative analysis. It is sufficient to note that if racial and ethnic minorities are defined in terms of boundaries, as was originally suggested by Michael H. Lyon (1972), this enables the student to look at the forces from both sides which define the social units involved. It also distinguishes culturally transmitted values from social practices, for a belief about the nature of race may be seen as sustaining a boundary while the boundary also sustains the belief. In much the same way, changes in the nature of a boundary may be related to changes in the groups involved.

By examining the kind of boundary and the justification put forward for it, we can proceed to define kinds of minority. A racial minority is created when opposition to the social incorporation of a minority is justified on the grounds of the minority members' hereditary characteristics, particularly those associated with skin colour and nineteenth century doctrines of racial typology. Attempts by an elite group to maintain political and cultural distinctions — as in South Africa — can result in the creation of a racial majority. Racial justifications could also be advanced for the maintenance of a purely voluntary, inclusive, minority, but in practice during the last century the chief sociological characteristic of relations considered 'racial' has been that they involve a category of people against whom social barriers have been erected. A national minority is comprised by people who are either citizens of another state, or regard themselves as such and want the political map revised so that this can be recognized and they can live with their fellow nationals. A nationalist movement is one pressing for the recognition of a new nation-state. An ethnic minority is one that cultivates a distinctiveness based upon common descent and wants this recognized within the state its members inhabit. A social class may also be a minority with inclusive and exclusive boundaries, as may a religious group. The formation of an ethnic minority depends upon a belief among the minority members that the nature of their common descent requires or justifies their coming together, and it will be easier for them to do so if the majority shares this belief. Here the nature of the state in which they live may be of the greatest importance. In some societies every citizen is expected to have an ethnic as well as a national identity but in others the ideal of common citizenship is thought to over-ride ethnic particularism and ethnic sentiment is expected to wither away. Where (as in Islamic countries and in Israel) the state is identified with a given religion, there will be less tolerance of separate ethnic organization. The formation of ethnic minorities and the scope allowed them, therefore depends upon a shared belief in the legitimacy of ethnic organization.

An important feature of the kind of classification being advocated is that it makes allowance for a minority's being both ethnic and racial, and for changes in the relationship of the inclusive and exclusive boundaries. The history of black Americans starts as the story of individuals captured from a variety of peoples in Western Africa and separated from their traditional culture. In the beginning they were a category, a racial minority constituted by white attitudes and behaviour. From their shared experience they built up a common heritage and a desire to identify with one another. They became a group. Discrimination continues, and a black American cannot join the white majority in the way that is open to the European immigrant, but neither can that immigrant join the black group. Black Americans have become an ethnic as well as a racial minority. On the other hand, Asians came to East Africa as a series of ethnic and religious minorities (Goans, Gujeratis, Sikhs, Ismailis, Muslim groups, etc.) marked off by inclusive boundaries. Their self-segregation contributed to the growth of African hostility towards them as a single category, so that in the last phase of their residence in Uganda all Asians together formed a racial minority. A different sequence is illustrated by the case of the Jews in Eastern Europe at the end of the nineteenth century who were both a racial minority (in that they were set apart and often persecuted by the majority), and an ethnic minority (in that they had their own institutions and regarded marriage outside the group as a cause for shame). Those who emigrated to New York found that their sense of identity was no longer reinforced by the hostility of others. They had to develop new institutions to respond to the novel threat of assimilation. As the exclusive boundary was weakened, so the minority members took steps to strengthen the inclusive one.

Though the United States is noted for the number of its ethnic minorities, the variety of kinds of minority is probably greater in the United Kingdom, so it should be a more searching test of the proposed classification to try it on British material. The United Kingdom is a state which contains three nations, English, Welsh, and Scots. The people who live in the province of Northern Ireland are culturally distinct from those in the larger island; they are divided politically, and religious (or sectarian) identification is often used as an indicator of political alignment. There are also cultural differences between the two sections. Though in Northern Ireland the unionists are a numerical and political majority, in relation to the United Kingdom they constitute an ethnic minority in that while they cultivate the distinctiveness of their group they are content to remain citizens of the state. The republicans are a national minority, since they wish to be citizens of the Republic of Ireland. There are also Catholic voters opposed to the unionists whose stance in relation to the Republic is more equivocal. From the standpoint of the belief that the six counties should be part of an Irish state, it is the unionists in the north who appear a national minority. The distinction between nationality and citizenship is worth maintaining for sociological purposes, even though it is not recognized when citizens of the United Kingdom apply for passports. Then they are told that their nationality is British rather than English, Welsh, or Scots. This practice reflects the assumption that nation and state are two expressions of the same body of people, but as current developments in the United Kingdom illustrate, the relationship of constituent nationalities to the state may be a changing one.

Substantial Asian minorities are now settled in England. Indian immigrants constitute a national minority which is divided into ethnic minorities like those of the Sikhs and Gujeratis. Pakistanis are a national minority with a slightly different constitutional status, since Pakistan has left the Commonwealth; they are divided into ethnic minorities (Mirpuris, Chhachhis or Campbellpuris, other Punjabis and Pathans). Englishmen will usually be unaware of the ethnic distinctions and may well regard all Asians as a single group. Nor will the immigrants necessarily unite at the level of the ethnic group. Ideas of ethnic origin and ethnic identity derive from a way of thinking about descent line are like the sections of a telescope which can be pulled right circumstances people identify with descent groups of varying scale, from the immediate family to the lineage or clan, so that segments of a descent lint are like the sections of a telescope which can be pulled right out or pushed into one another. In some circumstances it is just a small group of closely related people who come together, but at other times an external threat stimulates a whole series of groups to come together. The ethnic divisions of a national minority may also be identified with different positions in a scale of social status or be of different religion, so quite different alliances may be formed between groups depending upon the nature of the stimulus that is presented to them.

An underlying argument may now be apparent. It states that human societies utilize natural differences and natural relations as ways of organizing social relations (cf. Banton, 1967: 55–68). There is a sexual difference between men and women, and there are biological relations between parents and children. Human societies develop gender roles which go beyond the biological imperatives of sexuality. They create kinship systems which go beyond principles of genetics and the relationships necessary to child-rearing. In the same way humans utilize the physical differences that are thought of as racial to help create and identify social roles. They utilize the facts of common language, culture, and shared experience to develop notions of nationality. Some might say that they elaborate upon the division of labour to formulate ideologies of class relations, and though this suggests a somewhat different kind of relationship, there is sufficient similarity for it to be worth remarking.

A definition of ethnic minority has been proposed, but it remains to consider what ethnicity itself is. Like nationality, it should be seen as a shared quality, 'a condition of belonging to an ethnic group' (to follow the Oxford English Dictionary), but with the qualification that the significant members are *conscious* of belonging to the group. They believe the group to be ethnic in character and it is accepted by others as such. The stipulation that an ethnic group is a self-conscious group distinguishes it from what Soviet ethnographers call the ethnos or ethnic community, a group of people who share a common life but are not necessarily involved in competing for resources with other such communities. They regard these communities as 'basic units' existing prior to ethnic consciousness (Bromley, 1974: 19–23). In English, they could well be called ethne (the plural of *ethnos*) to capture this primordial sense. Contemporary examples may be found among some of the small societies in the New Guinea forests whose existence has only recently become known to the Western world. Being isolated and having little contact with other peoples or ethne, individuals in these societies cannot have had the same sense of conscious belonging that is found when several peoples are in regular contact. Earlier (page 144) reference was made to Africans who left traditional societies to join the heterogeneous society of the mining towns. What is called 'tribalism' is a manifestation of ethnicity that develops in the towns as a response to competitive social relationships.

No one is obliged to be a member of the same ethnic or religious minority as his parents, for if he is sufficiently determined he can always break away and identify himself with some other group. At times the opportunity to forsake the parents' ethnic identity may be negligible, or the costs of doing so almost prohibitive, but in general it is reasonable to regard religious and ethnic identification as springing from the choice of individuals, and as resulting in the creation of voluntary minorities. This is one of the main impulses behind changes in boundaries and takes us back to the discussion of the inter-relation between the two kinds of boundary. The level of ethnic consciousness is influenced by the action of individuals who seek to mobilize ethnic sentiment in order to achieve their goals, and these are frequently of a material kind. A good example is provided by the Choctaw Indians of

Mississippi, also mentioned earlier. Their history suggests that from 1830 to 1960 they retained a feeling of identity such that when opportunities improved they were able to organize as a distinctive group. The passage of the 1964 Civil Rights law and its provisions for fair employment opened the doors of local industries to Choctaws. Their industrial employment expanded. There was a great increase in the funds available to the Choctaw Agency and Choctaw Tribal Council, who initiated a programme which, for the first time, made available professional and managerial posts for Choctaws. In 1968 they regained the right to administer justice to their own people on their own land, and a tribal court began operating for the first time in almost 140 years. The formation of a United Southeastern Tribes bears witness to the increasing power of tribal governments and their people's growing consciousness of having a distinctive identity as Southeastern Indians (Peterson, 1971: 123; 1972: 1289. For a particularly instructive examination of the influence of class interest upon the formation of Chinese ethnic groups in Jamaica and Guyana, see Patterson, 1975).

The case of the Lapps in Scandinavia provides an example in some ways similar but uninfluenced by American developments. There are some 10,000 Lapps in Sweden, 22,000 in Norway, and smaller numbers in Finland and the Soviet Union. Since 1960 there has been a striking increase in Sweden in Lapp organization and ethnic sentiment which is as yet without any true parallel in Norway although in that country they constitute a large proportion of the population. The Swedish development is the more interesting because the Lapps constitute the only indigenous minority in that country and it is a major step for a homogeneous country like Sweden, that puts great stress on the constitutional equality of all citizens, to regard certain citizens as forming a special group meriting representation of a kind different from that accorded to other groups within the majority population.

The Swedish Lapps formed an association, *Svenska Samernas Riksförbund* (SSR) in 1950. Twelve years later there were two developments of particular importance to them. One was a reform of local government which gave all towns, including Lapp towns (for the term town is used even for fairly small settlements) the right to have their own councils. The other was the decision of the central government to appoint a special *ombudsman* for the Lapps and make him responsible to the SSR. This was important because plans to build hydro-electric power stations in the northern mountains, to construct reservoirs, to build a rocket base, to make new roads, open new mines,

and so on, deprived the reindeer-herding Lapps of pasture and
seriously interfered with the routes along which they have to coax their
herds in the journeys across the frontier between summer and winter
pasture. The Lapp ombudsman took some of these cases to court and
won settlements for his clients that would never have been obtained
under the old procedures. For example, a Norwegian proposal to
exclude Swedish Lapps from some of their traditional pasturage on the
western side of the mountains led to an action in which the Norwegian
Supreme Court struck down some of the official Norwegian proposals
as contrary to a codicil attached to a 1751 treaty. The success of such
actions stimulated Lapp morale and organization, which is the more
impressive because the Lapps have lived in small communities spread
very thinly over a vast territory with poor communications. The
Nordic Lapp Council, founded in 1953, to bring together Lapps
resident in the different countries, has gained wider recognition. The
ideology of the SSR has changed. Instead of seeing itself as a voluntary
association representing an interest group, it now presents itself to the
Swedish authorities as the body that should represent Lapps in all
matters concerning them as members of an ethnic group (Svensson,
1973). They sometimes talk of themselves as 'the Lapp nation' and in
recent times a Lapp political party has been formed. The rise in their
ethnic consciousness is clearly associated with distinctive material
interests though it is not fully explained by them. The actions of the
Swedish government in creating, even encouraging, a framework for
ethnic organization, are central to any explanation of the differences
between developments in Sweden and Norway.

The example of the Lapps is therefore important in another sense. It
is relatively easy for members of a minority to identify themselves as an
ethnic group if they live in a society that recognizes ethnicity and in
which people are expected to have an ethnic identity, as in, say, Nigeria
and parts of the United States. It is much more difficult for this to come
about in a society that defines ethnic divisions as illegitimate or
transitory. Though the resistance and the opportunities differ, the
main force behind movements such as those of the Choctaw and the
Lapps is that by organizing as an ethnic minority the members can
obtain material advantages for themselves. Minority organization
provides its members with services. It helps the Lapps to control a
particular ecological and economic niche by defending their legal
monopoly upon reindeer herding. In many industrial cities the work
force in particular sections of factories is largely from one minority and

people already working there are able to introduce their relatives and friends when job vacancies occur. By strengthening family ties (which can be a cushion in times of difficulty) and providing a basis for credit clubs and other forms of mutual aid, ethnic organization assists capital formation which is one of the most crucial factors in the upward mobility of minorities.

Members of smaller minorities like the Choctaw and the Lapps have shared a common class position, a common experience of differential treatment by the majority, and have a common sense of ethnic or national belonging. The black American had a weaker sense of natural distinctiveness and his best prospect of social advance appeared to lie in upward social mobility so that he might win acceptance because of his status even if his colour remained a disadvantage. But though individuals climbed, and though the formal barriers were removed in the 1950s and 1960s, the goal seemed no more attainable. Despite the growing income and status differences within the black minority, middle-class blacks turned away from the hazy prospect of assimilation and, helped perhaps by the positive image of black African leaders, began to identify themselves more along lines of colour. A tendency became apparent to refer to 'the American black' instead of the black American and this implicitly claimed that the black American had more in common with the black African than the white American. Implicit, too, in the emphasis upon their distinctiveness was a rather different use of the idea of race.

Nineteenth-century sociologists had good, though perhaps not sufficient, reasons for denying to national groupings an important place in their conceptual schemes. But they have been proved wrong. The new doctrine of nationalism whether for good or ill — and Kedourie at least thinks it was the latter — has captured men's imagination and nations have become important units. In a similar fashion, modern sociologists have denied that similarity of racial type leads naturally to the formation of a social unit, but the course of events here too may necessitate a reformulation. There is an important difference between the two cases because, by definition, no nation could be inherently better than any other, whereas races were supposed to be unequal. Races could become autonomous groupings in society only when the previously subordinated groups came to accept racial designations as they accept national ones and the presumption of inequality was overthrown. Such a process, I suspect, may have started around 1960. It was as if black leaders in the United States declared 'You define us as a racial group. Right, we will accept that label. We will show you that our subordinate position is not the outcome of our physical nature but of our social and political position. We will prove this by putting an end to our subordination while retaining our racial characteristics.'

There have always been some blacks who identified themselves racially. W. E. B. Du Bois in a lecture delivered in 1960 at the age of ninety-two years said that the situation when the Negro could claim complete civil and social equality was in sight. 'It brings not, as many would assume, an end to the so-called Negro problem, but the beginning of even more difficult problems of race and culture.' He went on to ask his black audience whether in such a situation they should simply adopt the ideals of the Americans.

'That would mean that we would cease to be Negroes as such and becomes whites in action, if not completely in colour . . . Physically, it would mean that we could be integrated with Americans, losing first of all the physical evidence of colour and racial type. We would lose our memory of Negro history . . .'

(Du Bois, 1975: 46)

Though racial identification was first employed by whites as a tool for putting blacks at a distance, Du Bois used it to evoke black solidarity. It seems as if some black Americans are now likewise inclined to use it to promote ethnic consciousness, as a basis for an inclusive boundary, and if this is so it may mark a further phase in the career of the race idea.

9

The idea of racism

It is probably a truism to remark that a key feature in the growth of knowledge in any field is the development of a battery of concepts of increasing range and precision. One feature of American writing in the 1960s was the display of impatience with the concepts and frameworks available for the sociological study of race relations; it was manifested in the attempt to formulate new concepts like 'internal colonialism', and in the tendency to interpret events in terms of oppression, exploitation, revolt, and similar evaluative expressions. In this period the word 'racism' was suddenly called upon to serve new purposes, becoming at times a political idea comparable to the claim of racial inequality earlier used by writers who adopted the opposite interpretation of much the same observations. If the word is given a wider meaning, is it a step towards a more penetrating mode of analysis?

The word 'racism' appears to have been introduced into the English language in the late 1930s, in order to identify the kind of doctrine that, in essence, asserts that race determines culture. One advantage of this usage was that it did not seek to comprehend other phenomena with which such doctrines are frequently, though not necessarily, associated. It made no presuppositions about the motives or intentions of the people who advanced or subscribed to such doctrines, nor the functions that they served in the wider society. Other concepts could be used to identify these. The words 'racism' and 'racist' were used by people who wished to attack doctrines of inequality and so, within the circles within which they were employed, they acquired strongly pejorative connotations which may help explain the recent attempt to extend their application. The best example is provided by two very influential black spokesmen who wrote 'By "racism" we mean the predication of decisions and policies on considerations of race for the purpose of *subordinating* a racial group and maintaining control over that group. . .'. They go on to distinguish between individual and institutional racism, stating that 'institutional racism relies on the active and pervasive operation of anti-black attitudes and practices. A sense of superior group position prevails: whites are "better" than blacks, therefore blacks should be subordinated to whites. This is a racist attitude and it permeates the society, on both the individual and institutional level, covertly and overtly' (Carmichael and Hamilton, 1967: 19–21). This approach rolls into one ball cultural assumptions, motives, institutions, attitudes, and beliefs about superiority: it may be politically effective, but it is not suited to comparative or historical analysis. Other authors have written about 'racist societies' and 'racist social structures'; they have said that Britain or the United States is a racist society without specifying (as they should have done) how a racist society is to be distinguished from a non-racist society, or how to determine the point at which either of these societies became racist.

Every concept needs to be seen both in isolation and as belonging to a particular family of concepts which inter-relate and support one another. 'Racism' used to belong with the family of concepts that includes nationalism, romanticism, and other doctrines associated with particular authors and historical periods. New uses of the word can perhaps be understood as part of an argument that doctrine is not now the key feature of race relations and that 'racism' should be located in another family of concepts. Some writers, indeed, identify racism with the history of Western Europe and North America in such a way as to put racism almost on a par with capitalism as a concept. Racism may be regarded as simply the way in which the forces of capitalist development express themselves under particular circumstances. Other writers favour a structural approach and may, for example, regard as racist any society in which racial distinctions are built into the social structure (there is a difficulty here comparable to the distinction between a society with slavery and a slave society: at what point does a society with racial divisions become a racist society?). All these proposals seem to run the risk of requiring the concept to perform too many separable tasks.

A leading concern of American social scientists working on race relations in the 1950s was with anti-discriminatory legislation, desegregation, and the application of psychological understanding to the reduction of intergroup tensions. Not surprisingly, they concentrated upon inter-personal relations and neglected the analysis of the macro-socio-logical aspects of racial conflict. The writers of the next decade preferred to emphasize that the incidence of racial discrimination cannot be understood in an inter-personal context but has been associated with broad historical movements that have shaped the form of the societies in question. As racial categories can be identified only when large groups share conceptions of others as significantly different, they must be located within cultural patterns. These categories are usually built into institutions that allocate resources to people, and this means that they are therefore social and economic phenomena as well. Because racial definitions are based upon immediately observable features of people's appearance and imply that members of different categories differ in their essential nature, they are easily incorporated into psychological processes and racial prejudice is often more deep-rooted and resistant to change than other kinds of prejudice. The influence of racial categories extends into so many spheres of life in multi-racial societies that these various features are almost certain to be supported by doctrines of racial difference or inequality. Much of the attraction of the extended use of 'racism' was that it drew attention to the way discrimination was inter-related with so many other features of social organization that it appeared to constitute a whole.

One way of determining whether it is more useful to locate 'racism' in one family of concepts or the other, is to examine a relevant text and see whether either usage permits the author to convey his arguments more satisfactorily or concisely. As authoritative a text as any is the Programme for a Decade for Action to Combat Racism and Racial Discrimination approved by the General Assembly of the United Nations on November 2, 1973. The Programme is set out in a document nearly 4000 words in length. Near the beginning it recalls that the United Nations has opposed all manifestations of racial discrimination, and apartheid in particular. It declares that any government whose policy or practice is based on racial discrimination contravenes the United Nations Charter. It next condemns collaboration with racist regimes, but as these are not separately defined it has to be assumed that racist regimes are those just designated, whose policy or practice is based on racial discrimination. There are subsequent references to 'racist dogmas', 'theories of racism', 'racist policies or practices', and 'situations that lead to racism', but considering the document as a whole it is difficult to see that in it the words racism and racist are given any meaning other than that of 'promoting racial discrimination'. On this test therefore the case for extending the application of the word 'racism' is not made out, but that in no way detracts from the need to improve the range of concepts suited to the analysis of the various phenomena associated with racial discrimination.

In discussing the use of the word 'racism' I am coming close to a statement I made on a previous occasion, and to what some sociologists have regarded as a controversy between Professor John Rex and myself. As I may be expected to dispel any doubts about the questions Rex has raised I had better recapitulate a little. In 1969 I delivered an address to the British Sociological Association in which I took as my starting point the definitions of racism to be found in dictionaries and leading tex-the definitions of racism to be found in dictionaries and leading textbooks, and identified the growth, at a particular point in time, of a nitions. I discussed three kinds of explanation of the origins of racism that were to be found, explicitly or implicitly, in existing writings on this subject. In preparing the address I contemplated the possibility of trying to describe the various phases in the history of racist doctrines — and referred indeed to a Mark Two racism — but I decided to concentrate on a question I thought should be of immediate concern. In previous generations people who would deny equal treatment to members of ethnic minorities often drew upon dubious biological arguments but in recent times, I remarked, they had been drawing upon observations from the province of social science. It seemed to me that if we were to extend the application of the term 'racism' to these new usages, without taking adequate account of the change in what was being designated, then we might encourage an error in diagnosis that could hamper the campaign against intolerance.

After reflecting on the reception my address received at the conference I made certain amendments, perhaps the most important of which related to the first of the three explanations, which I originally introduced, after having described racism as a scientific error, by saying 'the Marxist approach attempts to explain the mistake by showing the function it serves in capitalist society'. In order to make it clear that what concerned me was the use of functionalist explanations, I reworded this passage to say that racist theories were sometimes seen as a scientific response to the ideological needs of contemporary capitalism. I remarked that though this kind of explanation had been developed by writers influenced by Marxism, their approach was, of course, in many respects sharply opposed to functionalism.

From our two addresses to the conference it appeared as if there was a significant difference between Professor John Rex's conception of some of these topics and my own. Wishing to encourage conceptual analysis, I suggested that we exchange a series of letters to try to clarify the nature of the difference and that we send copies of them to our editor, Sami Zubaida. If the exchange proved interesting and successful he might then draw upon it in his introduction. Though at the time Professor Rex considered that this was not a public debate, and it was he who allowed it to lapse, he has since published one of the letters he sent me amended in several unmentioned, but mostly minor, respects. In the letter (1973a: 223–29), Rex says he felt required by his profession to consider a particular question. Many sociologists would have felt required on the same ground to explain the origin and editing of the letter.

Apart from this letter Professor Rex has commented on my address in a letter to *New Society* (April 17, 1969), one book (1970: 6), one article (1973b: 483), and in two other contributions to a volume of collected essays (1973a: 172–73, 221). Perhaps the first point to notice is that Rex regularly refers to the unrevised version of my address as published in *New Society* (April 10, 1969). While I do not retract the formulation in that version I naturally prefer the more polished one I prepared for the book (Rex took the opportunity to revise his paper for the book and has since revised it once again). The question therefore arises as to why he should do this when he had my revision at an early date. The evidence suggests that he was less concerned to discuss my arguments than to find grounds for castigating their author.

Professor Rex's chief references begin with a statement that in my address 'the view that racist beliefs might be explained in terms of function is associated with Marxist interpretation . . . and all such explanations are thereafter dismissed as Marxism' (1970: 6). Apart from observing that readers can evaluate for themselves the justice of this assessment, I would add only that in my view there is good Marxism and bad, and that in one of my letters to Rex referring to his extravagances about 'vilification' I remarked that I did not mind when one of the authors mentioned in my address greeted me as a fellow-Marxist. Some historians have used Marx's model of society to make additions to our knowledge of the greatest importance; others have tried to apply it in an over-simple and mechanical fashion. I know that this is far from his intention, but by his lapses into cheap point-scoring Rex puts himself in the position of defending poor Marxism and poor scholarship. He also remarks 'when racialism and racism became serious political problems in Britain, Banton used his scholarly knowledge of the history of racism to argue that Mr Peter Griffiths and Mr Enoch Powell should not be called racists' (1973a: 483). Such remarks in my view betray a cavalier attitude towards the importance to social reform of first getting the diagnosis right, though it may well be that we hold different views of the relationship of theory to action. My argument was that none of Powell's public statements fell within the authoritative definitions of racism that I quoted and that this required our attention, but I tried to guard against any misunderstanding on this point by saying explicitly that I did not imply that new-style ethnocentrism was any better than old-style racism.

Among Rex's other assertions one should be noticed in which he says that in my approach 'there is no basis left for considering whether doctrines advanced by Enoch Powell and Peter Griffiths . . . might not have the same function as racist doctrines . .' and another where he fathers upon me the contention that 'it was wrong to discuss what they said in the context of the theory of racism' (1973a: 173, 221). It is difficult to find any justification for such statements in either version of my address. If we are to discuss the functions of beliefs we need first to analyze these beliefs with care so we know what we are talking about. Neither Rex nor I have attempted any such analysis of Powell's statements but superficial acquaintance would suggest to me that, first, Powell has attempted to present race relations in Britain as primarily a problem of immigration. He states that he has never spoken on the question of race relations though I believe that even on his own terms, there is an exception to this in a speech delivered after our conference which I quoted in the revised version of my address. Second, Powell displays a central concern with the question of what, in the present generation, constitutes English nationality, and his appeal has an important component of nationalism. If this is the case, then my address made a modest contribution to the task of analysis. To describe my argument as Rex has done does not reveal any professional concern about the structure of argument and puts his own motives in question.

The possible functional similarity to old-style racism of contemporary non-biological doctrines is an issue important enough to merit independent examination. It is not a sufficient justification for stretching prevailing definitions. In view of the assertions that are made on this topic I find it surprising that there is so little research into what ordinary people believe about the nature of race and its place in human affairs. Such research requires not special grants but imagination and open-mindedness (for a small study of the consequences of belief about inter-racial sexual relations, see Pearson, 1973).

At the conference Professor Rex asked me whether my paper was about the history of ideas or a contribution to sociology. I replied that it was, as it said, a discussion of the diagnostic value of the concept of racism. I found the question surprising because I wished the paper to be judged on its own terms, to which my intentions (or classification of them) were irrelevant. But I have further reasons for rejecting any invitation to choose between two such simple alternatives and it will be disappointing if this book has not made them abundantly clear. In my address I distinguished between the problem of accounting for the origin of racist theories and of explaining how they were utilized politically. I remarked, as something not particularly contentious, that these theories were seized upon, magnified, and publicized, because they were convenient to those who held power in the Europe of that day. The element in my address that most irritates John Rex is my criticism of the loose use of functionalist explanations. His response has shown that this criticism was even more important than I believed it at the time.

The idea of racism — whether it be used to designate a doctrine or a larger constellation of institutions, values, and attitudes — is important to the subject of this book in another way. For it is sometimes argued that race relations are made into a distinctive kind of social relations by the quality of hostility and dissociation that racism introduces into them (cf. the references to maximal and minimal racialism in Schermerhorn, 1970: 73–7). This claim must be contested. Racial beliefs sometimes cause people to regard persons ascribed to a different racial category as more different than persons differentiated by class, nation, religion, or other criteria, and hostility or oppression may therefore be greater. But no one has provided good grounds for believing race relations as a class of social relations to be different in kind from the relations between other categories or groups of persons. All the features of race relations, except their label, can be found in some other class of social relations as well. This may be expressed briefly by stating that inter-racial relations are not different in kind from intra-racial relations.

The belief that race relations were in some important way distinctive was a mistake, but, as every sociology student knows, if men define situations as real they are real in their consequences. If people believe race relations to be different they will approach them differently, so that within a limited historical period the relations between people distinguished racially, but in different parts of the world, may show some special common features. Leo Kuper, for example, has argued that although there were class differences in Zanzibar and Rwanda after independence, and in Algeria prior to independence, when the revolutions took place in those countries they developed along racial rather than class lines. From this he concludes that though class conflict is the source of revolutionary change in many societies there are some where this is not the case, and he identifies 'plural' societies as being built round conflicts of a kind other than of class. The conquest of one people, by another of different race, frequently leads to the creation of plural societies in which 'it is the political relations which appreciably determine the relationship to the means of production, rather than the reverse, and the catalyst of revolutionary change is to be found in the structure of power, rather than in economic changes which exhaust the possibilities of a particular mode of production' (Kuper, 1974: 226).

As the relationship between class and race is often a source of controversy, it is of interest to notice Kuper's attempt to distinguish the two. Class structures, he says, are intrinsic to society, but race is not. 'Class societies may be viewed as arising directly out of the interaction of the members of the society', whereas race 'is in some sense extrinsic to that interaction. To be sure, the racial structure is also constituted by the interaction, but the racial differences which are societally elaborated, have preceded that interaction' (1974: 61). Such a formulation evokes many sorts of objection. The conventional view is that it is the division of labour that is intrinsic and gives rise to class in itself, but something else is necessary (which, unconventionally, could be called the idea of class) before class consciousness takes hold and a class for itself comes into existence. Class differences do not necessarily lead straight to class consciousness and it is well to heed the warning that 'it is no longer possible to believe that a class can be understood apart from its culture, or that most modern classes can be understood apart from their nationality' (Genovese, 1971: 21). In these terms it is scarcely meaningful to oppose class societies to other kinds of society. Kuper's claim that the conflicts in Zanzibar, Rwanda, and Algeria had or acquired a racial character also suggests that the revolutionaries were motivated by a racial consciousness, but this is to use categories of thought that may be taken for granted by a white scholar brought up in South Africa yet bear no relation to the way a Hutu in Rwanda perceives a member of the Tutsi elite.

A more valuable component of Kuper's work is the way he utilizes the later and more flexible formulation of the theory of the plural society, in which M. G. Smith emphasizes political structure rather than cultural difference and introduces as a central concept the mode of political incorporation (1974: 241). Following the later formulation it is possible to utilize the contributions that have sprung from the analysis of plural societies without accepting the assumption that they are a distinct societal type. The social and cultural units which are combined in South Africa and in the kinds of society that have been called plural, can then be seen as examples of the kind of grouping to which Max Weber gave the name *stand*, and which is best translated as estate (e.g. *inter alia*, Hughes, 1961: 346) rather than as 'status group'. One estate is differentiated from another on many criteria: class, status, party, self conception, religious practice, and its interpretation of the society of which it forms part (Bendix, 1959: 259–60). It is a kind of community and its collective behaviour cannot be explained without consideration of how its various distinguishing criteria are inter-dependent. Such a grouping may be identified by racial traits or it may arise because the majority treats its members as distinct. As Weber remarked in a passage which in the original is entitled 'The origin of "racial" qualities' (1968: 385–88) physical and cultural traits can be used to define people as ineligible for group membership and as the basis on which the group seeks to obtain a monopoly of particular roles. When cultural traits are used to define a minority individuals often have a choice as to the group with which they are to be associated, whereas physical traits allow few individuals any alternative.

Because race, class, nation, and other modes of differentiation are so much intertwined in particular communities, and because the ethnic structure of particular countries is always unique, a great deal of the work on race relations must be historical. The more the student is led into the examination of particular situations and sequences, the more difficult it is to conceive of race relations as a distinct field of study. It is here that the study of political structure in terms of the differential incorporation of minorities can marry the sociologist's questioning to the historian's approach. To understand the posture of one community towards another it is essential to review the circumstances in which its outlook has taken shape. For example, to account for the readiness of white workers in South Africa to support white capitalists in the exploitation of black workers, it is scarcely necessary to resort to theories about ideology. By utilizing their political power in the 1920s white workers were able to secure unusual economic advantages which they now seek to preserve when challenged by the blacks. They enjoy a monopoly over most forms of professional and skilled labour partly because they entrenched their position within the political structure before the blacks were able to mobilize such political power as they had. The South African scene has not been characterized by 'biological racism' to the extent to which outsiders assume, but this may not be of great significance since it can always be argued that the estates were so distinct and the challenges to the political order so weak that the whites were not under the sort of pressure that might have encouraged the propagation of quasi-biological doctrines. The processes by which the Afrikaans-speaking minority have become incorporated in the polity have made national consciousness more important, and racial consciousness less important, both for them and for the whole population. For the sequence whereby the Afrikaners came to feel themselves a *volk*, and to differentiate themselves from the English-speaking South Africans, led them to see themselves as a nation. They then interpreted the nature and likely development of other estates in the light of their understanding of themselves. No one had been able to prevent their achieving nationhood and similarly no one would be able to prevent the Africans doing likewise if that was what history had in store for them. Estates are defined in what to the outsider appear racial terms but the idea of race behind them is not that of the contemporary United States or of England. The whole policy of separate development may be seen as a means of controlling the supply of black labour. It seeks to rescue the disintegrating structures of the traditional African groups in order to maintain and control a cheap industrial labour force in or near the 'homelands'. The pressure for such a policy, it is said, will reinforce the tendency to describe the various estates as national rather than racial groups (Wolpe, 1972: 451) while the consciousness of the bulk of South African workers seems to be more nationalist (e.g. Zulu or Khosa or Venda) than racial.

The analysis of other multi-racial societies in terms of the differential incorporation of the various estates and the implications of the various modes of incorporation promises to bring sociological and historical interpretations into closer relation and to illuminate processes that have hitherto been neglected. John Rex has reinterpreted to the implications for the West Indian and Asian worker in Britain of his arriving as someone who had already been stamped with a colonial identity. It reinforced other tendencies to ensure that he entered the labour market and the other institutions of the majority society not just at the bottom but as someone regarded as different. This weakened his ability to enter coalitions with white workers and made them more unwilling to see him as someone who should be drawn into their institutions. Asian workers have now acquired monopolies over certain less attractive forms of employment in the foundries and in the textile industries; they are seeking to utilize the power that position gives them while white workers defend their monopolies over skilled posts. Racial, class, and nationality differences are interwoven. The weaknesses of the position from which black Americans started were even greater than those of the colonial worker in the metropolitan society, but their political power has recently been increased by the concentration of black voters in a number of key cities. The gains they have made in the field of employment have been in the areas (like federal and state government) most open to political pressure, and have been least notable in the craft occupations where white trade unionists have protected what they saw as 'their' opportunities. The black middle-class has been growing rapidly as its members have been offered a larger share in the rewards the established society can provide. Those rewards were sufficient to secure the assimilation of earlier white ethnic groups but the racial structures of the present day will not be so easily dissolved.

While, therefore, it may have originally been mistaken to believe that race relations had to be a separate class of phenomena, it looks as if there will be practical reasons for several generations at least to accept this as a special area for academic study: to clarify the nature of the error, to trace its consequences, and to examine the new forms in which it is implicated. In considering what this might entail it is best to distinguish two ways of defining a field of study. One is to define it descriptively, to identify its characteristics and the factors which make it a going concern. The other is to define it prescriptively, to state what it should be concerned with and to guide research workers towards particular sorts of problem.

Some writers have attempted to define the field of race relations by specifying its subject matter, which is like erecting a fence round the boundary and claiming the territory inside. Subjects are distinguished more by the questions they pursue than by the things which they study, and the latter are often common to several disciplines. Subjects are also distinguished by the people who participate in the research enterprise, by their shared experience, values, and interests. Any approach to definition that ignores the way in which the activities of students are organized and the character of the body that does the studying, must be deficient. I therefore contend that any descriptive definition of a field of study should be in terms not of the boundary fence, but of the nuclei: the core problems at the centre of the field. The best solution is therefore that outlined in the first chapter, which presents race relations study as defined by a tradition of enquiry. A number of scholars who share common interests comment on one another's work and draw others into their field of activity. Gradually a tradition emerges which changes shape and direction as the years go by (partly because of the accumulation of knowledge), often turning to new subject matter and discarding old material which seems exhausted. There may be distinguishable sub-traditions in some countries (when schools of thought contend) or in different countries, but nevertheless there are perceptible continuities which enable participants in different generations or countries to recognize one another as engaging in a common enterprise.

A prescriptive definition of the field of race relations study poses other problems. It is easy to complain that the intellectual heritage which the present-day student has received from his predecessors does not suggest solutions to many of the problems that beset him. The tradition needs to be widened or, some would say, re-directed. What should it become? There are scholars who insist that race relations should be regarded as constituting 'a sub-case of a theory of stratification' (Harris, 1969: 204; cf. Zubaida, 1970: 3–9). Some maintain that race relations situations can be distinguished from other kinds of situation and, because of their political importance, deserve to be made the objects of a special field of study. John Rex has recently tried to improve upon the work of Oliver C. Cox in this respect and has followed him (doubtless for similar reasons) in building upon the concept of a race relations situation. He has argued that the necessary and sufficient conditions for identifying such a situation are the presence of (i) exploitation and oppression; (ii) role ascription; and (iii) a deterministic theory of social groups (1973a: 203). This kind of delimitation is fraught with difficulties. Consider the postion of the Chinese in Malaya. The government has insisted that a certain percentage of employees in new industries must be Malay. It favours Malays when issuing licences for business (Mohamad, 1970: 41–7). Presumably this constitutes role ascription on the basis of racial criteria, in Rex's sense. Chinese merchants have done very well out of Malay cultivators and the Malaysian economy, but at what point can it be decided that this becomes exploitation? And who is oppressed — the Malays by Chinese economic activity or the Chinese by the government's use of state power? There is no deterministic theory. Does this mean therefore that a situation that has led to the sort of rioting that appears to be correlated with race is not to be studied together with race relations situations? Similar considerations apply in the case of the Asians immediately prior to their expulsion from Uganda, for there also it looked as if the exploitation and oppression operated in opposite directions.

The dangers of prescriptive definitions based on subject matter are two-fold. First, the difficulty of defining the boundaries promotes unproductive controversies. Whenever multiple criteria are employed there will be situations that exemplify many but not all of the features in question. Thus it has been maintained that the structure of sectarian strife in Northern Ireland fits Rex's definition of a race relations situation, but this scarcely reveals anything new about Northern Ireland. Equally it has been held that discrimination against women and ideologies of female subordination in some countries produce a form of racism which is basically the same as that directed against blacks. Such arguments remind the student that definitions and typologies cannot be properly evaluated in the abstract. They must prove themselves by showing that they have explanatory power. This leads to the second point, for the best way a scholar can persuade others to study the kinds of problem he considers important is for him to demonstrate what can be done. The general advice to study situations of oppression might discourage a young sociologist from studying intermediary minorities (especially one so small as the Chinese in Mississippi!). Yet a particularly valuable insight into the working of a social system can often be obtained from an examination of an anomalous category or an intermediary group. It is even more important to insist that the study of race relations may have as much to learn from research into situations in which relations appear good and tension low, as into situations of exploitation and hostility.

This view of the problem recalls the words of Max Weber at the conclusion of a speech in which he demolished the arguments for a racial interpretation of society advanced by the founder of the International Society for Racial Hygiene (and it should be remembered that Weber was himself a member of the nationalist Pan-German League). He said 'It does not seem to me useful to circumscribe domains of knowledge *a priori*, before that knowledge has been assembled, and to say: this belongs to our science, and that does not. That way we only multiply the most sterile quarrels' (Weber, 1924: 456–62). He believed that it was possible to understand the rational behaviour of human beings by reliving it in the mind, and in these chapters I have stressed the importance of understanding what racial categories have meant to individuals in different times and places. But there is more to sociology than this, and the problem of a prescriptive definition for the field of race relations remains. Scholars have now to answer new questions about the contributions made to patterns of race relations by the subordinated groups, by their perceptions of the situation, their senses of identity, their modes of mobilization, and their international links. They must question the previously taken-for-granted political structures within which conflicts are negotiated. They must seek the determinants in majority cultures of the kinds of evaluation that have reinforced the distinctions between privileged and unprivileged groups, for it is often the majority that is 'the problem'. And in particular they must examine regularities in social behaviour and social structures of which the participants themselves are unaware.

This study should have led the reader to reflect that if one begins by assuming that mankind is divided into races it is easy to organize the evidence on this basis and to overlook the importance and dubiety of the initial assumption. The study of race relations starts from an historical error and it cannot proceed unless that error is analyzed. If the student believes that the error was the product of the political and economic structure and that the origin of the race idea can be explained by the use that was subsequently made of it, he is led to quite a different view of the nature of the task than that which I have advanced. My essay on Charles Kingsley's racial philosophy is also relevant to this question, for Kingsley was a popularizer rather than an originator, and my essay demonstrates that the growing and rather diverse utilization of the race idea has to be set against the whole social background of Victorian England, and not just part of it.

The heart of the mistake about race lay in a doctrine formulated in the 1850s. I have argued that it is easier to understand that doctrine and its origins if it is seen as a theory of racial typology. This designation ciates the theory with the contemporary use of the concept of type in other spheres of enquiry. It has the advantage of identifying one version of racism which can be given a clear historical location and of reducing slightly the area of terminological confusion and dispute. Earlier writers had asserted that blacks and whites were different species without advancing any theory about the number and nature of the species of mankind. Once such a theory had been furnished in the form of racial typology, to say that blacks and whites were different species was to make a much more significant statement.

The typological conception of race was an error both in biology and in the social realm. In the first chapter I contended that the biologists overcame the error by putting in its place concepts with greater explanatory power, and that sociologists should seek to do likewise. Robert Park was one of the first to set out on this path, for he taught that there was no special category of race relations and employed other concepts for the elucidation of the problems thought to belong in the field. He presented race relations as the relations of people conscious of racial differences and emphasized the way of the idea of race put the maximum distance between parties to a relationship. Where the social Darwinists represented race relations as ultimately beyond man's power to influence, Park saw them as historical phenomena, the product of European expansion, and as lying within the realm of morality. The social researchers of the 1930s followed this up by showing that racial prejudice was not inherited but learned; that it was in part a reflection of personality weakness and was often irrational. They showed that the pattern of social relations between blacks and whites in the American South was not the outcome of the racial nature of the two groups, but was a feature of social system in which there were clear rewards and severe punishments to reinforce the modes of behaviour. They showed that the way people distinguished between racial and class norms of propriety was the product of past political struggles, and that prejudice served economic as well as psychological functions.

The men responsible for these advances were for the most part whites with a political commitment to reform. They concentrated, understandably enough, upon explaining the nature of white prejudice and upon addressing themselves to their fellow Americans. The limitations of this perspective became apparent in the 1960s when, taking advantage of changed circumstances, black Americans started to formulate their demands upon American society and revealed the inappropriateness of the conception of assimilation which had dominated so much of the previous thinking about race relations. Black Americans said, in effect, that they would make their own history and decide on what basis they were willing to cooperate with other groups in American society. The nature of the group to which they belonged was determined not solely by race, by their exclusion by whites, but also by ethnicity, by their voluntary identifaction with one another. This re-orientation, which was so significant in the United States, came at a time of rising ethnic consciousness throughout the world. Like whites before them, blacks from different continents now use their colour as a basis for entering alliances. If they think they can gain advantage from so doing African politicians will associate New World blacks with African institutions and international politics. Racial sentiments will be encouraged and the idea of race will enter into a new phase. The possibility of race being invested with new significance like this shows that for the sociologist one of the central questions of race relations studies must be the nature of racial consciousness and the explanation of the form in which it is manifested.

The variable nature of racial consciousness is one reason for believing that the key concept which for the sociologist must compare with the geneticist's 'population', must be 'minority'. A conceptual apparatus must be developed so that all the apparently special features of race relations can be explained within a framework that can comprehend the whole range of social phenomena. This can best be done, I have claimed, by distinguishing racial minorities from ethnic minorities and developing a conception of intergroup relations that gives equal weight to processes on both sides of group boundaries.

In diagnosing the problems requiring attention the intellectual has a role of the greatest importance. He has the equipment and usually more opportunity for clarifying what is at issue, but it is important that he preserve his independence and criticize all the prevailing interpretations, especially those advanced by the people who have his political sympathies, for criticism is essential to clear thinking. For example, it is at present customary in both the United States and Great Britain to refer to 'the Black community', 'the Polish community', 'the Chinese community', and even at times 'the white community'. The groups so designated have their own deep divisions and conflicts. They may be incapable of collective activity and the only 'community' may be purely sentimental. In Britain the kind of community that exists among immigrants from one locality in Pakistan is different from that among all Pakistanis or among all Asians. Only a small number of persons with a high political consciousness are sensible of a black community that includes both Asians and people of ultimately African descent. In these circumstances to designate almost any minority as a community is a political action, for it attributes to that minority a greater solidarity and potential for common action than they are likely to have. To tell an individual that he belongs in a particular community may be a way of suggesting to him where his allies lie and what sort of person he should be.

In the United States the adjective 'black' has been adopted by persons having any degree of Negro descent. There has been a tendency to import the adjective to Britain and, without any public discussion of the circumstances and groups to which it is appropriate, to apply it to all persons of ultimately African or Asian origin, even including Cypriots, Maltese, Arabs, and other people who are sometimes the objects of white prejudice. Blacks in the United States have recently come to a new consciousness of their shared identity but the same cannot reasonably be said of the various groups of so-called New Commonwealth origin who have settled in Great Britain. Many of the first generation settlers still look towards their homelands and, while the second generation will undoubtedly develop a different orientation, all the evidence indicates that there is very little chance of anything happening in Britain that will unify all New Commonwealth citizens in an alliance sufficiently coherent to justify its being called 'black' as an extension of the American usage. One possible justification for calling all New Commonwealth citizens 'black' derives from a theory of history. It maintains that the social and economic processes at work in the world are bound to make all these citizens come together in opposition to white exploitation. To call them 'black' is therefore to hasten an inevitable development. If this argument were simply a testimony to its proponents' political faith it might not matter, but if the fastening of a single label onto a very diverse collection of individuals constrains anyone's freedom to choose and fashion his or her own identity it is to be condemned. Social alignments change, and groups sometimes alter their character so that new names have to be found for them. When social scientists decide what designations to use they need to take their responsibilities very seriously and be on their guard against the urging of their personal political philosophies. They must criticize contemporary categories of thought just as they expose the weaknesses in earlier conceptions of race. It is the intellectual's duty to press the awkward questions, and he should never expect to be liked for doing so.

References

Note that the date refers to that of first publication. The name of the publisher indicates the edition to which page references in the text refer.

Aberbach, Joel D. and Walker, Jack L. (1970) The Meanings of Black Power: a comparison of white and black interpretations of a political slogan. *American Political Science Review* 64: 367–88.

Adorno, T. W., Frenkel-Brunswick, Else, Levinson, Daniel J., and Sanford, R. Nevitt (1950) *The Authoritarian Personality.* New York: Harper.

Altick, Richard D. (1957) *The English Common Reader: a Social History of the Mass Reading Public, 1800—1900.* Chicago: University of Chicago Press.

Aptheker, Herbert (1946) *The Negro People in America: A Critique of Gunnar Myrdal's 'An American Dilemma'.* New York: International Publishers.

Arnold, Thomas (1842) *Introductory Lectures on Modern History.* London: Fellowes.

Ball, Harry V., Simpson, George E., and Ikeda, Kiyoshi (1962) Law and Social Change: Sumner Reconsidered. *American Journal of Sociology* 67: 532–40.

Banton, Michael (1967) *Race Relations.* London: Tavistock Publications.

Barksdale, Richard K. (1957) Thomas Arnold's Attitude towards Race. *Phylon* 18: 174–80.

Barzun, Jacques (1932) *The French Race: theories of its origin and their social and political implications, prior to the Revolution.* Studies in History, Economics and Public Law, no. 375. New York: Columbia University Press.

Barzun, Jacques (1965) *Race: a study in supersitition.* New York: Harper (revised edition of 1937 work).

Bendix, Reinhard (1959) *Max Weber: An Intellectual Portrait.* London: Methuen.

Berry, Brewton (1972) America's Mestizos. In Noel P. Gist and Anthony Gary Dworkin (eds.), *The Blending of Races: Marginality and Identity in World Perspective*. New York: Wiley.

Biddiss, Michael D. (1970) *Father of Racist Ideology: the Social and Political Thought of Count Gobineau*. London: Weidenfeld & Nicolson.

—— (1976) The Politics of Anatomy: Dr Robert Knox and Victorian Racism. *Proc. roy. Soc. Med.*, 69: 245–50.

Blome, Hermann (1943) *Der Rassengedanke in der deutschen Romantik und seine Grundlagen im 18 Jahrhundert*. München & Berlin: Lehmann.

Blyden, Edward W. (1887) *Christianity, Islam and the Negro Race*. New edition (1967). Edinburgh: Edinburgh University Press.

Boissel, Jean (1971) Un Théoricien des races, précurseur de Gobineau: Victor Courtet de l'Isle. *Études Gobiniennes*: 203–14.

—— (1972) *Victor Courtet 1813–1867. Premier théoricien de la hierarchie des races*, Paris: Presses Universitaires de France.

Bolt, Christine (1971) *Victorian Attitudes to Race*. London: Routledge & Kegan Paul.

Brace, Charles L. (1863) *A Manual of Ethnology; or, the Races of the old World* (second ed. 1869). London: John Murray.

Briggs, Asa (1966) *Saxons, Normans and Victorians*. 1066 Commemoration Series, pamphlet 5. Bexhill-on-Sea and London: Hastings and Bexhill Branch of the Historical Association.

Broca, Paul (1864) *On the Phenomenon of Hybridity in the Genus Homo*. London: Longman Green for Anthropological Society (originally 1859–60).

—— (1874) *Mémoires d'Anthropologie*, 5 vols. Paris: Reinwald.

Bromley, Y. V. (1974) The Term 'Ethnos' and its Definition. In I. R. Grigulerich and S. Y. Kozlov (eds.), *Races and Peoples: Contemporary Ethnic and Racial Problems*. Moscow: Progress Publishers.

Bryce, James (Viscount) (1902) *The Relations of the Advanced and Backward Races of Mankind*. Romanes Lecture. Oxford: Clarendon Press.

Buenzod, Janine (1967) *La formation de la pensée de Gobineau et l'Essai sur l'inégalité des races humaines'*. Paris: Nizet.

Campbell, Ernest Q. (1961) Moral Discomfort and Racial Segregation—an examination of the Myrdal hypothesis. *Social Forces* 39: 228–34.

Carmichael, Stokely and Hamilton, Charles V. (1967) *Black Power: the Politics of Liberation in America*. Harmondsworth: Penguin.

Carus, Carl Gustav (1849) *Denkschrift zum hundertjährigen Geburtsfeste Goethes: Ueber ungleiche Befähigung der verschiedenen Menscheitstämme für höhre geistige Entwickelung*. Leipzig: Brockhaus.

Chatterton-Hill, George (1907) *Heredity and Selection in Sociology*. London: A. & C. Black.

Coleman, William (1964) *Georges Cuvier, Zoologist: a study in the history of evolution theory*. Cambridge, Mass.: Harvard University Press.

Coser, Lewis A. (1971) *Masters of Sociological Thought: Ideas in Historical and Social Context*. New York: Harcourt Brace.

Cox, Oliver C. (1948) *Caste, Class and Race: a study in social dynamics*. New York: Monthly Review Press.

Curtin, Philip D. (1964) *The Image of Africa: British Ideas and Action, 1780-1850.* Madison: University of Wisconsin Press, and London:Macmillan.

Curtis, L. P. Jr. (1968) *Anglo-Saxons and Celts: a study of Anti-Irish Prejudice in Victorian England.* New York: New York University Press for Conference on British Studies at the University of Bridgeport, Conn.

Davis, Allison, Gardner, Burleigh B., and Gardner, Mary (1941) *Deep South: a social anthropological study of caste and class.* Chicago: University of Chicago Press.

Demolins, Edmond (1898) *Anglo-Saxon Superiority to what it is due* (translated from the 10th French edition). London: Leadenhall Press.

Desmoulins, A. (1826) *Histoire Naturelle des Races Humaines.* Paris.

Dollard, John (1937) *Caste and Class in a Southern Town.* New York: Doubleday Anchor.

—— (1968) Hostility and Fear in Social Life. *Social Forces* 17: 15—26.

Douglas, David (1946) *The Norman Conquest and British Historians.* David Murray Lecture. Glasgow: Jackson, Son & Co.

Drake, St. Claire and Cayton, H. R. (1945) *Black Metropolis.* New York: Harcourt Brace.

Du Bois, W. E. B. (1975) An Address to the Black Academic Community. *Journal of Negro History* 60: 45-52.

Dumont, Louis (1966). *Homo Hierarchicus: the Caste System and its Implications.* London: Weidenfeld & Nicolson.

Edwards, G. Franklin (ed.) (1968) *E. Franklin Frazier on Race Relations.* Chicago: University of Chicago Press.

Edwards, W. F. (1829) *Des caractères physiologiques des races humaines, considérés dans leur rapports avec l'histoire: lettre à M. Amédée Thierry.* Paris: Compère Jeune.

Ellison, Ralph (1973). An American Dilemma: A Review. In Joyce A. Ladner (ed.), *The Death of White Sociology.* New York: Vintage.

Epstein, A. L. (1958) *Politics in an Urban African Community.* Manchester: Manchester University Press.

Essien-Udom, E. U. (1962) *Black Nationalism: a search for identity in America.* Chicago: University of Chicago Press.

Faverty, Frederick E. (1951) *Matthew Arnold: the Ethnologist.* Evanston, Ill.: Northwestern University Press (reprinted, New York: AMS Press).

Forbes, Duncan (1952) *The Liberal Anglican View of History.* Cambridge: Cambridge University Press.

Fredrickson, George M. (1971) *The Black Image in the White Mind: the Debate on Afro-American Character and Destiny, 1817-1914.* New York: Harper & Row.

Friedman, Lawrence J. (1970) *The White Savage: Racial Fantasies in the Post-Bellum South.* Englewood Cliffs, N.J.: Prentice-Hall.

Fyfe, Christopher (1972) *Africanus Horton 1835-1883: West African Scientist and Patriot.* New York: Oxford University Press.

Gasman, Daniel (1971) *The Scientific Origins of National Socialism: Social Darwinism in Ernst Haeckel and the German Monist League.* New York: American Elsevier Inc. and London: Macdonald.

Gellner, Ernest (1964) *Thought and Change.* London: Weidenfeld & Nicolson.

Genovese, Eugene D. (1969) *The World the Slaveholders Made.* New York: Pantheon Books.

—— (1971) *In Red and Black: Marxian Explorations in Southern and Afro-American History.* London: Allen Lane.

Ghiselin, Michael T. (1969) *The Triumph of the Darwinian Method.* Berkeley and Los Angeles: University of California Press.

Gobineau, Le Comte de (1853–5). *Essai sur l'inégalité des Races humaines.* Paris: Firmin-Didot. Page references are to the edition of 1967 (Paris: Belfond).

Gobineau, Arthur de (1915) *The Inequality of Human Races.* London: Heinemann (translation of Vol. 1 of Gobineau (1853—1855)).

Gregor, A. James (1967) Evolutionary Theory, Race and Society. In Robert E. Kuttner (ed.) *Race and Modern Science.* New York: Social Science Press.

Guillaumin, Colette (1972) *L'idéologie raciste: genèse et langage actuel.* Publ. no 2 of Institute d'etudes et de recherches inter-ethniques et interculturelles de Nice. Paris and la Haye: Moulton.

Gumplowicz, Ludwig (1875) *Rasse und Staat: eine untersuchung uber das gesetz der staatenbildung.* Vienna: verlag der Manzschen Buchhandlung.

—— (1881) *Rechtsstaat und Socialismus.* Innsbruck: verlag der Wagner schen universitaets-buchhandlung.

—— (1883) *Der Rassenkampf: sociologische untersuchungen.* Innsbruck: verlag der Wagner'schen universitaets-buchhandlung.

Haller, John S. (1971) *Outcasts from Evolution: scientific attitudes of racial inferiority 1859-1900.* Urbana: University of Illinois Press.

Halliday, R. J. (1971) Social Darwinism: a definition. *Victorian Studies* 14: 389–405.

Harris. Marvin (1964) *Patterns of Race in the Americas.* New York: Walker.

—— (1968) *The Rise of Anthropological Theory.* New York and London: Routledge & Kegan Paul.

—— (1969) Review of Banton's *Race Relations. Current Anthropology* 10: 203–204.

Hill, Christopher (1958) *Puritanism and Revolution: studies in Interpretation of the English Revolution of the 17th Century.* London: Panther.

Hofstadter, Richard (1955) *Social Darwinism in American Thought* (revised edition). Boston: Beacon Press.

Horton, James Africanus Beale (1868) *West African Countries and Peoples, British and Native . . . and a vindication of the African Race.* Edited (1969) by George Shepperson. Edinburgh: Edinburgh University Press.

Hughes, Everett C. (1961) Review of Reinhard Bendix, *Max Webe . Comparative Studies in Society and History* 3: 341—48.

—— (1969) Robert E. Park. In Timothy Raison (ed.), *The Founding Fathers of Social Science.* Harmondsworth: Penguin.

—— (1975) Colonies, Colonization and Colonialism. In John W. Bennett and S. Paul (eds.), *The New Ethnicity. Perspectives from Ethnology. 1973 Proceedings of the American Ethnological Society.* Minneapolis: West Publishing Co.

Hunt, James (1865) On the Negro's Place in Nature. *Memoirs read before the Anthropological Society of London* 1. 1863–64: 1–64.

Hunter, G. K. (1967) Othello and Colour Prejudice. *Proceedings of the British Academy* 53: 139–63.

Jordan, Winthrop D. (1968). *White over Black: American attitudes towards the Negro, 1550–1812.* Chapel Hill: University of North Carolina Press. Abridged edition (1974): *The White Man's Burden: historical origins of racism in the United States.* New York: Oxford University Press.

Kedourie, Elie (1960) *Nationalism.* London: Hutchinson.

Keith, Sir Arthur (1931) *The Place of Prejudice in Modern Civilization.* London: Williams and Norgate.

Klemm, Gustav (1843–1852). *Allegemeine Cultur-Geschichte der Menschheit.* 10 vols. Leipzig: Teubner.

—— (1851). *Grundideen zu einer allgemenen Cultur-Wissenschaft. Sitzungsberichte der philosophisch-historischen Classe der K. Akad. der Wissenschaft.* Wien.

Kliger, Samuel (1952) *The Goths in England: a study in seventeenth and eighteenth century thought.* Cambridge, Mass: Harvard University Press.

Knox, Robert (1850) *The Races of Men: a fragment* (second edition 1860). London: Renshaw.

Kuper, Leo (1974) *Race, Class and Power: Ideology and Revolutionary Change in Plural Societies.* London: Duckworth.

Lapouge, Georges Vacher de (1899) *L'Aryen: son role social.* Paris: Albert Fontemoing.

Latham, Robert Gordon (1850) *The Natural History of the Varieties of Man.* London: Van Voorst.

Laver, James (1966) *The Age of Optimism: Manners and Morals, 1824–1914.* London: Weidenfeld & Nicolson.

Leopold, Joan (1970) The Aryan Theory of Race in India, 1870–1920: Nationalist and Internationalist Visions. *The Indian Economic and Social History Review* 7: 271–97.

—— (1974) British applications of the Aryan theory of race to India, 1850–1870. *The English Historical Review* 89: 578–603.

Lewis, Bernard (1971) *Race and Colour in Islam.* New York: Harper Torchbooks.

Lewis, Hylan (1955) *Blackways of Kent.* Chapel Hill: University of North Carolina Press.

Loewen, James W. (1971) *The Mississippi Chinese.* Harvard East Asian Series 63. Cambridge, Mass.: Harvard University Press.

Lorimer, Douglas A. (1972) *British Attitudes to the Negro, 1850–1870.* Ph.D. thesis, University of British Columbia. Forthcoming: Leicester University Press.

Lyman, Stanford M. (1972) *The Black American in Sociological Thought.* New York: Putnam's.

Lyon, Michael H. (1972) Race and Ethnicity in Pluralistic Societies: a comparison of minorities in the UK and USA. *New Community* 1: 256–62.

Lytton, E. (1874) *Speeches of Edward, Lord Lytton.* 2 vols. Edinburgh: Blackwood.

Marx, Karl (1956) *Karl Marx: Selected Writings in Sociology and Social Philosophy* (edited by T. B. Bottomore and Maximilian Rubel). Harmondsworth: Penguin.

Mason, Philip (1962) *Prospero's Magic: some thoughts on Race and Class.* London: Oxford University Press.

Massy, Richard Tuthill (1855) *Analytical Ethnology: the mixed tribes of Great Britain and Ireland examined, and the political, physical, and metaphysical blunderings on the Celt and the Saxon exposed.* London: Ballière.

Medalia, Nahum Z. (1962) Myrdal's Assumptions on Race Relations: a conceptual commentary. *Social Forces* 40 223–27.

Meier, August (1963) *Negro Thought in America. 1880-1915: Racial Ideologies in the Age of Booker T. Washington.* Ann Arbor: University of Michigan Press.

Mohamad, Mahathir bin (1970) *The Malay Dilemma.* Singapore: Donald Moore for Asia Pacific Press.

Moore, F. C. T. (ed.) (1969). *The Observation of Savage Peoples by Joseph-Marie Degérando.* London: Routledge & Kegan Paul.

Moreau de Jonnès, A. C. (1861) *Ethnogenie Caucasienne: recherches sur la formation et lieu d'origine des peuples.* Paris: Cherbuliez.

Morton, Samuel George (1839) *Crania Americana; or, A Comparative View of the Skulls of Various Aboriginal Nations of North and South America, to which is prefixed an Essay on the Varieties of the Human Species.* Philadelphia and London.

—— (1844) *Crania Aegyptica; or, Observations on Egyptian ethnography.* Philadelphia and London.

Murray, Gilbert (1900) The exploitation of inferior races in ancient and modern times. In *Liberalism and the Empire*, three essays by Francis W. Hirst, Gilbert Murray and J. L. Hammond. London: Johnson.

Myrdal, Alva and Gunnar (1941) *Kontakt med Amerika.* Stockholm: Bonniers.

Myrdal, Gunnar with the assistance of Sterner, Richard and Rose, Arnold (1944) *An American Dilemma: the Negro problem and modern democracy.* New York: Harper.

Nott, J. C. and Gliddon, G. R. (1854) *Types of Mankind; or, Ethnological Researches.* Philadelphia: Lippincott and London: Trübner.

—— (1857) *Indigenous Races, or New Chapters of Ethnological Enquiry.* Philadelphia: Lippincott and London: Trübner.

Park, Robert E. and Burgess, Ernest W. (1921) *Introduction to the Science of Sociology.* Chicago: University of Chicago Press. ——

Park, Robert E. (1950). *Race and Culture.* Glencoe, Ill.: The Free Press.

—— (1973). Life History. *American Journal of Sociology* 79: 251–60.

Parsons, Talcott (1937) *The Structure of Social Action: A Study in Social Theory with Special Reference to a Group of Recent European Writers.* New York: Free Press.

Patterson, Orlando (1975) Context and Choice in Ethnic Allegiance: A Theoretical Framework and Caribbean Case Study. In Nathan Glazer and Daniel P. Moynihan (eds.), *Ethnicity: Theory and Experience* Cambridge, Mass.: Harvard University Press.

Pearson, Veronica (1973) Telegony: A Study of this Belief and its Continued Existence. Unpublished M.Sc. thesis. University of Bristol.

Peel, J. D. Y. (1971) *Herbert Spencer: the evolution of a sociologist.* London: Heinemann.

Perraton, H. D. (1967) British Attitudes towards East and West Africa 1880–1914. *Race* 8: 223–46.

Peterson, John H. (1971) The Indian in the Old South. In Charles M. Hudson (ed.), *Red, White, and Black: Symposium on Indians in the Old South.* Southern Anthropological Society Proceedings, no. 5. Atlanta: University of Georgia Press.

—— (1972) Assimilation, Separation and Out-migration in an American Indian Group. *American Anthropologist* 74: 1286–95.

Pike, Luke Owen (1866) *The English and their Origin: a prologue to authentic English history.* London: Longmans, Green & Co.

Piveteau, Jean (1950) Le débat entre Cuvier et Geoffroy Saint-Hilaire sur l'unité de plan et de composition. *Révue d'Histoire des Sciences* 3: 343–63.

Poliakov, Léon (1974) *The Aryan Myth: a history of racist and nationalist ideas in Europe.* London: Chatto, Heinemann, for Sussex University Press.

Popper, Karl R. (1957) *The Poverty of Historicism.* London: Routledge & Kegan Paul.

Powdermaker, Hortense (1939) *After Freedom: A Cultural Study on the Deep South.* New York: Atheneum.

Prichard, James Cowles (1826) *Researches into the Physical History of Mankind.* (second edition). London: Arch.

—— (1843) *The Natural History of Man.* London: Ballière.

Rawick, George P. (1972) *From Sundown to Sunup.* Vol. 1 of *The American Slave.* Westport, Conn.: Greenwood.

Rex, John (1970) *Race Relations in Sociological Theory.* London: Weidenfeld & Nicholson.

—— (1973a) *Race, Colonialism and the City.* London: Routledge & Kegan Paul.

—— (1973b) Sociological Research and the Politics of Racial Justice. *Race* 14: 481–88.

Rose, Arnold (1951) *The Roots of Prejudice.* The Race Question in Modern Science. Paris: UNESCO.

Salles, Eusèbe Fr. de (1849) *Histoire Génèralé des Races Humaines ou Philosophie Ethnographique.* Paris: Duprat.

Schermerhorn, R. A. (1970) *Comparative Ethnic Relations: a Framework for Theory and Research.* New York: Random House.

Semmel, Bernard (1960) *Imperialism and Social Reform: English Social-Imperial Thought, 1895–1914.* London: Allen & Unwin.

Singer, Lester (1962) Ethnogenesis and Negro-Americans Today. *Social Research* 29: 419–32.

Sinkler, George (1971) *The Racial Attitudes of American Presidents from Abraham Lincoln to Theodore Roosevelt.* Garden City, New York: Doubleday.

Smith, Anthony D. (1971) *Theories of Nationalism.* London: Duckworth.

Smith, Charles Hamilton (1848) *The Natural History of the Human Species.* Edinburgh: W. H. Lizars.

Sorokin, Pitirim A. (1928) *Contemporary Sociological Theories.* New York: Harper.

Stanton, William (1960) *The Leopard's Spots: scientific attitudes towards race in America 1815–59.* Chicago: University of Chicago Press.

Stark, W. (1961) Natural and Social Selection. In Michael Banton (ed.), *Darwinism and the Study of Society.* London: Tavistock Publications.

Stocking, George W. (1968) *Race, Culture and Evolution: essays in the history of evolution.* New York: Free Press.

—— (1971) What's in a Name? The Origins of the Royal Anthropological Institute. *Man* 6: 369–90.

—— (1973) From Chronology to Ethnology: James Cowles Prichard and British Anthropology, 1800–1850. In J. C. Prichard, *Researches into the Physical History of Man.* Chicago: University of Chicago Press.

Stone, John (1972) James Bryce and the Comparative Sociology of Race Relations. *Race* 13: 315–28.

Sumner, William Graham (1906) *Folkways: a Study of the Sociological Importance of Usages, Manners, Customs, Mores, and Morals.* New York: New American Library.

Svensson, Tom G. (1973) *Samernas Politiska Organisation: en studie av en etnisk minoritet i förhallande till storsamhället.* Stockholm: Akademisk avhandling.

Thomas, J. J. (1889) *Froudacity: West Indian Fables by James Anthony Froude* (with new introduction, 1969). London and Port of Spain: New Beacon Books.

Toll, Robert C. (1974) *Blacking Up: The Minstrel Show in Nineteenth Century America.* New York: Oxford University Press.

Turner, Sharon (1799–1805) *History of the Anglo-Saxons.* London (fifth edition, 1828).

Voegelin, Erich (1933a) *Die Rassenidee in der Geistesgeschichte von Ray bis Carus.* Berlin: Junker & Dünnhaupt.

—— (1933b) *Rasse und Staat.* Tubingen: Mohr.

—— (1940) The Growth of the Race Idea. *The Review of Politics* 2: 283–317.

Vogt, Carl (1863) *Lectures on Man: his place in creation and in the history of the earth* (edited by James Hunt). London: Longman, Green for Anthropological Society, 1864.

Wagley, Charles and Harris, Marvin (1958) *Minorities in the New World: Six Case Studies*. New York: Columbia University Press.

Watson, George (1973) *The English Ideology: Studies in the Language of Victorian Politics*. London: Allen Lane.

Weatherford, Willis D. and Johnson, Charles S. (1934) *Race Relations: Adjustment of Whites and Negroes in the United States*. Boston: D. C. Heath.

Weber. Max (1924) *Gesammelte Aufsätze zur Sociologie und Sozialpolitik*. Tübingen: Mohr.

—— (1947) *From Max Weber* (edited by H. H. Gerth and C. Wright Mills). London: Routledge & Kegan Paul.

—— (1968) *Economy and Society: An Outline of Interpretative Sociology*. New York: Bedminster Press (first German edition published 1921).

Westermarck, Edward (1927) *Minnen Ur Mitt Liv*. Helsingfors: Holger Schildt.

Willhelm, Sidney M. (1970) *Who Needs the Negro?* New York: Doubleday Anchor.

Wirth, Louis (1945) The Problem of Minority Groups. In Ralph Linton (ed.), *The Science of Man in the World Crisis*. New York: Columbia University Press.

Wolpe, Harold (1972) Capitalism and cheap labour-power in South Africa: from segregation to apartheid. *Economy and Society* 1: 425–56.

Zangwill, Israel (1917) *The Principle of Nationalities* (Conway Memorial Lecture). London: Watts.

Zubaida, Sami (ed.) (1970) *Race and Racialism*. London: Tavistock Publications.

Index